If I Am Found Dead

MICHIGAN VOICES
FROM THE CIVIL WAR

If I Am Found Dead

MICHIGAN VOICES
FROM THE CIVIL WAR

David Lee Poremba
Editor

All inquiries should be addressed to:
Ann Arbor Media Group LLC
2500 S. State Street
Ann Arbor, MI 48104

Printed and bound in the United States of America.

10   09   08   07   06   1   2   3   4   5

Library of Congress Cataloging-in-Publication Data
If I am found dead : Michigan voices from the Civil War / David Lee Poremba, editor.
    p. cm.
 Includes bibliographical references.
 ISBN-13: 978-1-58726-283-8 (hardcover : alk. paper)
 ISBN-10: 1-58726-283-5 (hardcover : alk. paper)
 1. Michigan--History--Civil War, 1861-1865--Personal narratives. 2. United States--History--Civil War, 1861-1865--Personal narratives. 3. Michigan--History--Civil War, 1861-1865--Regimental histories. 4. United States--History--Civil War, 1861-1865--Regimental histories. 5. Soldiers--Michigan--Correspondence. 6. Michigan--Biography. I. Poremba, David Lee.

 E601.I4 2006
 973.7'4740922--dc22

                    2006002456

ISBN-13: 978-1-58726-283-8
ISBN-10: 1-58726-283-5

Poetry at the beginning of each chapter is from *Michigan in the War*, originally written in 1882 by John Robertson.

To All Those Who Serve

Acknowledgments

There would be very little of the original historical record to study if it were not for the dedicated librarians and archivists who make it their duty to acquire, preserve, and make accessible the voices of the past. No less dedicated are the staff members of the Burton Historical Collection of the Detroit Public Library. This ninety-two-year-old collection is a veritable treasure trove of manuscripts and books.

Special thanks go to Mark Patrick, Mark Bowden, Barbara Louie, and Dawn Eurich for their assistance in making this book possible.

Extra special thanks go to my family, immediate and extended, who have had to put up with a preoccupied grump and a bunch of broken down vets in blue. Answering the call above and beyond were my daughter Theresa (with an "h") and my loving wife, Kate—because of you, I am.

Acknowledgments

Contents

Introduction

"THE BLOW AT LAST FALLEN. WAR! WAR! WAR! THE CONFEDERATE BATTERIES OPEN ON SUMTER YESTERDAY MORNING," screamed the headlines of the *Detroit Free Press* on April 13, 1861. The *Detroit Advertiser and Tribune* echoed, "THE CRISIS REACHED! CIVIL WAR INITIATED BY THE SOUTH. REBELS ATTACK FORT SUMTER. FIRING KEPT UP ALL DAY." These announcements and countless others signaled the end of the bitter sectional arguments occurring the length and breadth of the United States and the beginning of actual armed conflict that would cost the country more than a half million lives and a mountain of treasure.

Gone was the chance for peaceful reconciliation. On April 15, 1861, the day after Fort Sumter fell, President Abraham Lincoln issued a call for 75,000 militia to put down the insurrection and restore the Union, the Constitution, and the laws. These troops were to serve for three months—the maximum length of service by law. Michigan's quota in this initial request was for a single regiment of infantry, about 1,000 men. The First Michigan Volunteer Infantry Regiment was quickly formed from ten existing militia companies and was the first western unit to reach Washington, D.C.

Recruiting stations across the North were deluged with men clamoring to serve the colors, and on May 3, Lincoln called for 42,034 men to serve for three years, enough to form forty infantry regiments. In all, 208 regiments were accepted under the call, and in July Congress approved the President's request, allowing for 500,000 more troops to serve for three years or the duration of the war.

During the first year of the conflict, twenty-one Michigan regiments were organized. Before fighting stopped four years later, more Michigan men would don the Union blue, a total that just topped 90,000 souls. They would serve in forty-six regiments—thirty-one infantry, eleven cavalry, and one each of engineers and mechanics, artillery, colored infantry, and sharpshooters. Michigan also contributed soldiers to over fifty other military units and sent nearly six hundred men to serve in the Union Navy. Men flocked to the colors from all sections of the state and from all walks of life. Farmers, merchants, lawyers, doctors, laborers, college students, mechanics, and teachers answered the call to duty. They were well-to-do and not so well-off, from all ethnic and racial backgrounds: Polish, German, English, Irish, Scot, Native American, and African American. Their educations differed but the majority of them could and did read and write, often. They served in all of the major campaigns and battles of the war, from the occupation of Alexandria, Virginia, in May 1861, to the capture of Jefferson Davis in Georgia in May 1865. In fact, regiments of the Michigan Cavalry Brigade were sent west *after* the war ended to subdue the Indians, ending their last engagement at Willow Springs, Dakota Territory, on August 12, 1865.

Of the 90,119 Michigan soldiers who went off to war, over 15,000 never returned, placing the state sixth in most casualties, behind New York, Ohio, Illinois, Pennsylvania, and Indiana. In combat 2,800 Wolverines lost their lives, another 1,700 died of wounds, 700 of other causes, and 10,000 men died of disease. This uneven ratio of disease to combat deaths is typical of warfare throughout history until the middle of the twentieth century.

If I Am Found Dead focuses on the Civil War experiences of four soldiers: three nineteen-year-olds and one who just turned twenty; all are unmarried. George Vanderpool of Muskegon served in the 3rd Michigan Infantry. Charles Salter of Detroit served in the 1st and 16th Michigan Infantry. James Vernor, also of Detroit, enlisted in the 4th Michigan Cavalry. John Presley of Stockbridge, in rural Ingham County, served in the 7th Michigan Infantry. Vanderpool, Salter, and Presley served in the east with the Army of the Potomac and Vernor served in the west with the Army of the Cumberland. One of these men would not survive the conflict.

Vanderpool and Presley wrote diaries and Salter and Vernor wrote letters. The book is arranged chronologically throughout the four men's documents. The narrative shifts from writer to writer. Spelling is per the original documents, except where there would be confusion; words have been inserted, enclosed in brackets, when missing for clarification. As form was almost always ignored, especially when paper was in short supply, punctuation and paragraphing have been added, as needed, for a smooth flow of words. The correspondence is typical for Vernor as he is writing to family members—his mother, father, and brother; but Salter writes to Mrs. Duffield, the wife of a prominent Detroit minister, one Reverend George Duffield. One can only surmise the relationship between the two but the Duffields had a son, Henry, who was the same age as Salter, and perhaps Salter attended the First Presbyterian Church in Detroit.

The diaries were written in readily available standard pocket-sized, one-year diaries usually purchased from the local stationery store or the ever-present sutler who was stationed near every military camp in the operating theaters. Letters were written on large pieces of paper folded into 8½-by-11 sides. When that paper ran out or was not available, the soldiers used whatever was at hand, as in the case of James Vernor, who used an old account book for one of his letters. Not a space was wasted. The mail traveled via the Postal Service or was hand-delivered by a fellow soldier or civilian who was returning home. More often than not, it is the soldiers' letters home that have survived and not the letters they received. On active campaign, paper would not often survive in a man's knapsack.

The Burton Historical Collection, one of the country's richest collections of local history, acquires material either through outright purchase or donation and this material came to reside there in that fashion. The Vernor letters were donated by the Estate of Emily

Louise Vernor Davis; the Vanderpool diary was purchased from Fred Vanderpool; the Salter letters and Presley diary were both purchased as well.

An early testament to the performance of Michigan soldiers is the following letter written by Brigadier General Philip Kearney, commander of the 3rd Division, 3rd Corps, Army of the Potomac, to Michigan Senator Zachariah Chandler, barely one year after the fighting started.

> Headquarters, 3rd Division, 3rd Corps
> Army of the Potomac
> Harrison's Landing [VA], 16th July '62

Dear Sir:

I was sorry to see your remarks the other day in reference to our ungrateful silence as to the high merit of the Michigan Regiment, serving in the Eastern Army. I hasten to disabuse you of the idea, that those, who immediately command them, are insensible to their noble qualities.

Commanding the 3rd Division of the 3rd Corps of this Army, I am fortunate enough to count the 2nd, 3rd & 5th Michigan, in one of my brigades (Perry's). In each of the two great battles of Williamsburgh & Fair Oaks, I have personally led them into action—in each instance their duty was difficult, to retake ground lost, after arriving amidst panick stricken regiments, that had broken—it was thus necessary to deprive the enemy of his confidence from success; before gaining our impress over him, for victory—In each of these actions, by accident, that could not be foreseen, the brunt of the engagement was on this Michigan Brigade and their loss, consequently, has been fearful, unusual in European wars.

In the skirmishing of the 25th June, before the Lines of Fair Oaks, though material sufferers, they were in close support. At the Battle of the 30th, at the Charles City Cross Roads, where I defended the New Market road against the enemy's principal attacks, I intended my Michigan regiments as reserves, for their previous losses required sparing troops who were now steeled veterans, & whose numbers had been unduly diminished in the process. My division, indeed, has been much more frequently engaged than any other portion of this army. but even in this action, that bravest of brave Regiments, the 5th Michigan, under its dashing leader, Major Fairbanks, when night had closed in, sprung forth across the parapets to terminate the fight by an irresistible pursuit. It paid the price of its high valor by a loss, which as usual, was severe—And its leader, one of the last of my distinguished officers of Williamsburgh & Fair Oaks, was dangerously wounded.

Nor is it alone whilst on the field line that our troops suffer. At the Battle of Malvern Heights, their loss from the fire of the enemy's artillery was considerable—In this action, they were held ready to be launched on the enemy from whatever point he might assail us.

But it is not, sir, solely on the Battlefield that the Michigan Volunteer shines preeminent. It there [is] a dangerous picket to be held, it is given to him. It is known, that he is vigilant—that he is fearless, an unerring marksman, with rifle ever ready, to punish the assassin fire of any lurking foe—If information [is] to be gained, it is this knowledge of the woods, & high intelligence, that mark him as the accomplished scout.

Nor do his soldierly qualities end here; it is desired to strengthen some new site, it is again the care of the Michigan Volunteer, ever ready, & untiring, rivaling by labor the distinction of his courage—and when amidst repose, & the listlessness of the bivouac, you seek him out, the neatness & cleanliness of his camp attest the high self-respect & system of the man—Whilst an invariable cheerfulness of countenance close the most pleasing picture.

With many apologies for introducing myself a stranger to you, but without great sympathy, in genuine admiration for the Michigan Regiments, I have done so.

> I Remain, Sir, most Respectfully,
> Your Obt Servt
> P. Kearney
> Br. General, Commanding, 3rd
> Division, 3rd Corps

Kearney, a native New Yorker who inherited millions from his grandfather and father, was a career soldier with combat experience in Algiers with the French and in Mexico with the United States (where he lost his left arm at the Battle of Churubusco). He was a popular and certainly eccentric officer who was outspoken in his criticism of superior officers. He was, however, in Commanding General Winfield Scott's opinion, "the bravest man I ever saw, and a perfect soldier." Five weeks after sending Chandler his letter, Kearney was shot and killed during the Battle of Chantilly, Virginia.

To the Colors

"Come for your country! For all dear things come,
Come to the roll of the rallying drum!"

The 3rd Michigan Infantry, organized at Grand Rapids, Michigan, and accepted into state service on May 21, 1861, was mustered into federal service on June 10.

Company "H," under the command of Captain Emery D. Bryant, was made up largely of men from Muskegon. The company was raised as the "Muskegon Rangers," in which twenty-year-old George Vanderpool enlisted on April 17, 1861. A native of New York, Vanderpool moved to Michigan after 1860 and settled in Muskegon. Almost one month after his enlistment, he bought a diary or, in his words, a memoranda book. His first begins thus:

George Vanderpool was born in the year of our Lord 1840 in the town of Mayfield & the County of Fulton, State of New York. Should eny Accident happen [to] me or this Book be lost, the finder would Do a great favor by sending it to the following Address: F. Vanderpool, Mayfield, Fulton Co. NY. Or to Henry Vanderpool, Benson, Hamilton Co. NY.

1861

Memoranda book of George Vanderpool, kept from the day of his departure from the village of Muskegon as a Volunteer in the Company of Muskegon Rangers, Captain Emery D. Bryent [Bryant], 1st Lieut Charles D. Spang, 2nd Lieut William [L.] Ryan, all of Muskegon in Muskegon County, Michigan. This is a correct account of current events from the 14th of May, 1861, being the time we left the place of organization—I inlisted on the 17th of April & time up to our departure was spent on drilling.

May 3rd

Muskegon May the 14th 1861

14th TUESDAY—left Muskegon, Michigan on the tug Ryerson as a Volunteer; took dinner at Grand Haven; Arived at the Eagle Hotel, at Grand Rappids; took supper & logings at 7 P.M.

GEORGE VANDERPOOL
(MANISTEE COUNTY HISTORICAL SOCIETY)

15th WEDNESDAY—went to the barracks; it rained all day; returned that night to the citty for lodgings.

16th THURSDAY—Parraded through the citty and stoped at the Bransom House in the citty.

17th FRIDAY—stayed in the citty awaiting orders of Captain Bryant.

18th SATURDAY—went to the encampment of the 3rd Regt of Mich Infantry

19th SUNDAY—went to the Parrade-Ground to hear preaching

20th MONDAY—It was rainey; we drilled a little

21st TUESDAY—drilled and went on dress parade

22nd WEDNESDAY—took the State Oath in the army and drilled

23rd THURSDAY—drilled and wrote two letters; one home to my Brother Frederick, NY; one to Miss W in Muskegon, Michigan

24th FRIDAY—went to the City of Grand Rappids on a pass from Capt Bryant; staid until Dress Parrade

25th SATURDAY—bathed and put on clean clothes and drilled and staid in camp

26th SUNDAY—it rained a little in the morning; the 3rd Regt went to Grand River to bathe; one man drowned; at dress parade a large crowd of spectators

27th MONDAY—parraded and drilled

28th TUESDAY—drilled and parraded

29th WEDNESDAY—drilled & parraded & received our shirts, drawers and socks from the government

30th THURSDAY—drilled & parraded

31st FRIDAY—I was Colonel's Orderly; received our coats & pants

——————————— June ———————————

1st SATURDAY—staid in camp

2nd SUNDAY—received our caps, shoes, & guns from government

3rd MONDAY—the 3rd Regiment of Michigan Volunteers had a Banner presented to them by the Leadys of Grand Rappids. A large crowd of spectators on the ground, the largest ever known

4th TUESDAY—we commenced drilling at the Manuel of Arms

5th WEDNESDAY—received our knap-sacks & straps and drilled

6th THURSDAY—drilled and parraded

7th FRIDAY—drilled and parraded

8th SATURDAY—took the Oath for the United States Service in the Army of the U.S.A. I wrote to F.E.O.

THIRD REGIMENT OF MICHIGAN VOLUNTEERS MARCHING DOWN
JEFFERSON AVENUE, DETROIT, MICHIGAN. SKETCHED BY J. B. NANNERT.
(THE PICTORIAL BATTLES OF THE CIVIL WAR, NEW YORK, 1895)

9th SUNDAY—I went to the citty of Grand Rappids and bathed in [the] Grand River

10th MONDAY—received a letter from my brother Frederick; I wrote to Miss Mary E.
Van Renschler; I stood on guard

11th TUESDAY—rec'd orders to march & I wrote to my brother F

12th WEDNESDAY—was informed that we would get but half our pay; I mailed a letter to
EVR & my brother Fred

13th THURSDAY—left Grand Rappids, Michigan for Washington; arrived at Detroit;
parraded through the principal streets at 7 P.M. we took supper and went on board the
boats <u>Ocean</u> and <u>Concord</u> for Cleveland, in Ohio

The initial call for troops from President Lincoln made Michigan's quota one regiment. Governor Austin Blair and his advisors decided to offer the organized militia companies from around the state the opportunity to volunteer for the regiment. The Detroit Light Guard, a militia company descended from the Brady Guards, who were organized in April 1836, formed Company A of this 1st Michigan Infantry and was under the command of Captain Charles Lum, of Detroit. The regiment left Detroit on May 13, 1861, and arrived in Washington, D.C., three days later.

Private Charles A. Salter, a 19-year-old grocery clerk, shouldered a musket and fell in with his fellow Detroiters to do his duty to restore the Union.

CHARLES H. SALTER
(LIBRARY OF MICHIGAN)

Camp Willcox Alexandria
June 4th 61

Rev. Mrs. Duffield Detroit
Dear Madam

I received your kind note and the accompanying testament and golden treasury from friend Henry the day we left Fort Wayne and I can assure you I have never received any advice which has sunk so deep into my heart as that you gave me. I read a chapter in the testament and a piece in the Golden Treasury every day and derive great benefit from them. We arrived in Washington on the 16th instant and whilst there I improved all my spare time in seeing some of the beautiful public buildings of which that city has many.

On the morning of the 24th May we left for Alexandria and arriving there at 5 A.M. took the place with the loss however of the life of the gallant Colonel Ellsworth whose death we all sincerely mourn.

We are now encamped upon the Federal Hill, which is about one mile south of the city, and overlooks all the surrounding country. We can see Washington quite plainly from here.

It is also the spot where the parents of the great Washington resided and the place is venerated by us on that account. I have been in the Church which he was in the habit of attending and the old Hotel in which he received his commission also.

Our post here is one of some little danger however, as our picket guard is fired upon by the enemy almost every night and as I am called upon quite often to go out to that guard, I do not know but that I may be taken away at any moment but still if an overruling providence should see fit in His infinite wisdom to take away my life I hope and trust it will find me prepared. We have been throwing up entrenchments around our camp to protect ourselves in case of an attack. How long we shall stay here we do not know. It will probably be untill after the session of Congress which meets on the 4th July next unless some unexpected occurrence should take place to call us out.

I should be very glad to hear from you if you could spare the time to write me some good advice occasionally.

Please give my respects to Rev. Mr. Duffield and to friend Henry and also excuse me for intruding upon your good time.

I Remain
Your Obedient Servant
Chas. H. Salter

P.S. The Postal directions are Co. A 1st Regiment Michigan Infantry Washington Dist. Columbia. CHS

Camp Willcox. Alexandria. June 4th /61

Rev. Mrs. Duffield. Detroit.

Dear Madam.

I received your kind note and the accompaning testament and golden treasury from friend Henry the day we left Fort Wayne and I can assure you I have never received any advice which has sunk so deep into my heart as that you gave me. I read a chapter in the testament and a peice in the golden treasury every day and derive great benefit from them. We arrived in Washington on the 16th instant and whilst there I improved all my spare time in seeing some of the beautiful public buildings of which that city has so many,

On the morning of the 24th May we left for Alexandria and arriving there at 5 A. M. took the place with the loss havever of the life of the gallant Colonel Ellsworth. whose death we all sincerely mourn,

July 26th Friday
A pleasent Morning
I took a walk & Bathed
in the Potomac. Then done
Some writing & Bought
my Meals

27th Saturday
Mailed a leter to my
Brother Frederick & one
to M. E. R. & one to C. W.
I Bought My Meals today

28th Sunday
We were Alarmed last
Night by the pickets
fiering, Rested to day
& Bought My Meals

28th july Monday
I done Some writing &
at 4. oclock P. M. we pulled
up our tents & Martched
in the direction of Alaxandra
& we picked our tents on the
South side of the City of
Washington & between there
& Alexandra on the Bank of
the Potomac, it is a Beautiful
Spot Called Hunters place

30th Tuesday
The first thing I done was
to Clean my gun & then
Mailed a leter to Wm Owen
& I received one from him
today

GEORGE VANDERPOOL DIARY

14th FRIDAY—arrived at Cleveland, Ohio at 8 A.M. took the Cleveland & Pittsburg RR for Pittsburg, Penn; arrived at Pittsburg, Penn [at] 8 P.M.

15th SATURDAY—passed through the Great Tunnell in the Algoney [Allegheny] Mts. arrived at Harrisburg, Penn; rec'd our belts & 10 rounds of cartridges—took the cars for Baltimore

16th SUNDAY—at day break, we passed the burned RR Bridges; burned by the Secessionist. at 8 a.m., we arrived in the suburbs of Baltimore; marched through the citty; took the cars for Washington, then marched to Camp Blair at the Chain Bridge

17th MONDAY—fixed our tents a little comfortable; bathed in the Potomac River by the Chain Bridge

18th TUESDAY—wrote home and bathed in the George Town canale

19th WEDNESDAY—went to the citty of Washington and looked through the Capitol and around the citty; mailed a letter to my brother

20th THURSDAY—we all staid in Camp Blair

21st FRIDAY—went on guard the first time at Camp Blair

22nd SATURDAY—camp off guard and wrote some

23rd SUNDAY—was on police duty; wrote some

24th MONDAY—was excused from duty by the Doctor; mailed a letter to F.C. Odell

25th TUESDAY—was excused by the Doctor for Summer complaint; mailed a letter to Miss Cyrena Wilson; stood guard at night

26th WEDNESDAY—we shot at targets; mailed a letter to my brother John (the doctor)

27th THURSDAY—staid in camp and went on drills, parade

28th FRIDAY—went to the George Town canale to bathe

29th SATURDAY—received two letters, one from my brother Fred & one from John M. Miller

30th SUNDAY—I went to the Regimental Meeting

——————————— July ———————————

1st MONDAY—mailed a letter to John M. Miller; one to Wm Owen; a paper to my brother F

2nd TUESDAY—went to Washington and looked through the Patent Office and through the Smithsonian Institution

3rd WEDNESDAY—I went over the Chain Bridge; bathed in the Potomac River, then took a stroll in the Black Bery fields

4th THURSDAY—went to the Potomac to bathe

5th FRIDAY—wrote some, left my letter unfinished

6th SATURDAY—I helped to make a brick oven

SOLDIERS BLACKBERRYING DURING A HALT OF THE ARMY IN VIRGINIA
(THE PICTORIAL BATTLES OF THE CIVIL WAR, NEW YORK, 1895)

7th SUNDAY—was a pleasant day; I got a pass to go up the Potomac River two miles to get Black Berrys

8th MONDAY—I mailed a letter to Miss C Wilson; I wrote some; on dress parade

9th TUESDAY—I done some writing & parraded

10th WEDNESDAY—I mailed a letter to Miss F E Odell and one to Miss M E Van Raneschler

11th THURSDAY—I had a severe pain in the head; I done some writing & received a letter from my brother Fred & one from Miss C Wilson

12th FRIDAY—fixed up our oven out in the cook house & eat two meals of clean vitules on the ground; I rec'd a letter from Wm Owen

13th SATURDAY—rainey; I mailed a letter to my brother Frederick; I got vaxinated & was excused by the Doctor

14th SUNDAY—I was on police duty & done some writing

15th MONDAY—I done some writing & mailed a letter to Miss Wilson of Muskegon; it is <u>Pay-Day</u> in the army

16th TUESDAY—mailed a letter to brother F & one to Wm Owen; stood on guard in the A.M. & at 3 o'clock P.M., we joined the Briggade consisting of the Michigan 2nd, 3rd & Mass 1st & the New York 12th Regiments, all under [the] command of Colonel Richardson of Detroit; we crossed the Chain Bridge into Virginia at 4 P.M. and marched in the direction of Mannases Junction via Vienna, Fair Fax, Bull-Run; we reached Vienna at 8 P.M., where we joined General McDowell's Army; lay down in the open field

17th WEDNESDAY—arose & washed & took a walk and viewed the place where the Masked Battery fired on the Corps loaded with Ohio troops; we expected Battle today; at noon, we came in sight of Fair Fax & halted in a little grove to eat a bite; we expected battle to commence at one o'clock P.M. after eating a bite, we marched on & found the Secession Camps all deserted; we passed one mile to the right of Fair Fax & went through Germantown. The enemy had fled from their entrenchments only a few minutes before our arrival & the town was on fire; we halted a few moments to rest & while here a man was axcidently shot in the foot; an old Negro reported the enemy 1,500 strong— 6 P.M. we are laid down in an open field for the night; there is but little water here; what there is is muddy; the country through which we have passed so far is old & neglected.

First Blood

"Onward then our stainless banner
Let it kiss the stripe and star,
Till in weal and woe united,
They forever wedded are.
We will plant them by the river,
By the gulf, and by the strand,
Till they float, to float forever,
O'er a free, united land."

JULY 1861

18th THURSDAY—6 o'clock A.M. we are eating our scanty breakfast & unless we get provisions before night we expected to be attacted by cavalry—11 ok; we halted in a deserted camp about two miles from Bull-Run; we eat a bite here; we expect every moment to hear from the enemy—Centreville, 7 P.M. we came in sight of Bulls-Run at 12M. here our scouts came in & report the enemy just ahead & was making a stand for action. Then the order came to "Clear the Road" we did & the flying artillery went by at Rail Road speed. At 12.20 P.M., July 18th 1861, they fired three or four blank shots & was answered by the enemy in the distance. Our briggade was ordered to advance. The main army had branched off to the right back two miles at Centreville. We went ahead & heard the scouts firing sharply & we was ordered to rout the enemy.

The Massachusetts First Regt went in first & a masked battery opened on them & cut them badly & we was halted to wait for them to come around & load. Then the New York 12th went in & fired & retreated & two pieces of canon was sent in & the enemy charged on our battery & killed two horses. And with some difficulty we saved our canon & took them off the field. Our Regt was then ordered up to charge on them & while doing so, the enemy flanked us with one of their field pieces & fired two shots the whole length of our ranks. Then we was ordered to retreat. Luckily no one was seriously hurt. Some canon balls bounded & bit some of our men but broke no bones. We fell back to the top of the hill & our battery kept up a sharp cannonading untill about 4 o'clock. During this time we lay exposed to a heavy fire of shot & shell from the enemy's battery. Our boys was cool. Some spread their blankets & went to playing cards. I was sick, being nearly sun struck & hungry & tired & faint for want of water. I lay 16 feet from one of the New York 12th, when he had his face carried away by a canon ball & I set & saw many more brave fellows go to their last accounts. At 4 P.M. we fell back to Centreville for the night, having stood under a deadly fier for 8½ hours. Now I lay down on the ground to rest. I have hardly anything to eat, but rest I must have.

19th FRIDAY—We returned to the battle field in the morning & expected to have a bloody battle but we lay on our arms all day unmolested. We sent out scouts to inspect the position of the enemy. At 2 o'clock P.M. we had orders that eny man harming private property should be severely punished. Then there was a rumor that Gen'l Scott was coming with 30,000 men, but it proved to be falce. At 8 P.M. we took one stand on a wheat field (on the old battle ground), within musket shot of the enemy. We stood all night with gun in hand expecting an attact by cavalry, but no thing happened, except a few shots exchanged by the pickets.

20th SATURDAY—I eat a scanty breakfast consisting of black coffee & raw pork & hard bread. Then I lay down & took a short sleep & woke up & thought I would write a few lines to my brother Fred as I had a chance to send them direct to Washington. 8 P.M. It is a pleasant, moonlight night on the edges of the battle field. Troops are arriving from Washington. We expect an attack tonight. Rumor says that Richmond is taken. We are to try the Secessionist again tomorrow.

21st SUNDAY 5 o'clock A.M.—I suppose this will be an eventful Sabbath to me. 7 o'clock A.M. We are formed in line of battle, on the field used as a battle field [on] the 18th. We are awaiting action to commence. 7:30 A.M. We have just opened one of our batterys on the enemy. The Colonel of the NY 12th says he has not watered his horse yet this morning & he intends to water him in Bulls Run. 12 o'clock. We have kept up a sharp cannonading since 7:30. We got no answer to our fiering at this point. But at 9 this forenoon, they commenced a heavy cannonading on our right wing. General McDowell is having a hard fight there with 25,000 men. 1:15 o'clock P.M. The battle is still raging & we hear very heavy cannonading on our right. 3 o'clock P.M. The enemy has tryed twice to break in on us but a few grape shot scattered them. The canon on our right have slackened fier a little. A few men are detailed to cut down a strip of timber & throw up earth works across the road. Centreville, 6 o'clock P.M. One hour ago we retired from the field to refresh ourselves & we just stacked arms & took off our accoutrements, when we heard a heavy volley of musketry on our left & very near us. The order was immediately to "Fall-in." We just grabed our ammunition & guns & fell in as we supposed to meet the enemy (for retreat never entered no man's mind).

But instead of meeting the enemy, we were "About-Faced" and put on "Double Quick" back to Centreville, where we now are at 6 o'clock P.M. We are on a hill overlooking the country for miles around. Flying Artillery & Baggage Wagons are coming in on Double Quick time & they are falling in position to defend themselves. It is a splendid sight on our right as far as the eye can reach and can see just a living stream of men & Baggage wagons comeing off of the battle field. The skye is clear & the seting sun reflects on thousands of bayonets. There a cloud of dust shows that there is no end to the collums yet & now & then the report of a canon shows that there is men still on the battle field.

8 o'clock P.M. Now I am going to lay down. Numbers of the tired worn out soldiers come in every few moments. Among the rest are some of Elsworth's brave fier zouwaves. They look discouraged enough. I have ten dollars in gold in my pocket & I would give half of it for a quart of water & the other half for a loaf of bread. I have not eaten eny thing of eny account since I left Washington. I had nothing but hard bread & raw pork. I went without & today I have had no time to eat. & in our sudden flight, we left all behind except our gun & ammunition. I had half a cracker & a piece of raw pork gave me by a friend which tasted sweet. I have had no water to day, only what I sucked up out of a mud puddle & about a half pint that I saved with a table spoon in drops from between two rocks. How little people in this world realize their blessings of "Peace and Plenty."

11 o'clock P.M. For the last five hours, there has been a continuel rolling of wagons & artillery in the direction of Washington & for the first time we have heard that we were to retreat to Washington. Now we are to fall in & cover that retreat & guard the baggage train. I have got a hand full of green black berrys to chew for want of water. They moisten my mouth a little.

22nd MONDAY 7 o'clock A.M.—I am siting beside the road on my way to Washington. As I said last night, I lay at Centreville on the ground without eny covering except the broad heavens & the earth for a bed & nothing to eat or drink. We lay untill 11 o'clock & then commenced this Forced March for Washington. I am siting here awaiting the train to pass along. I am fatigued & worn out; still I am beter off than one third of the army. I have found a little dirty water to drink & to wash in, it being the first time for "four days" that I have enjoyed that privelage. Now it is forward march on the road to Washington. We have passed Fairfax & where we was alarmed by the cry of "Rebel Cavalry" in the rear. But they dare not atact us. Our captain had just told us if we could buy eny thing to eat in the country, we had liberty to do so. But the Colonel said shove through to Washington or we would all be captured as prisoners before night. But four of us companions left the road & went across the fields & came to a farm house & asked for something to eat.

They was poor but clever people & had lived a comfortable, easy life untill the commencement of the war, but since then all work had stoped & he was botherd to get to market; he said they had not much cooked but would give us something if we would wait a few moments. We went to a good well of water & washed & combed our hair & set down to a meal of hot hoe cake & buter & cold boiled ham & milk. We et a good meal & paid the lady of the house one dollar each & started on feeling like new men, although it rained quite hard.

We went but a short distance when we came to a halt & it raining very hard & we being wet to the skin, I concluded we had beter go in to a barn & lay down & rest & wait for the rain to slacken. We went into the barn & crawled into the straw & got warm &

steamed like a sweaty horse. We lay in that shape untill near night, when we held counsel as to what we should do. It still rained as if it never had rained before. Some was for visiting the slaves on the place & try to get some thing to eat & then sleep in the straw till the next morning. But the majority thought it unsafe to stay there over night on eny condition, as we were liable to be taken prisoners & ran off to Richmond.

As it was only five miles to Washington, we resolved if possible to get there that night. But when we got to the Long Bridge, we found that no soldiers were allowed to pass. There we were, hungry, tierd, cold & wet & no place to go to. So we saw a barn a little way off & went there where we found a part of our Regiment. They had a load of bread & I managed to buy a piece of raw ham & a cup of black coffee & made out a good super. I then got two bundles of straw & crawled under a wagon that stood under a shed. I lay there untill morning, when I waked up I found myself shaking with cold & sore & stiff as if I had grown older about 50 years.

23rd TUESDAY 8 o'clock A.M.—I have just bought some breakfast, consisting of bread, cheese & coffee & now I am laying in the sun to dry myself.

9 o'clock P.M. We have piched our tents today on Arlington Hights & I have just met my old friend George M. Van Renschler. He has just come from the Chain Bridge. Now I have seen him, I can go to sleep contented.

24th WEDNESDAY—I was awakened this morning by my friend George & I went & bought a meal of pie, cake, sausage & cheese. Stayed in camp & rested.

25th THURSDAY—I arose & took a walk & bought my breakfast & dinner & bathed in the Potomac. Supper.

26th FRIDAY—A pleasant morning. I took a walk & bathed in the Potomac. Then done some writing & bought my meals.

27th SATURDAY—Mailed a letter to my brother Frederick & one to M.E.R. & one to CW. I bought my meals to day.

28th SUNDAY—We were alarmed last night by the pickets fiering. Rested to day & bought my meals.

29th MONDAY—I done some writing & at 4 o'clock P.M., we pulled up our tents & marched in the direction of Alexandria & we piched our tents on the south side of the city of Washington & between there & Alexandria on the bank of the Potomac. It is a beautiful spot called Hunters Peace.

30th TUESDAY—The first thing I done was to clean my gun & then mailed a letter to Wm Owen & I received one from him today.

31st WEDNESDAY—I went down to the Potomac in the morning & bathed & then went out chopping 3 hours & forgot my jacket in the woods & went after it in the afternoon. I rec'd a letter from brother Henry.

———————————— August ————————————

1st THURSDAY—I stood guard & it rained hard in the morning & at noon, I parted with my dear friend George M.Van Renschler. It was hard to shake hands with him. We have been constant companions for the last ten months. he was discharged for inability.

2nd FRIDAY—came off guard & visited Colonel Hunter's grave; then done some writing & rec a leter from Mrs. F.E. Odell & one from Mary E.V. to me & one to her brother.

3rd SATURDAY—I was on police duty & I done some writing & mailed a leter to my brother Frederick.

4th SUNDAY—It was a pleasant morning & we had [a] meeting after which we were addressed by the Hon. Mr. Kelley, a Congressman.

5th MONDAY—I went to the river to bathe & picked some black berrys on the banks of the river. I rec a leter from brother Fred.

6th TUESDAY—I done three hours chopping & then mailed a leter to Mary E.V. & rec one from Schenectedy for George M. Van Renschler.

7th WEDNESDAY—I done some chopping & received a paper from Fred. I had a tooth ache.

8th THURSDAY—I mailed a leter to C.W. & at night stood on picket guard.

9th FRIDAY—Came off picket & done some writing; at night, we had a heavy shower.

10th SATURDAY—I was on police duty & done some writing.

11th SUNDAY—Had preaching by the Chaplain of the New York 21st Regiment.

12th MONDAY—I done some chopping & mailed a leter to my Sister & rec one from Mary E.V.

13th TUESDAY—I was off duty & done some writing.

14th WEDNESDAY—Done some chopping & mailed a leter to Wm Owen.

15th THURSDAY—I stood guard & rec a leter from Brother F.

16th FRIDAY—I came off guard & staid in camp & rested.

17th SATURDAY—done police duty & mailed a leter to Mary E.V.

18th SUNDAY—No labor done by the Regiment. I done some writing & reading.

19th MONDAY—We went on Battalion Drill & it rained all day.

20th TUESDAY—done some chopping & packed up & had our arms inspected. I mailed a leter to Fred & rec one from CW

21st WEDNESDAY—We pulled up our tents & marched up to join the briggade at Fort Albany on Arlington Hights.

22nd THURSDAY—I was excused by the Doctor. I done some writing.

23rd FRIDAY—I was excused by the Doctor.

24th SATURDAY—the Briggade passed in review before General McClellan & Lincoln & Seward. Rec'd a leter from Miss Ada Brigham & one from Mary E.V. & mailed one to C.W. Stood guard.

25th SUNDAY—We had rumors of an attact & we received knapsacks. I rec a leter from George M.Van Renschler. I done some writing & had a bad tooth ache.

26th MONDAY—We went on Briggade Drill & sent out some pickets to the lines at Baglies Cross Roads. I done some writing & had a bad tooth ache.

27th TUESDAY—Some of the pickets was brought in dead & wounded. At 3 o'clock P.M., news come that our pickets were being drove in, & the long roll was beat & 15 men from each company was sent out, with orders to stay untill forced in by the enemy. A fine orchard was cut today for being in the way. I rec a leter from George. I got the first tickets from [the] sutler.

28th WEDNESDAY—The long roll was beat this morning at four o'clock & we got up & eat breakfast & went to chopping down the woods so as to get a fair chance at the enemy. 11 o'clock A.M. We heard a sharp fiering of musketry & a few canon in the direction of Baylys Crossings. I mailed a leter to Ada Brigham & one to Mary E.V. I signed the Michigan pay roll.

29th THURSDAY—I stood guard & done some writing & received a leter from brother Fred & one from my Sister.

30th FRIDAY—Came off guard & we pulled up our tents & half of the Reg went up on Richardson's Hill to build a fort. This hill is about one half mile farther into Virginia.

31st SATURDAY—Stoped in camp & done some writing.

——————— September ———————

1st SUNDAY—I went chopping & we were visited by General[s] McClellan & Mansfield. The news came of the capture of Hattras Inlet. Today the tools come to build the fort with.

2nd MONDAY—was excused by the Doctor. I signed an order to get our Michigan pay. I mailed a leter to brother Fred & to George M. Van Renschler. Rec a leter from Mary E.V. I stood guard at night.

3rd TUESDAY—I had one day rest.

4th WEDNESDAY—Worked on the Fort in the forenoon & done some washing in the afternoon. And mailed a leter to E.R. & rec one from Wm Owen.

5th THURSDAY—went out to chop & it rained & we came in & rec the ballance of our State pay from Michigan.

6th FRIDAY—I got up unwell & went down to Fort Albany & bought a port folio.

7th SATURDAY—This is my birth day today. I am 21 years old. I done some writing & received a leter from C.W.

8th SUNDAY—Staid in camp & had parrade.

9th MONDAY—I help fix a box to sleep in & carried water to the hands on the Fort & mailed a leter to C.W., a paper to LW. We had a dress parrade.

10th TUESDAY—worked on the fort & had a parrade.

11th WEDNESDAY—I went chopping in the forenoon & got some fine grapes & I mailed a leter to Wm Owen.

12th THURSDAY—I went chopping & got some cucumbers & mellons & then mailed a paper to Fred & one to LW.

13th FRIDAY—I worked grubbing & we received our caps & I rec a leter from EV.

14th SATURDAY—I went chopping & grubbing.

15th SUNDAY—I stood guard.

16th MONDAY—I got my United States pay, $23.10 & went chopping.

17th TUESDAY—I went to the city of Washington & got some likenesses taken.

18th WEDNESDAY—I went to chopping & mailed a leter to my brother Henry.

19th THURSDAY—I went chopping & rec a leter from Fred & one from my old school-mate Wm Eglin.

20th FRIDAY—I went chopping & got some very fine grapes.

21st SATURDAY—moved our tents & rec a leter from George & one from CW

22nd SUNDAY—Staid in camp & rec a leter from ER.

23rd MONDAY—had a briggade drill & passed in review before General McClellan.

24th TUESDAY—I stood double guard & mailed a paper to Fred.

25th WEDNESDAY—In the forenoon, I mailed a leter to Fred with the 2nd likeness. At 3 o'clock P.M., Companys H & G went out on picket. 6 P.M. I am on post watching for "Secesh." I can hear them on Munson's Hill.

26th THURSDAY—I got up at dawn & was quite cold. I washed & eat my breakfast. I heard a good deal of fiering along the line. 8 o'clock A.M. One of our Co. G was just shot in the leg. I must go for the Doctor & ambulance. 4 o'clock P.M. I have just got in camp. I am pretty tierd.

27th FRIDAY—it rained all day.

28th SATURDAY—I piled & burned brush off the land of a new fort.

29th SUNDAY—We had orders to be ready to martch at a moments notice & we had inspection of arms and knap sacks. I done some writing.

30th MONDAY—The guards were doubled & I mailed a leter to C.W. & G.V. & Libie V.

——————————— October ———————————

1st TUESDAY—I stood guard & rec a leter from Wm Owen. I mailed a likeness to Mary E. Van Renschler.

2nd WEDNESDAY—We was in camp all day under martching orders.

3rd THURSDAY—I done police duty & some writing.

4th FRIDAY—I stood guard & mailed a leter to Mr. William W. Owen.

5th SATURDAY—I came off guard & received a leter from EV.

6th SUNDAY—I done police duty and some writing.

7th MONDAY—Staid in camp all day.

8th TUESDAY—Our Company was addressed by the Rev. Mr. Sinclair of Muskegon & a deep feeling was manifested by the company. I received a leter from brother Fred & I done some writing.

9th WEDNESDAY—we had orders to pack up & I mailed a leter to brother Fred.

10th THURSDAY—We martched from Fort Richardson to Fort Albany. I got wet by rain.

11th FRIDAY—I got up with a high fever and a severe pain in the head and had a bad cough and no apotite. I went to the Doctor and got some medicine and I was quite sick all day & night.

12th SATURDAY—We had orders to martch two miles below Alexandria. I fealt very weak and sick and went to the Orderly Sergeant and told him I was unable to martch and cary my pack. He said there were plenty just so when there was enything to be done. I asked him if he ever knew me to fail to do my duty when I was able. His answer was "No." he then told me to leave my baggage and try to get a ride in some of the wagons. But I found the wagons full. There was a two horse ambulance on purpose to cary the sick, but when I asked the driver if I could ride, he said the sutler & two clerks were going to ride with him so I started on foot. But I had to sit down every few rods to rest me as I was so weak. I went a little distance at a time and finely I came to a soldier's tent beside the road where they were guarding a cross road. I went into their tent and lay down and rested a little.

I suffered a great pain in the head & in my bones. I had a high fever. After resting about one hour, I started along a few rods at a time untill I got half a mile farther, when I began to look for a barn to stop in as I was confident that I could not hold out to get to the regiment. I found a barn and went in and lay down. And who can imagine my feelings as I lay there all alone in a Virginia barn suffering sutch pain & not a helping hand near to do enything for me. I lay for about two hours, the last hour of whitch I slept. I got up and saw the sun was fast sinking behind the hills. I thought I would go a little farther. I crawled along & at dusk I came in sight of the camp and never did it look so welcome. When I got into camp, I found that some of the tents were left behind, to come the next day, and among the rest was my tent, so I had no tent & not even a blanket to put around my shoulders. For once I fealt discouraged. I threw myself down upon the ground & lay untill a friend helped me into his tent, where I staid untill the next morning. Then I went to the Doctor.

13th SUNDAY—I went to the Doctor. He said I had Typhoid Fever. He gave me some medicine and said as soon as they got the hospital prepared, that I should come there. I had no apotite and was pretty sick all day.

The 1st Michigan returned to Detroit and was mustered out of federal service on August 7, 1861, its three months' enlistment having expired. The regiment had gallantly participated in the battle of Bull Run on July 21st, losing five killed, six wounded, thirty-two missing, and fifty-two prisoners. The unit lost four officers, including its commander, Colonel Orlando B. Willcox, who was wounded and exchanged in August 1862.

Many of the men reenlisted with other Michigan regiments, with quite a few of them accepting commissions as officers. So it was with Private, now Second Lieutenant Charles H. Salter, of Company E, 16th Michigan Infantry, who was commissioned on August 9 and reentered service on August 13, 1861.

Organized by Colonel Thomas B.W. Stockton of Flint, the regiment was known as "Stockton's Independent Regiment" until Governor Blair finally accepted it for state service and ordered it numbered "16th." The regiment left Detroit for Washington, D.C., on September 16, 1861, to join the Army of the Potomac. It went into winter camp at Hall's Hill, Virginia.

Head Quarters Stockton's Indt. Regt.
Halls Hill, VA Oct. 14th 1861

Mrs. Dr. Duffield

Esteemed Friend, I embrace the first opportunity I have had of writing letters since I left Detroit, to write a short one to you. We left in such a hurry that I had no time to even bid you good by. We arrived in Washington on the 20th Sept and went into encampment at Camp Casey on Meridian Hill about 2 miles from the center of the city. Here the regiment remained untill the 27th inst during which time we procured our muskets from the arsenal. On the 27th, Col Stockton received orders to move his regiment across the river, and in the afternoon we started but on arriving at the long bridge found that we could not cross, on account of a portion of the bridge giving way. The regiment therefore remained in camp on the grounds of the Smithsonian Institute over night, whilst the bridge was being repaired and started again at 5 the next morning. Crossing the Potomac, we passed the camp of the 2nd and 3rd Michigan regiments and continued up the river, untill we arrived at Fort Cocoran opposite Georgetown, where we pitched our tents and remained for four days, when we moved out to our present camp which is about 7 miles distant from Washington and on ground which was occupied by the rebels previous to the taking of Munson's Hill by the Union forces.

Since we have been here, we have been very busy in Drilling, Chopping down trees, being out on Picket Guard, &c. We are about 2 miles distant from Munson's Hill and 4 miles from Falls Church. The 4th Mich regt are encamped close by us. On the 9th inst. Captain Barry and myself were sent out with a party of 70 men to fell trees for the purposes of clearing a range for artillery on a hill near Falls Church. Arriving on the hill, we saw a large body of the rebels about ½ mile distant. We sent a messenger back to our brigade and in a short time Gen Butterfield came out with 2500 men and 3 cannon which caused the rebels to beat an immediate retreat without giving us a chance to give them battle.

The health of the regiment is generally very good, but few of them having been sick since we have been here. Rev. Mr. Brockway is our Chaplain and Postmaster. Every Sabbath morn we have church in a grove close by our camp and prayer meeting in the evening. Yesterday I was officer of our guard and in such a case I am kept busy all day. Therefore, it did not seem much like a Sunday to me or the men on guard with me. Those towels which you were so kind as to send to our company, they find to be very useful indeed, now that we are so far from home and I assure you we are truly grateful for them.

I presume that Col. Duffield's regiment is about ready to come on here by this time. I should like to hear from Henry and to know if he intends to come with it. I should like to see him if the regiment comes here. Please give him my respects and tell him to write if he has time. I had my photograph taken a few days ago and sent you one of them, for Henry. It is taken as I appear about camp, though not a very good one as it was taken in a hurry.

Senator Wilson's Massachusetts regiment arrived here today and are encamped near us. They are a fine looking set of men. We are looking anxiously to hear of some favorable news from Missouri and hope that the next battle that takes place there will result more favorably than that at which Col. Mulligan and his brigade were taken prisoner.

I should be pleased to hear from you at any time you could make it convenient to write. Please give my respects to Dr. Duffield. The direction of letters, &c use: Lieut C.H. Salter, Stocktons Indt Regt Mich Infantry, Washington, D.C.

> Yours Respectfully,
> C.H. Salter

14th MONDAY—I laid in my tent with a high fever & great suffering. I rec a leter from Wm Elgin but was to sick to read it. At night a friend [came] wit a cloth and put [it] on my head.

15th TUESDAY—I was carried to the hospital quite sick.

16th WEDNESDAY—I lay with a high fever all day. I thought of home & dear friends and thought if I only had a Sister to bathe my aching brow, I would be happy.

17th THURSDAY—I am fast loosing my strength.

18th FRIDAY—sick & weak.

19th SATURDAY—Still very sick. My old friend Lavelle [James] has been to see me and to bring me my mail.

———————— November ————————

2nd SATURDAY—I began to get some better.

3rd SUNDAY—No pain but very weak. I have good care.

4th MONDAY—Feel easy. Done some writing.

5th TUESDAY—My Captain's wife has been to see me & gave me some chicken broth.

6th WEDNESDAY—Feel quite easy.

7th THURSDAY—I got up and walked to the door and back to my bed. My friend came to see me and asked me to let him write for me.

8th FRIDAY—Set up a good deal and feel quite strong.

9th SATURDAY—Walked out side the door & began to have an apotite.

10th SUNDAY—I went over to the Captain's tent and eat some chicken soup.

23rd SATURDAY—Left the hospital and returned to my tent.

24th SUNDAY—Staid in my tent.

25th MONDAY—Done half duty, sweeping & cleaning.

26th TUESDAY—Went down to Mount Vernon and got caught in the rain.

27th WEDNESDAY—I stood guard and had a shake of the fever & ague from getting wet.

28th THURSDAY—Had a heavy shake of the ague.

  I had the ague every day for a number of days.

Camp Leslie Hall's Hill, Va Nov 1861

Dear Friend,

Your kind letter of the 4th inst. just came duly to hand, and I was truly glad to hear from one who has taken such an interest in the welfare of such a poor wanderer as myself, for such I must consider myself since this war has broken out, and also I was very glad to receive a letter from home as I have received but very few from Detroit since last leaving.

Our regiment is still encamped at the same place it was when I last wrote you. We are as busy as we can be in drilling every day, and have got to be quite proficient in all the manouvres of company and battalion drill. The NY 50th Regt., which was attached to our brigade has been sent to the Navy Yard at Washington as they were a regt of mechanics and the government can make better use of them there than here. The People's Ellsworth regiment from NY state also has been sent to supply their place. This is a regt composed of picked men taken from every township in the state and number 1200 men, but probably they are also called the Ellsworth Avengers.

We had another review of our division by Genl McClellan and staff on the 9th of this month. It rained quite hard that day, but the review passed off the same as if it had been fair weather, though to be sure it was not quite as pleasant for us. As the General entered the field, the artillery saluted him and three times three cheers from the whole division greeted him. In fact, he is very popular with all the troops here and they all received the news of his promotion to the command of the army with great enthusiasm.

We have a great deal of rain here during the last few weeks but the weather has been quite mild so far. There is a good deal of sickness in our regiment, more I think than in any other regiment in our division, and no less than thirteen of our men have died since crossing the Potomac. Last Sunday, we buried a young man named Wellington, of Capt. Fisher's Saginaw Co. He had a brother die in the hospital at Georgetown only a few days before this and today another man belonging to the St. John Company was buried. They were none of them sick but a short time. Fever and the measles appear to be the principle complaints amongst the sick. I have not lost any in my own company, however, and hope we shall not lose any by disease at least.

Capt. Martin and his company arrived here yesterday from Detroit. They are rather a small company, numbering only 43 men, but then every little helps. I have not been able to visit the 5th Mich regt as yet, as they are encamped near Fort Lyon at Alexandria, with the 2d & 3d Mich regts and that is 9 miles distant from our camp and I cannot spare time to go down there. We are rather anticipating a forward movement to be made by our side in a few days. As this great naval expedition will probably draw off quite a number of the rebel troops from this state to defend the more southern states and, in that case, we shall certainly close down upon them from this side, so that the rebels in this state, at the present time, do not know which way to turn, being between the two fires.

I am very glad to hear that the Ladies of Detroit have established a soldier's aid society. We had an account of the meeting held by the society in the Woodward Ave. M.E.

Church on the 2d inst. and have no doubt but that it will accomplish much good under the efficient management of the ladies at the head of the movement. The society is certainly something that has been needed for some time. Our regiment is very well provided with about everything they need with the exception of towels.

I am very glad to hear that friend Henry has succeeded in getting such a good position as Adjutant in the 9th Mich regiment, for I assure you it is a much pleasanter place to be in than to be a company officer with not anything near as hard work to perform. From all that I can hear we shall probably see some stirring times in Kentucky before long. I saw by the accounts in the papers from Detroit that Col. Duffield left with his full number of men. In this he was more fortunate than Col. Stockton, as we have only 800 men and quite a number of them should be discharged, as they are not fit for duty and the best that could be done for them would be to send them home.

By the way, some of the regiments from our division are to be sent on the next naval expedition. Probably the next time will be the Mich 4th and our own. There is to be a grand review of all the troops in this section of the country, where there will be about 40,000 appear in one large field, one manouvre. We pass through all these reviews partially prepares the men for actual service. It is this; we advance in line of battle and at a given signal, the men all lie down and the artillery come up and fire directly over our heads. This is done in order that if the enemy either cavalry or infantry attempt to charge upon and take the cannon, we can rise up and protect them or charge upon the enemy if necessary.

We have raised $150 by subscription in our regiment for the purpose of buying a large tent for a chapel and we will have it in a very few days. This will be a great inducement for the whole regiment to attend divine service, as heretofore we have been obliged to hold our meetings in the open air, and when the weather is cold, that is rather unpleasant for us, and sometimes it rains on the Sabbath, in which case the service had heretofore been dispensed with. But now the weather will not make much difference with us. Genl McClellan has issued an order giving permission to any regiment that chose to buy a chapel tent to have transportation furnished them whenever they move, which is, I think, very considerate in him. By the way, I have noticed that the bad habit of swearing had become quite common in the army, or at least it is growing very fast in this portion of it. Our Chaplain and most of the officers are doing as much as they can to put a stop to it. And Genl McClellan has issued an order to prohibit the practice, which order is published and a copy given to each soldier.

As my sheet is nearly full, I shall have to close now. Please give my respects to Dr. Duffield and any other enquiring friends. I shall be very glad to hear from you whenever you can spare time to write.

> Yours Respectfully,
> Charles H. Salter
> direct letter same as last.

————————— December —————————

10th TUESDAY—We martched out to the picket line and piched our camp & the Old General (Richardson) called for volunteers to scour the country in front. I went out and had a hard tramp. Came in later hungry and tierd.

11th WEDNESDAY—Orders to fall back. We came back two miles and camped. We had been out too far. I had the ague.

12th THURSDAY—I had the ague bad.

13th FRIDAY—I fealt very bad. Weak and sick.

14th SATURDAY—Wrote a leter. The dipthera apeard in my throat. The Doctor sent to Alexandria for medicine.

Had dipthera 7 days. 5 days only could swallow a little milk. Burned the canker with caustick and swabbed out my throat every hour. I done picket & camp duty all winter. We had skirmishing and reconitiring up to the 14th of March.

Head Quarters Stockton's Indt. Regt Mich. Inf.
Camp Leslie Halls Hill Va. Dec. 1861

Rev. Mrs. J.G. Duffield Detroit, Michigan
Dear Madam,

Your kind and motherly letter of the 4th inst. is at hand and I am truly much indebted to you for taking so much trouble as to write to me whilst you are so busy. Also, I am much pleased to hear of the promotion of your two worthy sons and only wish that Col. Duffield will be made an actual Brigadier General, as I know that he is better able to fill the position than a goodly number of others that hold it. It must have been a very careless sentinel that fired at Henry, especially as it was right at the camp of a regiment.

It was alltogether a mistatement about my being sick as I have not been the least unwell since last leaving home. You speak of having cold weather in Detroit, but at the same time we were having weather here as warm as it is in Michigan in September and it certainly is much pleasanter than a person would suppose it would be at this time of the year here but the last two days we have had a cold north wind which is the first intimation we have had of the coming of winter. The statement in the papers that our regiment is under orders to march to S. Carolina is entirely untrue and without the least foundation in fact. It was got up by the Lieut there recruiting for the purpose of getting recruits. I think it a perfect sham that anyone connected with this regiment should put such statements in the papers, and the whole regiment feels very indignant that he should have done so, as it must cause considerable anxiety on the part of the friends and relatives of all, both officers and men of the regt.

We have had on an average from 150 to 200 sick in our regiment since we have been here which is not near as many as your son has in his regiment, but still is a good many more than we like to have. It is so in about every regiment in the army, and this naturally largely decreases the number of men in the army that can be of service. However, there is fewer sick in our regiment now than there has been for two months past.

Since last writing to you we have had nothing unusual occur here. On the 20th Nov we had a grand review of 90 regiments, near Munson's Hill, by the President and Genl McClellan, which I presume you have heard of through the papers. It was undoubtedly the largest review that has ever taken place in this country. Thanksgiving day passed off in our camp without any difference from any other day, but otherwise we would not have known that it was Thanksgiving.

On Dec 1st we had a general inspection of our brigade. Our regiment was inspected by Col. Lansing and Adjutant Taylor of the NY 17th regiment, and they pronounced my company the A no1 of the regiment in regard to the soldierly appearance of the men, the cleanliness of their clothes, the brightness of their arms and accoutrements, the arrangement of their tents, as also the cooking for the company. The Colonel passed by our company cook room just as the men were eating dinner. He tasted their soup and pronounced it as good as could be obtained at any hotel in New York and better than he had at his own table. We have, in fact, a first rate cook for the company. Co. A., Capt Barry, stood next on the list, at the monthly inspection previous. Co. A had stood first and our Co. second, so that I was highly pleased with the result of the last inspection, seeing the captain was away and I had command of the company at the time.

On the 8th inst (last Sunday), seven companies of our regiment were ordered out on picket duty. The day was as warm as it is in summer in Michigan and we started at early dawn. The morning was quite foggy, but the sun rose clear and bright and as we were passing over the hills we had some splendid views. The fog below us in the valleys would make them look like so many rivers, and the country is nothing but hill and dale in this vicinity. We marched out eight miles and then halted at Barratts Hill, so called from the gentleman that lives on it in a splendid farm house. We there separated in four parties and established a line of pickets about three miles long. The party I went out with comprised Capt. Meyers, myself and two other lieutenants and 160 men. We had a line about one mile long to guard. We established our head quarters at the house of a captain in the rebel army named Ashford, who had been justice of the peace but had fled to a warmer climate on the morning after the taking of Munson's Hill by the Union forces and since then he has raised a company and joined the secessionists. We found the house pretty well furnished and in charge of some darkies he had left behind. We established our office in the parlour and, dividing our men into four reliefs of 40 men each, who were to take turns in standing 2 hours at a time, each officer took charge of a relief and then settled ourselves as comfortable as could be in the secesh captain's house.

We boarded at Mrs. Barrett's house about ½ mile from our station. Whilst there, and as the people of that house are good Union people, we fared better and had everything more like home than we had seen since leaving Detroit. We had also another house to guard or rather to guard the inmates thereof, which consisted of a man and three ladies who were addicted to the bad habit of sending information of the movements of the Union forces whenever they could get a chance. We had sentinels stationed around their house and none of the people were allowed to leave the house unless accompanied by one of the guards, and no one allowed to approach or speak to them without being watched or heard by the guards. Whilst there, we had no sign or appearance of the enemy at all, but as two surveyors came towards our lines, the sentinel at one of the posts gave him the signal by which we challenge everybody whilst out on picket, but although the surveyors were in the employ of the U.S. government and had a pass signed by Maj. Genl. Porter, they did not understand the signal, and the sentinel fired at them but not hitting them. They took refuge behind a large tree and called lustily for the officer of the guard. When I came out and, finding who they were, admitted them. We remained out there untill Tuesday afternoon, when we were relieved by a force from another regiment and returned to camp. But whilst we were out there the change from the monotony of camp life to picket duty was so sensibly felt by all, that we would liked to have remained a week.

Our colonel is at present absent in Washington, being engaged in the court martial of Col. Kerrigan of the NY 26th regt., who is accused of being a traitor, and also of disobeying his superior officer General Martindale. So that in his absence, we do not drill much and have quite easy times.

But as I must have fatigued you by this time with my long letter, I will bring it to a close. Please give my respects to Dr. Duffield and any other enquiring friends, and write whenever convenient and I shall write to you as often as I have anything interesting to write about.

> Believe me
> Yours most respectfully,
> Lieut. C.H. Salter
> Co. E, Stockton's Indt. Mich. Infty.
> Washington DC

3

Winter Quarters

"Let the flag of our country be flung to sky;
Our arm shall be bared for the glorious fight,
As freemen we'll live, or like freemen we'll die!
Our Union and Liberty! God and the right!"

Camp Porter
Hall's Hill, Va.
Jan. 14th 1862

Rev. Mrs. Duffield. Detroit
My Dear Friend

Your kind note of the 5th inst. came duly to hand and I assure you I was very glad to receive such an interesting letter from home and also to hear from friend Henry once more since I last wrote you.

We have had very pleasant weather here, with the exception of a day or two occasionally when the weather would become suddenly cold or windy. On the 21st Dec. we had another grand review of our division by Genl. McClellan. The day was quite cold and it was then that Genl. McClellan took a severe cold and was quite sick for about two weeks, but I presume you have seen accounts of this in the papers. On the 23rd we had a great storm and gale here. My company was on camp guard that day and I took a severe cold and sore throat, by reason of exposure to the weather and have not been able to get over it yet, however, I have attended all drills &c, the same as usual.

Christmas Day passed off very quietly here in camp. Our chaplain was yet in Michigan at that time, so we amused ourselves as best we could. The men had a mock fancy dress parade in the afternoon, electing officers of their own, and conducting the parade in the manner best calculated to ridicule the usual form of the regular dress parades. New Years eve we, the 83rd Penn. Regt. (in our brigade), gave a grand supper to all the officers of our brigade and it was one of the most beautiful sights I think I ever have seen. They had several large tents joined together and trimmed up very neatly with evergreens, flags, Chinese lanterns, &c. Chandeliers trimmed with bright bayonets, which gave them a novel and unique effect. The supper was got up by C. Gautier, the most celebrated caterer in Washington and take it altogether the supper was a complete success.

On the 7th, our regiment went out 7 miles from camp on picket guard and remained three days. Whilst there, Gens. McCall, & Smith went out with 22,000 men on a reconnaissance towards Drainsville and returned without meeting the enemy, but succeeded in procuring a large quantity of forage, provisions, &c. We are now in daily expectation of having to move. We have made every preparation for it. All extra baggage has been sent to Washington to be stored. I sent my trunk last Saturday. All the quartermasters' stores have also been sent away. It is the intention to leave our tents standing as they are, ready for some other troops to occupy. What our destination is we do not as yet know. Perhaps it may be we are to be sent on some naval expedition or we may go on the advance by land, but it is certain we shall move in some direction.

You spoke about my men purchasing a library. I should be much pleased if we had one in our company, but we cannot do anything with it untill we get moved and settled, wherever we may have to go. I think that in a few days you will hear of something important from this portion of the army as three divisions of the army here, viz, Porter's, Franklin's & McCall's have received the same orders to prepare to move. Perhaps the situation may be to have us follow up Burnsides expedition as soon as it reaches its destination, but wherever we may go, Porter's division will give a good account of itself.

I see by the papers that the great Mississippi expedition has finally got under way. I sincerely hope that they will push their way straight to New Orleans. I see also that it is anticipated Gen. Buell's command will shortly advance. I see no reason now, why they should not clear Kentucky entirely of rebels in the course of a few days.

Last night we had quite a snow storm here. The snow is about 4 inches deep and continues falling fast. It is very unpleasant for us, situated as we are in canvas tents, but we have to grin and bear it, in hopes that we may be sent so far south in a few days that we shall not be exposed to the extreme cold after that. It seems to me that the southern army within a few miles of us must suffer exceedingly in this weather as they are said to be quite destitute of clothing and cannot bear the cold as well as we northerners can anyway.

But I must close now, not having any more news to write. Please give my respects to Dr. Duffield and Mrs. Stewart. Also please remember me to your son Henry, next letter you write him. If we move, I will, if possible, write you as soon as we reach our destination.

Yours Truly and Respectfully,
C.H. Salter

BALLOONING IN THE SIGNAL SERVICE AND FOR RECONNOITERING
(THE PICTORIAL BATTLES OF THE CIVIL WAR, NEW YORK, 1895)

——————————— March 1862 ———————————

14th FRIDAY—Broke up our camp and moved to Alexandria and lay near Fort Lyons. We had to await shiping. It rained and we had nothing but shelter tents to sleep in and the water run all over the ground. I went back to the old camp and built a fier in the old shanty and slept untill next morning.

15th SATURDAY—We saw plenty of vessells in the Potomac River and we still waited.

16th SUNDAY—We moved out of the mud.

17th MONDAY—Went on board of the John Brooks; lay out in the stream.

18th TUESDAY—Sailed down the Potomac.

19th WEDNESDAY—Came to Fortress Monroe. I saw and had a good view of the Monitor lying in the harbor.

20th THURSDAY—Came ashore and encamped near the ruins of the once beautiful village of Hampton. I went and saw the residents of President Tyler & a splendid house owned by a Secesh Colonel. Our boys got some oysters from the bay.

From this time, 20th of March to the 4th of April, we lay doing camp duty & we could plainly see the Rebels over on New Port News. We were quite busy unloading Armey stores from the boats.

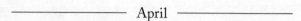

April

4th FRIDAY—Took up our line of march for York Town. Encamped over night near Big Bethel. I saw a lot of old Rebel papers and talked of war with a lady that lived in a house near where we camped.

5th SATURDAY—Marched on slowly towards York Town. It rained some & General McClellan passed us with a private's over coat on, but the men knew him and cherrd him loudly. We had a quick march and heard heavy canonading & as we neared the scene of action, I heard musketry. I supposed we were to take part in it but found we were to late for enything except a good shelling. We were close to the Rebel works and at sundown Leow went up in his baloon and the Rebels threw shells at it.

6th SUNDAY—The baloon went up today. I went over to it and saw General Porter go up and come down. He said he could see every thing. Our rations are short today & the men have killed some cattle running here. But it is poor meat, it tastes of leaks.

7th MONDAY—It rains today & it is a cold, bad day & we have to move our tents to get out of the mud.

8th TUESDAY—We are encamped around among little ponds of water. Today I have gathered some pine boughs and peeled some elm bark for a floor in my little tent. My little tent is not quite long enough to lay in with not exposing either my head or feet.

9th WEDNESDAY—It still rains and every thing is very wet. There is some guns either large or small going all the time. The roads is so bad that the trains can hardly get through, and today we only got two crackers each.

10th THURSDAY—I am wet and have been for the last three days. I have neither been dry or warm for the last three days. I have stood and shiverd day times & lay and shiverd nights for the whole three days, and yesterday and today we only received two crackers per day. That is what I call pretty short rations. There is signs of good weather again. I hope so as we are to go on picket tonight.

11th FRIDAY—On picket guard & we saw the Rebels busy repairing their Forts and could plainly see the Three Bared Flag of Secession. We have one canon fiering every fifteen minutes, day & night. We came off picket duty tonight.

12th SATURDAY—We were called out three times last night and had to sleep with our belts on. The Rebels tryed to take our fifteen minute gun but failed.

13th SUNDAY—Once more we have a clear day. Evening I went out today to see what I could find to eat. I was very hungry and saw a Negroe cooking something in a kettle for an officer. Now, as the officers had the privlage of buying meat at the Quartermasters & we had not, I concluded to examine the contents of the kettle. So when the Negroe went in the tent, I took the kettle up to our tent & found it to contain a beef's hart, which I finished cooking and eat.

APRIL—From this date to the 4th of May, we were hard at work building works to siege York Town. We worked a great deal nights & we had some very bad weather.

Camp of Stockton's Ind. Mich. Regt.
Near Yorktown, Va. April 21st 1862

My Dear Friend

Your kind letter of March 28th was duly handed over by Lieut. Partridge on the 16th inst. and I can assure you I was very glad to hear from you once more, particularly as I have received but very few letters from Detroit lately.

The past six weeks have been full of important events, to our own as well as other portions of the army. We marched from Hall's Hill on the 10th to Fairfax Court House and remained there untill the 15th, when we marched back to Alexandria, and on the 22nd, our division embarked on transports and arrives at Fort Monroe on the evening of the 23rd. We landed and marching through Hampton village, or rather the ruins of it, we pitched our camp about 4 miles west of Fort Monroe. On the 27th, our brigade was sent out on a reconnaissance as far as Big Bethel, and we entered the rebel fortification there without meeting any opposition. This is the same place, you will recollect where, some of our troops under Gen. Pierce were defeated with such a heavy loss of life last fall. After examining the country about there and finding that the rebel pickets were three miles beyond, we returned to camp after a march of twenty miles that day. On the 4th April, our division as well as all of the army here under Gen. McClellan, marched at daybreak and, next day by noon, found ourselves only one mile from the rebel forts around Yorktown and immediately our artillery opened a brisk fire upon them and kept up the game of ball with them untill darkness put a stop to it at night.

Our brigade has ever since then remained encamped about ¼ miles from the rebel forts, and as a necessary consequence, we have brisk skirmishes with them every day. Our picket line is only ½ mile from one of their forts and the riflemen of the rebels kept up a constant firing with our men all the while. Our regiment was out there for 24 hours last Tuesday and whilst we were there some of the riflemen of the rebels were concealed in rifle pits about 400 yards from our line, and our pickets were concealed near the edge of a wood. They kept up a brisk firing every time any of either party showed themselves in sight, and two of the rebels were shot, whilst none of us were hit at all. The rebel fortifications here are eight miles in extent and extend in the form of a horseshoe from the Ojook River across the Peninsula to the James River. They have been at work upon them almost ever since the war broke out, and it is said that their entrenchments here are the strongest they have and that we will have a hard task to take them. The rebels have 500 pieces of cannon and over 100,000 men here, and are sending in more men every day. Their men here are the best drilled that they have, being the entire force that has composed the rebel Army of the Potomac and have already been in the service about a year.

Gen. McClellan is putting forward every endeavor to get heavy siege guns here and have them put up, so as to open upon the rebels as soon as possible and we have an army of nearly 150,000 men here that are already camped right in front of the rebel entrenchments and keep the rebels cooped up inside of their works. We shall soon have 200 siege guns here and mounted in position and besides a larger number of field artillery, and when all these are roaring together, we shall have quite a lively time of it, I suppose. There is also several gunboats on the river holding themselves in readiness to assist us.

We have been busy most of the time building bridges, breastworks, &c. There is a creek lying between us and the rebel forts at this point. Across this creek we have thrown a large number of bridges, of all kinds, pontoon, floating and solid bridges, so that a large number of troops can cross it at one time. The 15th and 50th NY Regts., both engineer corps, have been busy making buckets to be used for bastions in the entrenchments.

Last Friday night, the 18th, Capt. Woods of Co. E [C], 4th Mich., was killed whilst on picket guard. It appears he was going the rounds of the line and getting outside of the line. One of the sentinels, supposing him to be one of the enemy, fired upon him, killing him instantly. The Capt. had just returned from Michigan, where he had been absent on a furlough on account of his health. It is very dangerous business to be on picket here, as the lines keep up a constant firing night and day and every detachment that is sent out takes surgeons and ambulances with it.

But I must close now. I have but very little time to write. Please excuse poor writing as I have no fit place to write in. please give my respects to Dr. Duffield and any enquiring friends. Direct all letters to Washington, DC, the same as formerly and believe me,

> Most Respectfully Your
> Humble Servant
> Charles H. Salter

——————— May ———————

4th SUNDAY—I set [to] writing a leter to my Brother. I was surprised to hear drums and bands playing. It was something that had not been allowed before while there. Soon the news came that the Rebels had evacuated their works. We had orders to fill our haversacks and be ready to martch at a moments notice.

1 o'clock P.M. We left our camp & saw every thing rushing along—Artillery, Cavilry, Baggage Wagons & Infantry, all hurrying after the flying armey. We passed the Rebel's Forts at 5 o'clock P.M.; saw a large burying ground & read quite a number of names of Rebel soldiers. I saw a number of dead horses and some men that had been blown up by torpedoes burryd by the Rebels & I saw some sticks with a red cloth on to mark where the torpedoes were. & at dark, we made some fier and encamped about two miles from York Town.

5th MONDAY—Early in the morning, we were awakened and called out and it was raining very hard. We found our blankets wet and no fier yet. We had to pack up every thing. Our little shelter tents were wet and heavy. But we could dry them. We had orders to fall in and I saw some cavalry going back with some prisoners. We were soon on the march, the mud growing deeper at every step. We could hear the booming of canon at Williamsburg & our Major rode along and said we would have to make a forced march & he hoped we would all do our best for there might be a great deal depending on our movements that day.

We quickened our pace and soon we were rushing along, passing Baggage wagons, Artillery, Ambulances &c I saw Artillery sunk in the mud nearly to the hubb on. On we rushed, passing every thing, and the rain still pouring down as if it had not rained for six months. about two o'clock P.M. we came to a halt and unslung knapsacks and piled them up in heaps and we primed our guns. Then Forward was the order. On we went at double quick. We could plainly hear the clash of battle, booming of canon, bursting of shells and the rattle of musketry. We passed a rifle pit, then we met Captain Mott of "Mott's Battery" with General Heintzleman, he said he wanted our regiment to support his battery as we had done on the first Bull Run battle field. Heintzleman said to our band, "Strike Up," give them "Hail Columbia" or "Yankee Doodle" or something quick. Here we turned to the left of the road into a wheat field & went around untill we met a column of Rebels coming around to flank our armey. Then fighting on the road in the woods. Our battery was not long getting into position. Then the 3rd & 4th Maine came to our support & the Rebels fell back to their works.

Then we were ordered to join our briggade then fighting very hard on the road in the wood. We came in and found them charging back and forth over a rifle pit. The Rebels saw us and heard us cheer our reinforcements and they began to give way. We only had a chance to fier three rounds & dark put an end to that struggle. O, who can picture that night. No one can form eny idea, without seeing. There we stood, the rain pouring down & wet, cold, tierd & hungry, all covered with mud. Standing there in the mud, dark as tar & all around lay the dead and dieing. We stood waiting orders and all was still, save the groans of the wounded.*

Soon came orders to march back to our knapsacks. I could scarcely stand but had to stager back through mud ancle deep every step. We got back and I threw myself down on the ground and slept.

6th TUESDAY—I awoke early and was shaking with cold. I made a little black coffee and eat a couple of hard crackers. I fealt sore & stiff and we fell in the ranks & marched along towards the battle field. We soon met an officer who told us that the Rebels had fled. Soon we came to the ground that had been so hotly contested. There lay the Dead, all covered with mud, some lieing right in the road & the artillery & cavalry were treading almost on them. Most of the dead lay just as they fell, some with the wild look of excitement still in their countenance.

We halted there a short time and looked for wounded men in the brush. Then we passed along inside of their works and encamped on a little green field. We found all of the buildings filled with the wounded Rebels, & talked with a number of them and they seem sick of secession. I found a number of rebel knap sacks and found a great many interesting leters. I dried my blankets and cooked some ration.

7th WEDNESDAY—I got up & found myself sore & we cleaned up our guns & went with a train of wagons to get corn from a mill but found the mill burned. I then went with my friends to a family in the village of Williamsburg. We went to see if we could get some dinner. We entered a fine looking house near the large and beautiful lunatic asylum. The house was occupied by an old lady and her daughter and her niece. They said they would get us some dinner. While sitting there, the daughter stood by the window looking at the Union flag flying on the asylum. She remarked that it was a larger flag than waved there the day before. I added, yes, and a better one. She said she did not know as to that, but she hoped so. The old lady began crying. I asked her what was the trouble. She looked out at our passing armey and said Oh, our (Rebel) Armey will have so much blood to spill. She then said her husband & two sons were in the Rebel Armey. We got a diner of warm buiscuit and honey and tea and peach sauce and cold boiled ham.

8th THURSDAY—Lay in camp all day and when night came, got a leter from home.

9th FRIDAY—Marched at noon & halted and eat a hard tack at the village. Then in the afternoon, we marched very fast and untill late in the evening.

10th SATURDAY—Got up early and our Captain had the Company "fall in" and he pronounced my friend Levelle & my self Corporels. But I declined the office. We marched that day and encamped near a fine spring of water. I was very sore and tierd. I done some washing.

11th SUNDAY—I was doing some writing and we lay still all day.

---

*The Battle of Williamsburg, Virginia, fought on May 4–5, 1862, began as Confederate General Magruder started the withdrawal from Yorktown, prompting Union General Hooker to attack.

12th MONDAY—We lay still all day and the Rush Lancers passed us.

13th TUESDAY—We marched at 11 A.M. Was all day going two miles and encamped on the dirtiest place in a long time.

14th WEDNESDAY—We began cooking rations & we had orders to march. It rained and we camped five miles from Kent Court House. I rec a leter from Ada F. Brigham and we had to stand picket in the rain and we brought some cherries at 50 cents pound.

15th THURSDAY—We were turned out early and it rained and we had to pack up wet blankets. We marched all day in the rain & I allmost got asleep walking. We marched to Cumberland Landing and bought some mouldy soft bread for 25cts a loaf. Saw an old friend, Thomas Van Valkenburg.

16th FRIDAY—Got early breakfast. Went down to the Landing. I saw a good many boats. Got a pint of sugar and paid half dollar for it. I rec a leter from M.W.

17th SATURDAY—Got up, done some writing and went down to the Landing and had inspection.

18th SUNDAY—Done some washing and writing And had inspection.

19th MONDAY—We had early roll call. Orders to be ready to march at 7 o'clock. We marched at 8 o'clock, on the back track and at night we camped a half mile back. It rained all day.

20th TUESDAY—Was turned out early with orders to be ready to march at 4. But did not march till 5 o'clock. We encamped in a nice field where [there] was a fine spring and they call the place Baltimore Cross Roads.

21st WEDNESDAY—Stoped in camp all day and had a dress parrade. Had orders not to write leters to our friends that would give information to the enemy. I done some washing.

This is the last diary entry for George Vanderpool. Although he would take an active role in the 3rd's campaigns up through the bloody battle of Fredericksburg, he did not keep up with his diary. After suffering through typhoid fever and diphtheria, George was discharged for disability (inability) at Alexandria, Virginia, in February 1863.

Camp of Gen. Morell's Division
Near New Bridge, Va. June 17th 1862

My Dear Friend

Your kind letter of the 11th came to hand on the 15th and I was very glad to hear from you, and also to hear from my friend Henry. I ought to have wrote you a letter long before this. However, I have been so busy since we left Yorktown and have had such little accommodations for writing purposes, that I have unintentionally neglected it untill the present occasion.

Our division embarked from Yorktown on steamers May 8th and proceeded up the river to West Point, landing on the south side of the York River, at the mouth of the Pamunkey, and in consequence of taking this route, we missed the battle of Williamsburg. General Franklin's division had preceded us one day, and upon landing, had met a large body of the rebels, and had quite a sharp little battle with them. However, there were no signs of the rebels about upon our landing there. We remained camped there untill our wagons came up and then on the 13th May, commenced our "Onward to Richmond" march. The roads were in very bad condition and we made very slow progress. However, we arrived at our present camp on May 22nd, having marched only 45 miles in 9 days. We then found ourselves at New Bridge, on the Chickahominy River and only 7 miles distant from the rebel capitol. Upon our arrival here, our former commander of the division was promoted to the command of a corps de armee, which consists of General Franklin's division, a division of regulars under command of Gen. Sykes and our own. This corps forms the right wing of the army before Richmond. We were all sorry to have Gen. Porter leave the division, still we were glad he was promoted. Gen. Morell, who formerly had command of the 1st Brigade, now commands the division.

On the morning of the 28th, our division was called out at 5 A.M. and received orders to march immediately. We did not know where we were to go, but supposed our destination to be Richmond, but on starting, we took a northwestern direction and soon made up our minds that some particular business had been laid out for our division to do. The rain poured down all the morning untill about 10 o'clock and the roads were very bad to march over, and then when the rain ceased, the sun came out very warm and it was actually worse for us than the rain, but we knew we were going to meet the enemy and everyone done the best they could to keep up with their regiments and a good many even threw away their coats to lighten their load. About 1 P.M. we had arrived within 5 miles of Hanover Court House, when suddenly the roar of artillery and musketry burst upon our ears, announcing that the right of the division had already met the enemy and were engaged with them. Our regiment was in the rear of the division, therefore, we were the last to get to the scene of conflict. We were going through a wood and upon nearing the battlefield, we came out into a large open space where we had a full view of the battle.

We saw Benson's battery engaged with a rebel battery right in front of us and Gen. Martindale's and our own brigades engaged in fierce conflict with two brigades of rebel infantry. As we came on the field we were exposed to the full fire of the rebel battery. However, we marched steadily on and took the position which our Gen. Butterfield assigned to us. We were then ordered to charge through a piece of wood there and then come out in the field again upon the right of the rebels. We did so and when we came out in the field again we found our troops had already put the rebels to flight and captured one of their cannon. We joined in the pursuit, arriving near Hanover Court House. The rebels faced about and seemed determined to make another stand. However, a few well directed shots from our battery and the appearance of our long line of infantry, charging upon them seemed too much for them and they broke and run three times, not to rally again, and then the regt. of lancers with us charged upon them, scattering the rebels like a flock of sheep and taking a good many prisoners.

Our regiment was then ordered over to the railway station to hold possession of the place. We found there a train of cars loaded with tents, provisions, &c., belonging to the rebel government. We had been there but a few minutes, however, when we heard firing in the rear of us. It seems another force of the rebels, about 20,000 of them, had been sent up by rail from Richmond to assist the other force that had been in possession of the place, and these attacked us in the rear, thinking perhaps to surprise us, but our general had left the KY 44th and 2nd Regts. there to guard against any such movement and these two regiments nobly stood their ground untill others came to their assistance. Griffin's famous battery hurried back to the rear and opened a terrific fire upon the rebels, mowing down large numbers of the rebels at every discharge. The infantry also done very well. The two regts. first left there were soon joined by the 14th NY, the 9th Mass., the Duryea Fire Zouaves and others, who charged upon them and, after a fierce conflict of about two hours, drove the enemy from the field.

In the meantime, when the firing of the second engagement first commenced, the Penn. 83rd and our own regiment were taken across the railway and to the right of the rebels, Gen. Butterfield leading us himself. In joining there, we had a swamp to go through, which delayed us considerable. We then got over that and into a wood, where we found the 9th Mass. had already been making a charge through the place, leaving the ground behind them covered with dead and wounded rebels. We then went still more to the right and came out upon them as our troops were making their last charge. Whether the rebels were unable to resist that charge, or that the sight of our two new regts. upon the right determined them, I do not know, but they broke in confusion at that time and fled. We succeeded at that time in taking over 300 prisoners without losing any after our regiment came into the field.

The battle was thus ended and, as the sun went down, the last echoes of our artillery ceased. We had marched 25 miles before arriving at the scene of the first fight and 6 miles since then, and after marching over to the place where the battle had commenced, our regiment stacked arms and then threw themselves upon the ground to snatch a few hours sleep. Early next morning, I went over to some houses next by where the wounded had been placed and found there a large number of wounded men, both of ours and the rebels, but one of the first I saw was Lieut. Halpin of Co. K, 25th NY Regt. his regt was in the advance of all and his company thrown out as skirmishers. The first they discovered of the enemy was they run right upon a whole regiment of rebels and they had a desperate struggle for their lives. About 30 of them were taken prisoners by the rebels, most of those being wounded. Lieut. Halpin, whilst leading his men, fell pierced with four bullets. Some of the rebels then advanced to take him prisoner, when he drew his revolver and shot two of the rebels dead and they then left him lying on the ground. He lived untill noon the next day. We thought he would get over it but he died. He was one of my best friends.

During that day we were busy in burying the dead and taking care of the wounded. And in going over the field, the appearance of the dead left lying on the ground was very sad to behold. The mutilated state of those killed by the artillery was the most shocking to behold of anything I have ever seen.

Our cavalry were out all day scouring the country for rebels and brought in a large number of prisoners. The result of the battle was 53 killed, 296 wounded and about 30 taken prisoners on our side and over 500 killed, over 1000 wounded and between 1200 and 1300 prisoners. Lieut. Perkins of Gen. Butterfield's staff was taken prisoner and exchanged on the 8th of this month and returned to us.

On the 29th at 3 P.M. we fell in and started back for New Bridge, arriving here at 4 A.M. next morning and here we have had our camp ever since. On the 31st May and 1st June, whilst the battle of Fair Oaks was being fought, our regt. was out on picket duty. Our pickets are stationed about ½ mile beyond the Chickahominy [River] towards Richmond, and about 1 mile beyond that the rebels have a strong line of earthworks. Fair Oaks is about 4 miles southeast of our picket lines. As soon as the firing over there commenced, our whole division came out to the line, and were drawn up in line of battle. The rebels opposite also were ready to receive us, but we were not called upon, for the reason that our forces were not prepared to take Richmond, and therefore, we only wanted to drive back the rebels, who had attacked the left of our line.

Since that time, we have been busy in preparing for the advance upon Richmond. Our division has built several bridges across the river, and made roads all through the country here. On the 13th, a band of rebel guerillas crossed over to the Pamunkey River and at a place called Garlick's Landing , destroyed 40 wagons loaded with forage and other government property belonging to our division. They killed our Quartermaster Sergeant, a young man named Potter, and several other men belonging to other regiments. They also went over to Jamedall Station and fired from the bank down upon a train of cars passing and killed a colonel and three other men and wounded 7 others. However, our cavalry are now stationed through there to catch any more of the rascals that attempt such things again.

I cannot say when the attack upon Richmond is to be made but I think we are now waiting for more reinforcements, as the rebels have a very strong force here and they are all the best and oldest troops. However, when Gen. McClellan gives us the word we shall be glad to go forward. Well, I have now wrote a much longer letter than I intended to when I commenced, and have to beg your pardon for taking up so much of your valuable time. Please remember me to Henry when you write to him next, and to any enquiring friends in Detroit.

> I Remain
> Most Respectfully
> C.H. Salter

> Camp of Morell's Division Porter's Corps De Armee
> Harrison's Landing, on James River, Va. July 12th 1862

Dear Friend

Since my last letter, wrote you from camp near New Bridge, we have passed through more battles and skirmishes than I had seen before since the war broke out, and, although at times I have thought that I could not go through with the severe fighting we had and not get killed or wounded, I find myself uninjured and in as good health as ever.

On June 26th, whilst our division was camped near New Bridge, we heard that the rebels were coming on to attack McCall's Division, who was at that time camped at Mechanicsville, and soon we were called out and marched up there. During that afternoon, our brigade was held in reserve, and we therefore did not take part in any active fighting. Next morning at daybreak, we moved back to about ½ mile this side of New Bridge, and formed our line of battle from Woodbury's Bridge to beyond Coal [Cold] Harbor; Gen. Sykes' division, on the right at Coal [Cold] Harbor and our division upon the left in a line from that place to Woodbury's Bridge; McCall's division, being held in reserve, the whole being under command of Gen. Porter. About 8 o'clock, the rebels were seen advancing upon us but during the forenoon, they done nothing but play upon us with their artillery from a distance, and send out their skirmishers to find out our position. And then about 1 P.M., they advanced upon us with their whole force, and now the real battle just commences. The rebels had Jackson's army and other troops from Richmond, to the number of 80,000, whilst our force was only 25,000. They assailed us with great fury all the afternoon, making no less than 6 bayonet charges on us, with their whole force of infantry. At the same time, their artillery kept up a heavy fire of solid shot and shell, all the while, but could not force us to give way a single inch, untill about 6 P.M., when some regiments to the right of our line, getting out of ammunition, gave way and retreated. The rebels then rushing through the gap thus made, in immense numbers, soon had us outflanked, and slowly regt. after regt. of our troops gave way, and retreated before none of ours left but our brigade, who were on the extreme left of the line.

We stood our ground for a half hour after that keeping up a rapid fire upon the enemy, untill finding that the rebels were upon our front, right & left, and there was

CAMP LIFE—SHOWING A SOLDIER'S HUT ON THE JAMES RIVER
(THE PICTORIAL BATTLES OF THE CIVIL WAR, NEW YORK, 1895)

great danger of our being surrounded, we retreated in good order, keeping up our fire as we did so, untill we had gone about ½ mile, the enemy pressing us closely all the while, when word was brought us that Meagher's Irish Brigade & Sickles' Excelsior Brigade had crossed the river and were charging the rebels on our right. And soon we saw the Irish Brigade with their coats off and sleeves rolled up, charging the rebels and driving them back in confusion. We then rallied and, charging upon the enemy, drove them back and regained our original position. But it was growing dark and as we had held our position longer than it had been intended we should, therefore, as the rebels were still pressing upon us with overwhelming numbers, we retreated over across the Chickahominy, after having fought one of the hardest battles, for the numbers engaged that ever was fought on this continent. Our loss in this battle was 3,000 in killed, wounded & missing, whilst the rebels had over 8,000 killed and wounded.

My regiment suffered severely. We had 237 killed, wounded & missing, a good many that are missing, having been wounded and unable to get off from the field. Our Col. Stockton was wounded and is supposed to be a prisoner in the hands of the enemy. Capts. Carr & Fisher & Lieut. Williams were killed; Capt. Mott wounded and left on the field; Capt. Meyers and Lieuts. Chandler, McGraw & Eddy were all severely wounded, but were brought with us, however. Our assistant Surgeon, Dr. Seeley, was taken prisoner. All the other regts. of our division suffered equally as bad as we did. The 9th Mich. had their Col. Woodbury killed, and a number of other officers killed & wounded. The 1st Mich. suffered also in the same manner, although the report, which was published in the Detroit papers that Col. Roberts was killed, was untrue. He has been with his regt. and attending to his duties every day. The 83rd Penn., in our brigade, had their Col. McLane and Major Nagle both killed. Also, they lost about the same number that we did.

As we were now across the Chickahominy, we were with the left wing of the army and next morning we commenced the march for this place. The rebels, after having drove us across the river, re-crossed it again at New Bridge and then pressed down upon us with an army of over 200,000 men. We were retreating and fighting with them every day untill the 30th. We had reached the Malvern Hills. There we halted and formed line of battle in a good position, then waited for the coming of the enemy. They soon discovered our position and came down upon us on all sides, except one and that was the river. Our brigade was stationed on the left centre to support some batteries there. The rebels were soon seen coming down the river road in immense force and soon their artillery was planted and throwing shell right amongst us. Our artillery was not idle either, and as we had the advantage of position, they caused great havoc amongst the rebels. Presently they came up with immense numbers of infantry in a long line, preparing to charge upon us, and advancing across the open plain that lay between us; there seemed to be no end to their numbers. But, suddenly, from the direction of the river, we heard heavy firing. The gunboats had now a chance to assist us and right well they improved the opportunity. At the first discharge from their immense cannon and mortars, the shells burst in every direction amongst the rebels. Hundreds of them fell to the earth, never to rise again. The long line wavered and shook with terror, but they had plenty of men and the gaps made in their ranks was soon filled up and on they came.

But our gunboats did not cease and our field artillery kept up a rapid fire upon the advancing enemy. About this time, some of our heavy siege guns were also brought up and commenced firing, untill from the combination of all the slaughter in the rebel ranks was awful. No troops in the world could stand it and they soon retreated, having thousands of dead upon the field and that without our infantry having fired a shot. The gunboats that came so opportunely to our assistance were the Galena, Arostook, and Jacob Bell

On the side furthest from the river, however, the fighting had been more desperate and the loss on our side considerable. And it was on this side that the rebels determined to make their principle attack. Next morning, July 1st, our division was moved out there to the front and also Kearney's & Sedgwick's divisions of Heintzelman's Corps, Sumner's Corps and

Sykes division & McCall's division of our own Corps. The balance of the troops being held in reserve. The rebels had a large number of cannon, planted around in every direction they could possibly, to bring them to bear upon us. They had also more than double the number of infantry that we had and a great many times during the day they would charge upon our line, with their troops in such large masses that it seemed as if nothing could withstand them. They had the cover of a wood about a half mile distant from us. Whilst our division with their batteries were stationed right upon the front of a bulge of high ground with a sloping field laying between us and the wood. When the rebels would advance from the cover of the wood, our artillery would open on them with canister & grapeshot, mowing down immense numbers of them at every discharge, and when this failed to drive them back, and they advanced to musket range of our line, we would commence by rapid firing of musketry and end it by a bayonet charge, driving them back to the woods again.

The hardest fighting of all took place after 6 P.M. About that time, the enemy advanced upon us in greater numbers than ever before. They came out of the wood with a long line in front that looked splendid, whilst after this came large numbers of them from the wood like a swarm of bees. We had brought up some of our siege guns, and these being placed about ½ mile in the rear of our field artillery, soon opened upon them with their 100 lb shell, and our lighter field pieces also kept up a very rapid fire. The 5th US (regulars) Battery [artillery] was with our regiment and having had a number of their men killed, the balance could not work the guns fast enough; so we detailed 50 men from our regt. to assist them, and the firing was very rapid, at every discharge immense gaps were made in the ranks of the rebels but no sooner seen, than they were instantly filled up again and on they came apparently determined to crush us at once. When they had approached to within close musket range, our artillery gave out of ammunition and the cannon were drawn to the rear. And everything looked dark enough for us, but our Gen. Butterfield soon remedied this error. "Charge," he shouted and we did charge with terrible effect upon the enemy. At this same time our whole line charged upon them and we soon had them drove back to the woods again. And now it was growing dark, so we took up our original position again, and then the artillery opened again upon the rebels in the woods. Keeping up a tremendous fire untill 11 P.M. At this time the firing ceased and the greatest battle of the war was at an end.*

For two days had the enemy, with a force of over 200,000 men, assailed with great fury our army of 95,000, but had not succeeded in forcing us to give way a single inch, whilst the rebels had lost more men in killed and wounded than they did in the great battle of Shiloh and Fair Oaks! All those that were in the battle estimated this loss to be over 20,000, whilst our loss was not over 3,000. It was certainly a terrible retribution upon them for our losses in the battle of the Chickahominy.

---

*The Seven Days' Battle, fought from June 25 to July 1, 1862, in Virginia, included the following conflicts: Mechanicsville, Gaines' Mill, Frayser's Farm, Savage's Station, and Malvern Hill. The 16th lost 230 men at Gaines' Mill, the regiment's first serious engagement.

Our regiment went on picket duty that night and next morning, 3 o'clock, we left there and started for this place, 7 miles further down the river. It rained hard all that day and next night. The mud was knee deep. We had lost all our tents in the retreat and the men had thrown away their knapsacks before going into the first battle, so that we were entirely destitute and had to stand around fires untill the rain was over, which was not untill the next morning. On the morning of the 3rd, the rebels came down and shelled our camp but we soon stopped that for in less than 1 hour, we had taken their battery and the balance of them run away and we have not seen anything of them since. Our division then went back into the woods to bivouac. Since then we have been furnished with what new clothes were wanted, and expect to get tents very soon, but it is very uncomfortable when it rains, being situated as we are without shelter. On the 3rd inst we had 20,000 men arrive to reinforce us. They were composed of Gen. Shields division and other new troops from Washington. They were immediately sent out to the front to relieve the tired & worn out divisions that were there. And then Gen McClellan promised us we should have plenty of rest after our 7 days fighting and that new reinforcements would come up sufficient to do all the work untill we got in good order again.

But I must now close. A rain is coming on and I cannot write any more. I will write you again as soon as I can and give you a few more of the particulars of the great events of that memorable week. Give my respects to all enquiring friends & remember me to friend Henry when next you write. I RemainYours Respectfully

> Lieut. C.H. Salter Co E
> Address 16th Regt Mich Infantry
> Porter's Corps Army of the Potomac
> Washington DC

P.S. I am much obliged to you for your kind invitation for assistance in case I should get wounded and return home, but at the same time, hope that there will be no occasion for my returning home before this war is completed and I think, that when we have captured this place or drove the rebels out of it, we will have accomplished the hardest task we will have in conquering Virginia and here we do not, any of us, feel discouraged or lonely, as everybody is too busy here, to scarcely spare time to think of such things. As for myself, I know that I am doing my duty here and doing more for the benefit of my country in my present situation than I could in any other, and therefore never think of whether I am appreciated up North or not, and I think that is about the way most of us think about it, or rather we do not think anything about it. But also those kind friends, who are interesting themselves in our behalf, such as the Soldiers' aid society. I do not think there are any of us that will ever forget their kindness. I see by the papers that they have a bloody battle in Tennessee, but have not as yet heard whether Col. Duffield's brigade were in the battle or not. I presume you must be very anxious to hear from your sons, in the present crisis. I hope they will return home safe after the war is over and hope that will not be at a very distant day either, for I can assure you no matter how grand it may be for people up North to read accounts of splendid victories, it is not very pleasant for those engaged in it.

The weather here has been very rainy for the last two days, and this makes it very unpleasant for us here, as we are but very poorly protected from the rain. But generally, the weather has been quite pleasant since we have been here, but I have wrote more than I intended to, and I suppose you have not much time to read, in these busy times, so I will close.

Yours Respectfully
C.H. Salter

Camp of Morell's Division Army of the Potomac
Near Harrison's Landing, Va Aug 1862

My Dear Friend

Your kind letter of the 22nd inst came duly to hand and I was very glad to hear from you and to hear from Detroit once more. I have heard accounts through the papers of the disaster to the 7th Regt and the wound Gen. Duffield received and was very sorry to hear of it. However, it must be a great deal of consolation to you to know your sons were not taken away by the rebels. Although it seems to me very strange that the Union force in Murfreesboro could have been so completely surprised as they were and would suppose they either had no pickets or else the pickets were all asleep.

Since I wrote you last we have remained near the landing, only changing our camp from the woods to a fine airy place on the top of a high ridge here, from which we have a fine view of the surrounding country and of the James River, with its broad bosom covered with large numbers of steamboats & vessels and also a few black looking craft that keep continually moving up and down the river, to keep the banks on the other side clear of rebels. On the 20th, we had a review of our corps by Gens McClellan & Porter. There were on the ground McCall's division, Sykes' division & our own; this forming the 5th Army Corps, under command of Major Gen Fitz John Porter. The regiment all appeared very small in numbers. Our own regiment numbers 340 men, that being all we could turn out for the review. I suppose we had about 160 sick, left in camp. Our regiment at Yorktown numbered 1040 men and was the largest in our brigade. This is quite a reduction in our regt in three months. Of the balance, 300 have been killed or wounded in the different battles we have been in, and the rest, are some sick in northern hospitals, some prisoners in Richmond, and the others we do not know what have become of them.

On the night of the 31st July & 1st Aug at 12 o'clock, we were suddenly aroused by a heavy firing upon us from the opposite side of the river. We had not had any troops on that side of the river, and did not suppose the rebels would dare to make their appearance there because we supposed the gunboats would keep them away but in the night they run down about 24 cannon to the bank of the river and opened a very rapid fire upon us. At that time, most everybody except the necessary sentinels were asleep and were of course quite startled by the firing from such an unexpected quarter. We had only one gunboat in front of us, at that time, but this soon got ready for action, and our artillery were soon run down to the river bank and firing across at the rebels, and after about an hour, the rebels skedaddled, the only damage they had done to us was the killing of 1 man and wounding about 20 beside sending a couple of balls through one of the steamboats lying here. One of the rebel batteries had been planted on a high bluff opposite us close to, or rather, right amongst the buildings of a nice plantation. And so last Friday, 200 of the 1st regulars, the same number of the 4th regulars and the same of our own regiment were detailed to cross the river and destroy [it]. So, taking axes, as well as our arms, we got aboard of 3 light draft steamers at 4 p.m. and, darting across the river, sprang ashore and climbed the steep bank. The rebels had had some pickets stationed there but they fled when they saw us approaching and we quietly took possession and proceeded to business. Stacking arms, [we] then cut down all the trees, fences, &c and burnt the buildings. The place had been a very beautiful one. The house, being situated on a bluff overlooking the river and surrounded with the most beautiful grounds I have ever seen. For fences they had box wood hedges and, I must say, they were much prettier than any I have ever seen in Detroit. There were 12 other buildings there, used for darkies' quarters, barns, &c. We finished our work and by sunset we had every building afire and the entire place was made a desert. At dusk, we got aboard the boats and returned to our camp by the lights of the burning buildings.

By the way, you spoke of Dr. Wixam of our regt going to Richmond with our wounded. It was not Dr. Wixam but Dr. Seeley, our Asst. Surgeon, that was taken prisoner and Dr. Wixam has now resigned and gone home, leaving us without any doctor for the present. I suppose you are having a good deal of excitement in Detroit now about enlisting and raising new regiments. I suppose from the accounts we have that Col. Morrow's regiment will be raised in a very short time and I hope to see it here in less than a month from this time. But I think after all the governor of Michigan is pursuing the wrong course in not filling up the old regts. first, for it is a fact, well known, that recruits can be drilled and made good soldiers of in the old regts. in one fourth the time they would require in the new regts. to learn their business.

We have eight Michigan regts here and these eight regts require not less than 5,000 men to fill them up to their full numbers. Now if Michigan would send this number on here to fill up these regts, they would be worth more to the government than 10 new regts, because if a battle should occur in only a week of their arrival, our old veterans would keep order and keep the new recruits in their places. But the new regts will require 3 months to drill before they will be fit to go into the field of battle.

The weather here is very warm, and we are badly annoyed by immense numbers of flies, & mosquitoes. There are a great number of our troops sick, about ⅓ of my regiment is sick now. A great many of them have the scurvey & we have to send a whole boat load of sick from the different regts of our army north every day. On the 1st inst, Corporal

George Lauder of my company died from the effects of a wound received at the battle of Malvern. He was a very well educated young man and was formerly a clerk in stores in Detroit. He was buried on the morning of the 2nd inst with military honors.

I must now bring my letter to a close, as we have not much news to write about here. I will write you again as soon as I can if anything important occurs. I shall be glad to hear from you as soon as convenient.

Yours Truly
C.H. Salter

P.S. I suppose you have heard of the new ironclad gunboats the rebels have been building. It seems they have a little Merrimac, called the Richmond and 4 or 5 other iron clad gun boats, as well as a few wooden ones, and on the 30th, these boats came down to Fort Darling, and have remained in that neighborhood ever since. Our iron gunboats are at City Point, about 8 miles above this place and there they are waiting to give the new rebel fleet a proper reception whenever they choose to come down. The rebels are even now constantly receiving reinforcements from the more southern states and from all we can learn, I believe, it is their determination to advance upon us by a combined movement of their land and naval forces and try to destroy our army at once. We have only received 5,000 men to reinforce us since we arrived here and those came on the same day that we reached this place, and I know that since we have been here fully that number have been sent north, sick, besides the wounded men that were first sent away from here. Our actual force here altogether is only about 95,000, whilst the rebels have fully 250,000 to attack us, and leave a sufficient force opposed to General Pope to keep him at bay. And you need not be surprised to hear of some terrible fighting here in a few days; but the rebels cannot surprise us or any portion of our army. It has now been a full month since they commenced recruiting to reinforce us and as yet the northern states have not sent any reinforcements to us at all. The trouble seems to be that the volunteer system is too slow. They should have commenced drafting at once and drafted the men & sent them on to fill up our old regts and then we would have been ready to march right on to Richmond. But we will not now before 3 months. I should really like to see every young man between the age of 18 & 30, that is unmarried in Michigan drafted and sent right on here, especially those behind the counters of stores, measuring tape, &c and keeping books, and all such work that might just as well be done by the Ladies. And I think the young ladies of Detroit ought to take some measures to drive these cowards off to the war. If they would do so, they would do more for the benefit of the brave men who have fought so long, than they could in any other way. But I must now close, as I have wrote most too much, I am afraid I will weary you, so I will close. Please give my respects to Dr. Duffield and all other enquiring friends.

Yours Respectfully
C.H. Salter

Carver Barracks Hospital Washington DC Sept. 20th 1862

Dear Friend

You have began to think, I suppose, that I am either dead or have forgotten you, but circumstances have been such that for a long time I have been unable to write. But now I will try to give you a short account of what I have been doing since we left Harrison's Landing, Aug 15th. At 2 P.M., our corps left that place and, marching through Williamsburgh & Yorktown, we arrived at Hampton on the evening of the 18th, having marched 80 miles in four days. Next morning, we crossed over to Newport News, and that day our division was shipped aboard of transports, and, on the 20th, sailed to Aquia Creek, where we landed, and, taking the cars, proceeded to Fredericksburgh.

On the 22nd & 23rd, we marched to Kelly's Ford and were now in the extreme left of Gen. Pope's army. The next four days were spent in watching the fords along the Rappahannock to prevent the rebels from crossing and turning our left flank. But contrary to our expectations, they advanced upon the right, and on the 27th, we marched to Warrenton Junction, 18 miles. The next day we marched to within 2 miles of Manassas Junction, 15 miles that day. Next morning, we marched out 7 miles west of the RR and had a smart little skirmish with the rebels with but little loss on either side, and that night, we marched back about half way to the RR, and then north untill we came to the old battlefield of July 21st/61, and there, on the morning of Aug 30th, we took our position in line of battle.

Our corps were in the centre, Gen Sigel's corps to the right of us, also in the centre. Gen Heintzelman's corps on the right and Gen McDowell's on the right. Our division had but 2 brigades in it, the third one, in which the Michigan 4th belongs, having by some mistake gone to Centreville. The battle commenced about 8 A.M. and during the day Gen. Sigel's Corps and ours drove the enemy, slowly but steadily back untill at 4 P.M., our division were 2 miles in advance of the place where the battle had commenced and we were in a wood, in front of which was a ridge where our skirmishers were posted. Beyond that was a large open field, beyond which was a ridge where the enemy had their batteries planted. In another place was a R.R. embankment, behind which the rebel infantry was concealed, or rather, protected as I should say. Our artillery were in the rear of us, on high ground from whence they were firing at the rebels over our heads, during all the day.

So far we had noticed that McDowell had not advanced nor had he even fired a gun so far, and we had not seen Gen. Pope at all but McDowell seemed to exercise command, as the next officer in rank. About this time he sent an order to Gen. Porter to send our division to charge the rebel batteries in front of us. But Gen. Porter sent back word it was useless to attempt to take them in that manner, that they should first be flanked upon the right, which could very easily be done by the troops to the right of us. However, there came another preemptory order to charge, and Gen. Porter had to order our two brigades to do it. Gen. Butterfield, who had command of both brigades, formed us into line of battle, and then we advanced upon the double quick. As soon as we came out of the wood, we were exposed to the full fire of the enemy. But we advanced steadily on, keeping up a continual fire upon the rebels as we advanced. Meanwhile, we soon saw, we were getting into a very bad place, for the enemy's batteries were planted in the form of a half circle and we were advancing right into that, and the rebels upon three sides of us, were pouring into our ranks a perfect rain of grape shot & canister, solid shot & shell and even R.R. iron, besides the fire from a force of infantry larger than our own. But still we kept steadily on, expecting our batteries to be advanced and also that we would be reinforced by infantry. But our reinforcements came and when we were about ½ mile in advance of the wood, we found that our artillery had not advanced and could not reach the enemy, but many of their shells were bursting in our ranks, and as we had nearly one half of our force killed or wounded, we were ordered to retreat, which we did in good order, firing as we retreated, untill we fell back behind the first line of reserves where we halted to rest and reform our shattered columns.

And now the rebels attacked our left wing where McDowell's Corps were stationed. It appears that McDowell had not even had skirmishers thrown out in front of his troops, as officers of his Corps afterwards informed me, and the rebels had brought up their artillery and placed it in positions where they could fire right into his troops, and also brought up large numbers of infantry, so that when they did commence the attack, they took them by surprise and in a few minutes, McDowell's entire Corps were in full retreat. And we received orders about sundown to fall back to Centreville. We marched across Bull Run at Blackburn's Ford and reached Centreville that night about 10 P.M., where we threw ourselves upon the ground to obtain a few hours sleep. And thus ended all that I saw of the battle of Manassas, a battle that has been the most disastrous of any that has occurred to us during the war and it is the universal opinion in the army that it was lost to us by the treachery of McDowell. The officers and men of his own corps in particular denounced him as a traitor. But his case is, I believe, soon to be investigated by a court, and then we are in hopes he will be dismissed the service, or at least not allowed to command a corps again, as long as this war lasts.*

The loss in our own regt. was 96 killed & wounded out of only 290 we entered the field with. Besides this, between 30 & 40 were taken prisoners & afterward released on parole; Capt Ransom, Lieuts Chittick & Ruby were killed and Capt Barry and Lieut Swan wounded. The loss in the other regts. of our two brigades was fully as much and in some regts more than in ours. The day after the battle, it rained hard all day and we lay under arms, ready to receive the enemy in case they should attack us. And that night our regt went out on picket duty, returning to the village the next day. And Sept 2nd at 2 P.M., we marched from Centreville, passing through Fairfax. We went north to Vienna,

---

*Major General Irvin McDowell was severely criticized for his performance at the Second Battle of Bull Run. Relieved of command, he demanded a court of inquiry, which ultimately exonerated him. McDowell then served on various boards and commissions in Washington, D.C., before going west to command the Department of the Pacific in July 1864.

then east to Lewinsville and halted at night near the Chain Bridge after having marched 34 miles that day. Next morning, we marched to Hall's Hill and bivouacked in the same old place we had occupied for a camp all last winter. About as soon as we arrived there I was taken very sick with fever and have been sick ever since then. On the 7th, our division marched to Alexandria, and on the 8th, marched back again to Fort Corcoran, opposite Georgetown. At that time, I was so sick as to be unable to walk and had to be carried in an ambulance. However, I would not leave the regt as I was in hopes of getting well in a few days. But on the morning of the 12th, our division crossed the river and marched to join McClellan at the present seat of war. And I had to be left behind and was brought to this hospital the next day.

Since that time I have not heard anything from the regt, although I know that they are with the rest of the army in pursuit of the rebels. They numbered when they left here but 166 men, so that they cannot be expected to do a great deal of fighting this time. Our brigade of 5 regts was so much reduced in numbers by the many battles they have been in, that when they left here, they only numbered 750 men altogether, less than any one of the new regts. By the way, I see by the papers that the 17th Mich regt almost annihilated a brigade of South Carolina troops in the battle of South Mountain, though I suppose that brigade must have been an old brigade, and, like our own old brigades reduced in numbers to less than one full regt as the 17th was. However, it speaks well for a new regt as the 17th to fight so well as they did there, and I think they have taken all the feathers out of the cap of their more favored rival, the 24th Mich. The news that we have today is that the rebels have been drove entirely out of Maryland, across the Potomac and Gen. Sigel with his Corps is at Leesburgh to attack them on that side. But we have not much particulars as yet. I am now getting much better than I was and hope to be able to rejoin my regt in about a week from this. I received a letter from you when we arrived at Hall's Hill, but have not been able to write untill this present time. I hope you will excuse my poor writing as my hand is very nervous and weak as yet. This hospital is situated on 14th street, about 1½ miles from Pennsylvania Ave. It is composed of a number of bar-racks buildings that were used as quarters for a brigade of troops last winter. In one of the buildings there are a number of wounded officers, amongst them Lieut. Merriam of the 1st Mich Cavalry. He is wounded in two places, besides being badly bruised by a fall from his horse. The doctor says he will not live but a short time now, and we are expect-ing him to die every day.

But I must now bring this long letter to a close. When you write again, direct to the regt as I shall probably join them in about a week unless I should become worse again. Please give my respects to Dr. Duffield, and remember me to your son Henry when next you write to him, and believe me

As ever
Yours Truly and Respectfully
C.H. Salter

Back in Michigan, other regiments were organizing, cavalry as well as more infantry units, in response to the President's call for more volunteers.

Among those mounted units was the 4th Michigan Cavalry, authorized July 11, 1862, with Colonel Robert Horatio George Minty, formerly Lt. Col. of the 3rd Michigan Cavalry, as regimental commander. Minty, a 37-year-old Detroiter, was a former British army officer. In mid-September 1862, he started his regiment, some 1,200 troopers, south for Louisville, Kentucky. All except one of the hospital stewards, who missed the train.

James Vernor was born in Albany, New York, in 1843 and was brought to Detroit five years later. At the age of fifteen, he was employed as an errand boy in Higby & Stearns drug store; his chemical knowledge gained for him his hospital steward appointment when he enlisted in August 1862.

JAMES VERNOR
(BURTON HISTORICAL COLLECTION, DETROIT PUBLIC LIBRARY)

September 25 [18]62
Jeffersonville [IN] Sunday

Dear Mother

We arrived here this morning safe & sound. I don't know when I ever enjoyed myself so much in so small space of time. Dr. Bacon is a first rate traveling companion. He was just as full of fun as he could be & it was eat, eat, eat until we could not stuff any more down but it cost me some thing for my fun. Dr Bacon & I went through Laport to see if we could not get some thing to carry along with us & he bought just what he had a might to & when he came to pay for it he found out he had not got any money & so you see I had to the bill to foot but never mind that, it was not a very large Bill, so I did not grumble.

Wasn't that a good joke about my getting left by the train but I soon made it up for I took the 8 O clock train & met the Regt at Laport where they stopped to feed the horses. We had quite a little excitement this morning. They was a soldier riding upon the top of the cars & where we went under the Bridge about 2 or 3 miles from here it struck him & cut his head open just above the left temple. The cut was only about 7 inches long, broke his jaw in 3 pieces & bruised him in several places quite badly & in spite of this he lay there & swore like a trooper at us while we were sewing him together. I tell you I will soon be quite a surgeon. There was 5 or 6 came near fainting just watching us work at him. I have heard of scalping men but never saw one before this & the Dr says he is going to get well if Congestion of the brain does not take place.

But I must stop. We expect to go across into Kentucky the first thing in the morning. I don't know if we will go very far or not. The rumor is we are to go into the interior the first thing but I don't see the idea of sending them without Carbines or Pistols. Nothing but those government Chees knives but I can tell you better when we get there. So good bye. Be sure & write to me every time you get a chance.

Jimmie

Camp off Jeffersonville, Tuesday
[c. September 30, 1862]

Dear Brother

How do you do [?] I am mighty tired. I never knew what it was like to move a camp before but I have found out now, its every man for himself. The best man gets his tent up first & that was not me, I can tell you. In the first place I could not find my tent when we arrived here so I took the first tent I could lay my hands on & made quite a good thing of it, for the one I got was 3 times as large as the one I had. I have had to work like a horse ever since I have been here but I enjoy myself, I tell you.

In my letter to mother I told her we expected to move right across the river to Louis-

Camp Rosencrang
Near Nashville
Saturday
Dec 20/1862

Dear Mother
            I received your
very welcome letter written
in great haste on Monday
Morning lamenting in
strong terms the loss
of all your letters but
I begin to think they
were not all lost for
I have received quite
a number lately I have
answered all of them
but one from Jerry
& one from Libbie so
you can tell wether
I have got them all
or not you said you

ville but the order was changed & we went into camp about 1½ miles out of Jeffersonville. It is a very pleasant place but we might as well have stayed in Detroit for all I can
see. This is a little better place to drill to be sure & there is not quite so many Boys wants
to go down town so they can have a little better discipline. There is a man owns a corn
field the next field from the camp & he went to the Colonel to sell the field to him for
he said he would rather sell it to him than have his Boys steal it all. The Colonel asked
him if he had lost any of it by our boys. He said no but the Pensylvania Cavalry, which
was camped here stole every thing they could get. The Colonel politely informed him
that this was not Pensylvania Cavalry but Michigan & he wanted him to understand that
Michigan Boys did not steal but paid for [what] they wanted to eat. I rather think he
would have changed his mind if he had seen what I did Sunday. I saw a God Sized Hog
& 2 or 3 Geese used up in ½ hour. I never saw Foraging carried on in earnest before.
They made short work of it I can tell you.

I suppose you heard all about the shooting affair across the river here Jeff Davis shot
Genl Nelson. I don't suppose you heard the particulars though. Davis went to Nelson
after orders & Nelson, being a swearing man, swore at him considerable & told him that
he had no orders for him. Davis said he did not come there to be swore at. When Nelson
struck him in the face, Davis turned and went down stairs in the street & met an officer
& asked him if he had any weapon. The Officer handed him a Pistol. He turned round
& went into the Hotel. Nelson saw him coming & went to meet him. Davis met him
coming down & said Genl Nelson, you have insulted me, defend your self. Nelson drew
a pistol & Davis shot him through. He turned, grit his teeth, went into his room & died
in 10 minutes. Davis went & gave himself up to the authorities.

The Colonel is across the river & sealed orders have come to move immediately. He
went over to see where to report around camp. Says we go to Cincinati but there is no
telling. We have heard firing all the afternoon, quite a distance but very heavy. There was
a shell thrown into Louisville this afternoon. They report the Rebels in force 20 miles
from Louisville. We may go there but there is no telling. There is a Captain just went by
says we will make a good show with nothing but dull chees knives to fight with.

Armstrong wants to be remembered to the folks. Remember me to all the girls & be
sure to write soon. Send me some papers. I want to see some news from Home.

> Your small Brother
> Jim
> Direct your letters & etc
> James Vernor
> Hospt Steward
> 4th Mich Cav
> Jeffersonville Ind

P.S. give my love to all the folks. Father & Mother in particular & excuse mistakes.

> Jim

Danville Tuesday
[c. 14–16 Oct 1862]

Dear Father

Here I am way down among the Secesh & the further I get the better I like it. I think this is the prettiest country I have ever seen & the further we get into it the better we live. We left Jeffersonville Friday evening & my usual luck did not desert me for I got left behind at Louisville & could not find my way out. It took me about 1½ hours to catch up with the Regt. When every thing went all right we marched until 11 oclock at night & stopped. Started again at Day Light & marched all day Saturday until after dark. In the evening, we had a grand supper. Pigs–chicken–geese–turkeys & squash. That is what we call living on half rations & we like it better than full rations.

We started on time Sunday morning. This looked to me the hardest of all marching. All day Sunday is something we have not been used to & to prove it was all wrong. We stole a pig at just dark & put it on our wagon & started to catch up with the other wagons. It got so dark that we got rather mixed up & finaly finished the Job in a hurry by turning the whole concern over in the mud. I took a leap for luck & struck headfirst in the mud & rolled over once or twice. When I picked the mud up I found myself was inside of it. I got one of the Boys to scrape me off or rather dig me out & then we all went to work & filled up the wagon & caught up with the other wagons; made a big fire & cleaned ourselves off. In the morning I went to a house that was near by & had Breakfast. We had Corn Dodgers, Pork Steak (part of the cause of our accident) & coffee with Sugar & cream. It would have done your goose to have seen me eat.

We started on Monday [at] 8 o clock & Passed Perrysville after noon thereabout. 300 Rebels dead on the Battle field of last Wednesday. I asked some of the folks why they were not buried & they <u>oh, they are Secesh</u>. I think if I lived around there I should want to get them out of sight for they are any thing but pleasant to look at.

Our Boys caught sight of the rebels yesterday & came very near having a time of it. The Rebels sent 2 or 3 shells whistling over our heads but did not hurt any body. There is many of our men getting this new disease. It is the Gunpowder Disease. We are going to move on this morning. I cant tell you how far we will go. We are to be held in reserve & most likely shant see any fighting in a few days. Tell Charlie that I came across his friend Paxton here & he wanted to be remembered to him. Direct your letters to Louisville, Ky. I have not heard one word from home yet. Your affectionate son

Jimmie

Thursday morning

I did not get a chance to send this letter so I thought I would let you know how far we have moved on. We are 15 miles past Danville. We stopped last night & ever since there has been a continual stream of Soldiers passing here. Every kind is represented. I thought that I had seen some large crowds at home but you would miss them in this crowd. We

Breakfasted this morning on Sweet Potatoes, Hard Bread & coffee. Tell Mother that she must make some sweet potatoe cake. They make it here & I tell you. It is not bad to take. It is made ½ sweet potatoe & ½ Flour; boil the potatoes very soft & mash them; tell her that is all the information I could get & if she goes by guess work she will get it about right. If she does, you will like them.

Jerry told me to write after every little Battle but it is impossible to do it for there is no way to get the letter home. I will write though as often as I can, so you must not be alarmed if you do not hear from me every day. If I don't hear from home soon, I shall think some thing must be done. I miss the Papers very much. We cant get any news here. I hope to get a letter tonight or to morrow for the rest of the Regt will be here then. About ⅓ of the Regt did not start till a day or two after we did & we are expecting them to come on every day. It is next to an impossibility to get any Post Stamps here. Tell Jerry to send me some. I got a chance to send this letter by a friend who is going to Louisville & he says he will drop it in the office for me. Tell Ben Lieut. Montgomery of the 23rd stopped to see me & wished to be remembered to him. When I wrote home he is acting Brigade Adjutant. Good Bye & give my love to all the folks & don't be afraid to send me to many news paper.

Jimmie

Camp of the 16th Regt Mich Vols
Near Antietam Iron Works Oct 13th 1862

My Dear Friend

Your kind letter of the 23rd containing your photograph was received on the 6th inst, and I was very glad indeed to hear from you as well as Dr. Duffield and Henry, and also to receive the likeness. I shall keep that to remember you with. As you will see by this I have returned to my regt again. I left Washington on the 3rd and reached the camp on the 6th inst. I think that I am fully recovered now and that there is no danger of my being troubled with fever again. When I arrived at the camp, I found my regt lying opposite Shepardstown. But on the 8th, our brigade moved 3 miles down the river, and our camp is now situated just below the mouth of Antietam Creek, near the Iron Works of the same name. Burnsides corps was camped here, but moved down the river on the 7th, although I do not know where they have moved to.

We are kept here for the purpose of guarding the forts along the river. Our pickets are stationed along the bank of the river, whilst the rebel pickets are about 2 miles off, though they were stationed on the opposite bank of the river a few days ago. There are no other troops within 2 miles of our brigade in any direction in consequence of which we are kept very busy, in doing picket and guard duty. We are about 2 miles southeast of Sharpsburg and the same distance west of the Elk ridge Mountains. Our camp is pitched on a high piece of ground from which we have a fine view of nearly all of the battle ground of Antietam, and a very beautiful scene it is too.

A person coming here now can scarce realize that it was so recently the theater of such a heavy battle but for the graves that are so thickly scattered for miles around Sharpsburgh and the works of cannon balls and shells upon the houses of the village. There has been a great many of the bodies of Union soldiers taken up by their friends and sent north to be interred. The Union soldiers who were killed were all buried properly with head boards to designate their names but the rebels were buried with large numbers of them piled in one large grave.

The 24th Mich is camped on the other side of Sharpsburgh, about 3 miles distant from us. They think the living here is pretty hard, and most of them are already sick of soldiering. The weather has been very rainy and cold here for the last three days and it continues to rain yet. It is very unpleasant, the more so that our regt has but very few tents and have no over coats, and very few blankets. The tent I live in is a small one, called by us a poncho tent. It is 6 feet long, 4 wide and 3 high. I have cedar boughs spread on the ground to sleep on and here I live all alone and most of the officers have to live with 2 or 3 in equally small tents.

For the last two days we have been watching for the rebel cavalry that have been visiting Pennsylvania, so that if they came this way we might give them a proper reception. But we have seen no signs of them as yet, and it is not likely that they will venture this way at all, for they know very well they could never get through here. I have not heard the particulars of this last raid of theirs, but it cannot be for any purpose but that of procuring forage and cutting off railway communication between Harrisburgh and Hagerstown. I hope that the troops on the river above us will succeed in capturing the entire body of them because it would be a disgrace to our army to allow them to go back without being punished.

At present there does not seem to be any indications of an advance being made by our army this fall, and if it is not made very soon, it will then be too late to do anything this winter, because when the rainy season sets in, it is impossible almost to move an army in Virginia over such roads, as there are in that state. And I think the intention of our government is to wait untill the new troops are drilled, before they commence doing any more than is actually necessary here. There has been one new regiment added to each brigade of our corps. The 20th Maine had joined ours, and the other day, when the President reviewed us, their line was longer than that of the five old regiments and that regt is no larger than each one of the old ones were when they were first organized. So from this you can see how much we are reduced. My regt has but 200 men here in camp and but 17 officers out of 38 that we had six months ago. Our Colonel now proposes to fill up the regiment by allowing men in Michigan to bring on recruits and to give them the vacant offices to pay them for bringing on the recruits, whilst the officers think that the vacant places should be filled by the promotion of the officers and such non-commissioned officers as deserve it, and to recruit the regt by sending officers from the regt to enlist men in the State and send them on. And quite a number of us have made up our minds to resign and leave the regt unless justice is done us. For my part, I think that after having served for a year and a half, and, having fought in a dozen battles, if I cannot get the promotion that belongs to me, but have some man—that has never seen a battle and knows nothing about military affairs—sent on from Michigan and placed over me—I would be disgraced by remaining in the regt and, although I do not wish to leave the army as long as the war lasts, yet I shall resign if I am imposed upon in that manner and then enter a new regiment, if there is anymore to be raised in the State. As it is, I am only sorry that I did not resign and leave this regt before, whilst there was plenty of new regiments being raised in the State, because I know very well that they needed officers of experience in those regts. However, I will wait patiently and see what our colonel is going to do before I take any hasty action in the matter.

Your letter was forwarded to the regt and never came to the hospital at all. Therefore, I did not receive it untill I joined my regt or I would have answered it before this. I had very good care whilst I was in the hospital and commenced to get well from the very day I entered it. The Capitol and the Patent Office and several other public buildings are now used as hospitals in Washington. There are about 30,000 sick and wounded soldiers lying in the hospitals of Washington, Georgetown, Alexandria, and vicinity. I went through the Capitol before I left the city. It seemed very strange that the Capitol of our country should be used for a hospital, but in my opinion, it is doing a great deal more good than it was last summer when the politicians were in it, plotting how they might best prevent our army from taking Richmond. But I must now bring this letter to a close, so you will please remember me to Dr. Duffield and my Friend Henry, as well as any other enquiring friends, and believe me, as ever,

Most Respectfully Your Friend
C.H. Salter

Saturday Nov 8th [1862]
Mitchellville Tenn

Dear Mother

Here I am way down in Tennessee, just one mile over the State line & 27 miles south of Bowling Green [Kentucky]. I have been so busy for the last week, moving, that I have not had time to write home. I received a letter last week from George & he said that you were all well & that is all the news I have heard from home since I left except one Paper. I would have had some no doubt if I had been with the Regt, but I have not been with them since they left me at New Market, in charge of 60 men, all sick, about 2 weeks ago. I left there last Saturday & have been on the move ever since, part of the time in wagons & part in the cars. I only had to leave about 15 men behind. The rest were all able to come along with me.

The Regt was encamped about 2½ miles from here last night. I expected to go there this morning with my men but didn't. The Regt has gone on to Nashville & when the Railroad is opened we are to come on, which may take perhaps 2 weeks. No telling, though. You must continue to direct your letters to Louisville & they will be sent to the Regt. I expect to get about a peck when I get there. I am enjoying myself here. You may be sure of that. There has been very few Soldiers through here & live stock is very plenty. We have Geese, Chickens & Pigs whenever we want them. Potatoes are very scarce, some sweet but very few Irish. It would make you laugh at the way the boys (that is some of them) get their dinner. They will go at night & help themselves to a man's chickens & the next day they will trade them back for their dinners. It takes a man with a straight face to do it. I have not got so far as that yet.

I slept in a Secesh house night before last. You don't know how easy it is to get lodging here, the way we done. One of our Lieutenants & 3 of us went into the man's house & he was sitting by the fire. He was on the left side of the fire. The Lieut. told him to move to the other side of the fire. He moved & didn't say a word. We made up our beds on the floor & went to bed. Rather unceremonious, to be sure but we slept just as well for all that.

I am getting quite fat on camp fare. It agrees with me first rate. I have not been sick a day since I left Detroit. The 21st Regt is camped near here. I went over to see Col Whipple. [He is] in first rate health & wished to be remembered to Ben & all the folks. When I wrote home I saw Benny Briscoe at New Market. He is the only Officer left in his company. They have all died except him. I expect he will be Capt of the company. He is as fat as he can be just like all the rest. He likes [the] Military better than any thing he ever tried before. That's my fix. I guess it is because it is such a lazy business.

How did my photograph look[?] I suppose you have answered that question in some of your letters that is with the Regt. If you have not sent them to me, send me some of them for I would like to see how I look when I have my good clothes on. Keep on writing & may be I shall see some of them by & by. Give my love to all the folks. Good Bye.

From your affectionate Son
Jimmie

Hookers Army Corps
Camp of the "Light Brigade" Butterfield's Division
Warrenton, Virginia Nov. 14th 1862

Dear Friend,

I have not heard from you since I wrote you last on the 12th Oct at Antietam, but as I suppose you are willing to read a letter that may give you some information about our army here, and more particularly our division, as the 1st and 4th Mich belongs to it as well as ours, I take this opportunity of writing you a few lines.

We remained at Antietam, guarding the fords there untill the evening of the 30th Oct, when our corps fell in and marching to within 2 miles of Harper's Ferry, halted for the night to rest. Next morning, crossing the Potomac on a pontoon bridge, we passed through Harper's Ferry and, crossing the Shenandoah on another pontoon bridge, we then marched up over the Blue Ridge Mts. and southeast to Lovettsville, where we halted at sunset. Resting the next day, and on the morn of the 2nd inst at 6 A.M., fell in and marched that day to Snicker's Gap, in the Blue Ridge about 25 miles distant from Harper's Ferry. We reached the place just in time to prevent a large body of Rebels from crossing. They were advancing from the west side, but we reached the place first, a fact which they soon discovered and, without coming up to range of our artillery, they faced about and retreated towards Winchester. We remained there untill the 6th, when, at 6 A.M., we again fell in and commenced our march, taking a southeast direction, we passed through Middleburg, then halted at sunset, about 1 mile south of the village, after having marched about 20 miles that day. Next day, we marched to White Plains, and that day we experienced the pleasure of being out in the first snow storm we had yet seen this winter. We commenced our march again early the next morning and passing through the Bull Run Mts. at Thoroughfare Gap. We then marched south untill within 3 miles of this place and then we halted for the night after having marched about 20 miles that day. And next morning, Sunday, the 7th, we moved close up to the village, where we pitched our camp and where we yet remain.

During our march to this place, we passed through a better portion of Virginia than we had yet seen. We saw a great deal of beautiful mountain scenery, and the country was more thickly settled, and in a better state of cultivation than any we had passed through previously. Warrenton is a village that did contain about 2,000 inhabitants before the war, but now, it is almost deserted, there being no one left of the whites but a very few old men, women and children, and fewer still of the blacks. In fact, this portion of Virginia we have passed through has been entirely drained of every man capable of bearing arms, or working for the rebel government in any way, and many of the families have left for more peaceful climes. There are about 12 or 15 churches in the town, some of them very fine buildings but now, they are all used as hospitals. We found about 300 wounded rebels in them when we arrived here, most of whom have been wounded ever since the Battle of Manassas plains. Also, we find about 1,000 new graves in the cemetery, all being rebel soldiers who have been killed in the battles that have taken place in this vicinity.

When we arrived here, we found the graves decorated with flowers, that had probably been placed there by the rebels before they left here, for effect.

There are several very fine private residences in the place, and it will compare very favorably with any northern village of the same size. Gen. Burnside has his Head Quarters in a hotel on the main street. There are no stores open or any business done except by our suttlers. On the 10th inst, there was a grand review of all the troops here by Gen. McClellan, who issued his farewell address to the army, of which he has been so long the Commander-in-Chief, and after the review was over, all the officers of our corps assembled at Gen. Porter's Head Quarters, where Gen. McClellan met us and bid each one good by, took each one by the hand and spoke a few parting words, saying, that whatever should be his fate, he should always remember that he belonged to the army of the Potomac, and he hoped that we would only do as well in the future as we had done in the past and we would reflect honor upon our corps. The scene was very affecting and many of the old officers who had been through the campaign on the Peninsula with him, were seen to be in tears.

On the 12th, we had a review of our corps by Gen. Porter, who has been relieved from his command and ordered to Washington. As he passed our Division, the soldiers manifested their sympathy for him by cheering vociferously, and throwing their caps in the air. It seemed to us as if we were losing our best friend. Gen. Hooker has been assigned to the command of the corps, so that hereafter we shall be known as Hooker's Corps, instead of Porters'. Gen. Hooker is now second in command to Burnside, as the command of our corps is considered in that light, for the reason that we are the reserve corps. There has been a change also in our division. Gen. Morell was transferred last month to the command of another division, and Gen. Butterfield was given the command of this division. He was formerly our brigade commander. Col. Stockton now has command of the brigade.

There has been a number of commissions received in our regt., from Gov. Blair for promotions, and amongst others I received a com. as first lieutenant and have been transferred from my old company to Co. B by order of the Colonel. This company was raised in Ionia, Michigan, by Captain Sibley, who resigned in September when the former First Lieut. GW Fuller became captain. My com. dates Aug. 30th 1862, the day of the Battle of Manassas Plains. I prize it very highly, as it is a promotion made on the field of battle, and the only one in our regt that dates from the day of the battle.

Our army feels great confidence in our new commander, Gen. Burnside, and will go into battle as willingly for him as they have done for McClellan, and with the army we have now, if he only handles the troops with skill and good judgment, we shall succeed in every thing we undertake, at least I think so. A portion of our troops have been advanced as far as the Rappahannock for the last six days, and we are every hour expecting an order for the entire army to advance, and when we do advance again, we shall have another great battle, for we cannot advance much farther without being met by the rebels in force. Our troops are all anxious to meet the enemy and have the war settled as soon as possible. In fact, we do not wish to halt at all, but, to press right on and finish the war without delay.

The weather so far has been quite pleasant for this time of the year. We have had but very little rain, and the roads are in fine condition at present. But we cannot expect this will last much longer, the cold rainy season will soon set in and then we shall suffer considerable from exposure if we are in an active campaign. We hear cannonading every day down towards the Rappahannock, but as yet no serious engagement has taken place. A portion of our cavalry made a dash into Fredericksburgh the other day and created quite a commotion amongst the rebels there, killing a number of them and taking a number of prisoners.

But I must now bring this letter to a close, as I have but very little time to write. Give my respects to Dr. Duffield and any other enquiring friends. Also please remember me to your son, Henry when next you write. Hoping to hear from you soon

> I Remain
> Yours Truly and Respectfully
> C.H. Salter
> Co. B 16th Regt Mich Infy
> Washington, D.C.

Nov 15th. We are to have another review of our corps this afternoon. This is to be before Gen. Hooker, our new commander. We have just received orders to be ready to march early tomorrow morning. Today, Gen. Sumner's corps is moving out to the front. Probably before you receive this letter, you will have heard of another battle being fought near the Rapidan.

> Camp of the "Light Brigade" Gen. Butterfield's Corps
> Six miles from Fredericksburgh, VA Nov 27th 1862

My Dear Friend,

Your kind letter of the 16th has just arrived today and I am very glad to hear from you once more. My last letter was wrote on the 14th inst, at Warrenton, and, of course, you had not yet received it when you wrote. We remained encamped there untill the morning of the 17th, when our corps fell in at daybreak, and marching through Warrenton Junction, we halted 5 miles southeast of that place at night. Next day, we marched about 14 miles in the same direction, and on the 19th, we marched about 5 miles and then pitched our camp on a large open plain about 8 miles NW of Fredericksburgh.

We were then encamped on a plantation, owned by Negroes, whose master had willed it to them and given them their freedom when he died. The plantation consists of 900 acres and there were about 80 darkies on it. They appeared to be better off than any Negroes I have ever yet seen in Virginia. We remained there untill Sunday, the 23rd, when we marched again, this time moving directly east. The roads were very bad and our artillery had such a hard time getting through that, at 7 P.M., we had only marched 7 miles and had to halt for that night within 1½ miles of our destination. Next morning, we moved to our present camp, which is pitched in the midst of what was a thick pine wood, but it is fast disappearing now, for as there are no fence rails near the camp, the men are obliged to cut their own wood for the first time since we left our camp at Antietam.

Our camp is on the rail road, 6 miles from Fredericksburgh and 9 miles from Acquia Creek landing. Our army, or rather that portion of it which is under the immediate command of Gen. Burnside, is situated as follows: Gen. Sumners' Grand Division, of two corps, on the Rappahannock at Falmouth; and, opposite Fredericksburgh, Gen. Hookers' grand division, to which our corps belongs, is camped along the R.R., from there to this place; and, Gen Franklin's grand division lies between us and Acquia Creek landing, along the R.R. also. The last we have heard of Gen. Sigel's corps, they were yet at Centreville. Whilst our corps was on the march from Warrenton here we were followed up pretty close by a large force of rebels, who kept at a respectful distance from our rear guard, and appeared to be only watching our movements.

What our future movements are to be is a mystery to me. The rebel papers prophecy that we are going to move our army by water up the James River, but as yet I cannot see any indications of anything of the kind. That we are to have a winter campaign and a pretty hard time in roughing it, is very apparent, but I suppose it will be the last one of the kind, as this war must be closed up before another winter. Our new commander, Gen. Burnside, is well liked by the entire army. There were quite a number of officers as well as soldiers who are dissatisfied that Gen. McClellan should be removed, but at the same time, they like Gen. Burnside. For my part, I am much better pleased with the new commander than with the old one and I am satisfied that the war will now be pushed ahead with a great deal more vigor than it ever has been heretofore, and also satisfied that McClellan is not as good a general as the army had always supposed him to be. With our own immediate commanders, Gens. Hooker and Butterfield, our corps is more than satisfied. Gen. Hooker we know from reputation to be a very skillful general, and a very active one also, whilst Gen. Butterfield is reputed amongst us to be the bravest and most gallant of all the generals of the Army of the Potomac. He had command of my brigade, untill the removal of Gen. Morell from the division, when he assumed command of it. And when Gen. Porter was removed from the command of the corps, he was made commander of the corps. And now, being in a position where he can display his abilities, I believe he will yet make a reputation for himself second to none in the army.

Lieut. Col. Welch, who has been absent in Michigan on recruiting service, rejoined us yesterday and now has command of the regt as Col. Stockton yet continues to command the brigade. Col. Welch has been absent about 3 months and we are very glad to have him come back as we have more confidence in him than in any other officer who ever commanded the regt. Capt. Brockway of our regt left us on the 16th to return to Mich as he has been promoted to 1st Major in the 9th Mich Cavalry. Our Chaplain also Mr. Brockway, left us on the 24th, as he has resigned his position in the regt. Several company officers have sent in their resignations, but they are returned, not accepted, and so they go, untill now, in consequence of losses in battle, resignations and so on. We have not one half of our old officers left now.

It must have been a severe trial for Col. Duffield and Henry to have been kept away from service as long as they have, but I see by the papers that those taken prisoners at Mumfordville last September were exchanged, so, I suppose, the Ninth must be by this time also. And if so, Henry will have a chance to go into active service again.

The weather for the last week has been quite cold and very rainy, so much so, that the roads are getting very bad, and when we advance again, I fear we shall make but slow progress through this Virginia mud, which is the worst I ever saw anywhere. The result of the elections up north are rather discouraging to the army here but if the soldiers had been allowed to vote in all the states, as they did in the Wisconsin and Iowa regts.,* there would have been a very different result, for it is a fact well known that a large majority of the soldiers are Republicans and I believe that had the soldiers voted, the Democrats would not have carried the few states that they did. I know that about ¾ of the soldiers of the Mich. Regts. here are Republicans. And if, after all our fighting this war is to be broken up by such Disunionists at the North as Gov. Seymour of New York, it would have been better never to have fought the war at all, but to have given up to the Rebels in the first outbreak of the war without having lost as many lives as we have. But, perhaps it may come out all right yet, at least I hope so.

But I must now bring this letter to a close as I have but little news to write. Please give my respects to Dr. Duffield and any other enquiring friends. Remember me also to Friend Henry. Hoping to hear from you again soon, I Remain As Ever

> Respectfully Your Friend
> Lieut C.H. Salter
> Co. B 16th Regt Mich Infy

P.S. There is a rumor in camp that there has been a large force of our troops sent from Washington and landed at the White House Landing on the Peninsula and, in that case, it must be the intention of Gen Burnside to send a large force up the Peninsula, and as soon as that force is ready to operate, we should move down the R.R. from Fredericksburgh to Richmond. Gen. Burnside himself will take command of the force on the Peninsula and Gen. Hooker will take command of this force here, which consists of about 100,000 men, and Gen. Sigel has at Fairfax and Centreville about 40,000. And now, in a few days, I think you will here of greater and more decisive battles being fought, than any that have yet taken place during the war. CHS

---

*The 1864 election was the first in which soldiers in the field were allowed to vote, although this was not the case for all states. Each state determined on their own the process by which soldiers' votes were to be handled. Some states passed legislation allowing absentee ballots and others arranged for voting in the field. In Michigan, legislation was passed to permit soldiers to vote in the field through absentee ballots. For those soldiers who were residents of states without new voting legislation, they could be granted leave to return home to vote.

Mitchellsville [Alabama]
Wednesday
Nov 26 [1862]

Dear Mother

I received your letter nearly 3 weeks ago & I am ashamed of my self for answering the other one first but I will answer it now & here after I will try & do better. What makes you think it will be labor lost to write to me? I ain't out of the world yet. Why, it is only about 700 miles down here & I guess there is not much danger about letters getting lost coming here if they are directed to one via Louisville. At any rate, I hope you will keep trying. If you do lose one now & then, why all you have got to do is to write it over & try it again.

Well, Mother, it is two months to day since I left Detroit. Does it seem as long as that to you? It don't to me. The time passes much slower here than it did when I was with the Regt, to be sure. But it goes fast enough. Anyhow, if I had known that I was going to stay here I should have Telegraphed to you for a box to be sent to me by express. But no telling now how I shall leave here, there is only about 40 men now too sick to go on to the regt. I think we will all be able to go in a week or two. I hope so, for I want to get there & get my letters. I think there must be a big heap there by this time. You asked me to give your love to Armstrong. I will when I write to him. I don't expect to see him again for some time, if ever before the war stops. He is at Danville in a post hospital. He most probably will stay there during the war. They came very near putting me in one at Lebanon. When I left New Market, I had to go to Lebanon with my men to get on the cars. We went there Saturday & had to stay in Lebanon till Monday before we could get on the cars. We had very comfortable quarters in an old barn with the sides all taken off (to half ventilate, I suppose). Sunday afternoon there was a surgeon came to me & asked me if I was a good hospital steward. I told, of course I was & he said you are just the man I want. I told him I guessed not, but he said come along with me & I will see about it. So he took me to the head surgeon at Lebanon & told him he had found just the man he wanted & I told him he had found just the man that was not a going to stay in Lebanon. Oh well, he said that don't make any difference. I told him I rather thought it did with me.

The head surgeon spoke & told him that he had been having his eye on me for some time for him, but had come to the conclusion that he could not have me, so I about-faced & marched. I was glad to get outside of that building, you may be sure.

The folks in this country are a regular set of fools. They don't know beans when the bag is open. I went to get some butter of the best educated man there is in this place. The butter was 30 cents a pound & I wanted 50 cents worth & he had to figure it out & then he said he could not get at it exactly so he gave me 1¾ pounds of it. They don't know enough to last them over night. Milk is worth 10 cents a quart here; coffee 50 cents; brown sugar 25 cents & every thing in proportion.

But I must stop. Write as often as you can. Give my love to all the folks & tell them to write & when they write, tell me just how long it takes this letter to get through.

Good bye
Jimmie

Gallitin, Tenn.
Monday Dec 15 [1862]

My Dear Father

You will have to excuse ink this time for it has give out. I arrived at this place Saturday morning with 20 men. I put part of them in hospital yesterday & the rest in barracks & am writing for Dr. Bacon to come on with the Hospital stores, when we will go direct to Nashville. We were ordered to bring our sick here & to report immediately to our regiment for further orders, which I shall be most awful glad to do for this being left behind is not the kind I like. Genl Rosencranz has issued an order that no sick men should be sent on to their regiments without they were able to go on active duty.

That looks some like hot work. I should not wonder if we had a fight near Murfreesboro very soon. I hope I shall be there in time, for Dr. Frick is not very well & he is the only one with the regiment. The regiment numbers about 500 men fit for duty. We have a great many sick; we have them all along the route from Louisville to Nashville. This place (Gallitin) is one perfect hospital. Nothing but soldiers in the street—citizens are very scarce. I don' think I have seen 15 citizens since I have been in the place. Stores & dwelling houses are all occupied by sick soldiers. We are in the 2nd floor of a once large shoe store. It makes it very nice for the boys, the dirt don't track in & we can keep it much cleaner than we could on the first floor. The court house is full from steps to cupola & it is about the size of the Post Office in D[etroit]. One of the churches & a large school house are full of wounded from the battle of Hartsville, about 1,700 of our men, paroled at that place, passed through here Saturday—yesterday 1,800 rebels passed through on the way to Louisville captured 6 miles this side of Murfreesboro.

I expect the rebels have quite a force near that place & I know we have. I think we will hear from there soon. I received a letter from Nashville just before we left Mitchellville, mailed back to me. It contained a letter from Mother, Jerry & Libbie & Mother's picture that looked quite natural. I don't think I shall get into Nashville in time to see Mr. Willard. I should like to very much. I am very much obliged for those stamps you sent me. I just begin to think of franking my letters, but shant be under the necessity now. You must excuse this miserable scrawl, but take the will for the deed. I would do better if I could. I suppose it will be about Christmas when you receive this, so I will wish you & all the rest of the family a Merry Christmas & a Happy New Year.

From
Jimmie
Write

Nashville, Tenn.
Dec 17th 1862

Brother Charlie

Here I am at last with the regiment, after being absent over 2 months & I am glad of it. I found all the boys all right & fat as butter. Ed Owen is the fattest one in the crowd. You ought to see him & for that matter you ought to see me, for I am just about as fat as he is.

I left Gallatin yesterday afternoon at ½ pass–4, & arrived here at 6, then I had to start & find where my regt was stationed. I traveled up one street & down another to find [the] director for the information I wanted. Then commenced another hunt. I could not get any intelligent answers from the citizens, but every darkey I met could answer questions & I got my directions principally from them. They are the sincerest people in the city. You ask a white man he will tell you to go on a piece & ask again, any body up there will tell you where it is. You ask a darkey & he will tell you to go up 3 blocks & turn to the right & it is next door to the corner. When they tell you a thing, you know a little more after they tell you than you did before.

But to continue my story, I found the army director & he told me my regt was 1 ¾ miles from the city on the Lebanon Pike & that I should have to wait till morning & get me a pass from Genl Mitchell to go to my regt. Well, I went back to the depot & took my men to the barracks & put up for the night. This morning, I went to visit the tomb of President James K. Polk. It is in the front yard in front of his house. I went over the grounds. The house is a very nice one & the grounds are laid out very neatly. There is a great many very nice residences in Nashville. It put me in mind of home more than any place I have been. When I was going to the Chief of Police, the bells began to ring for 6 o'clock, the only place I have heard the bells since I left Louisville. This morning I got my pass & to show you how much good it done me, I will send it to you. I was so good looking, nobody asked me for it but it was all for the best for I should not have seen Polk's tomb if I had come out to the regt last night.

George Clark has had an attack of dysentery & it has run him down a good deal. But I must stop for my candle is getting low & I must make my bed before it goes out. I find all my papers here, about 25. Among the rest, your paper, which had that article on Our Balcony & Ten-cent Jimmy. Remember me to all my friends. If you get a chance, you must send me Hatties' photographs. She asked me if I had got one yet. Be sure & send me one. I expect Armstrong every day & will tell him what an impression he has made. I wonder if you are drafted yet? Think of me New Years Day, when you go calling. I wish you could have me to go with you.

Good Bye
From Jimmie

Camp Rosencranz
Near Nashville
Saturday Dec 20 1862

Dear Mother

I received your very welcome letter written in great haste on Monday morning, lamenting in strong terms the loss of all your letters, but I begin to think they were not at all lost for I have received quite a number lately. I have answered all of them but one from Jerry & one from Libbie. So you can tell wether I have got them all or not. You said you would like to send me a box of good things; if you still feel that way, you may do so. I wrote to Mattie last night about it. We expect to stay in this camp some time, long enough to send me a box by express, if it is sent pretty soon after you get this letter.

You said I was not to laugh when I got your first letter. You need not be afraid of that for I was to near broke to laugh at such things. I don't want you to rob yourself sending me stamps for Uncle Sam's paymaster is expected around pretty soon & I shall have lots to get stamps with. When I wrote for some I was where I could not get them for love or money, but here it is different. We can get all we want at Nashville.

I wish I could have been there to help you dispose of your Thanksgiving Dinner, as it was, I did not think any thing about it until or 3 days after it had passed. I am much obliged for your picture. It looked as natural as life when it dropped out of the envelope. I wrote a letter to George Maurice to night telling him that I expected to go on with Dr. Fish to the battle field tomorrow. We have heard heavy firing all the evening & signals have been moving from hill top to hill top.

But our regt have returned; they were out in a different direction & consequently we won't have to go. Give my love to all the folks & write soon to

Jimmie

Camp of the Light Brigade, Butterfield's Corps
Near Potomac Creek, Va. Dec 21st 1862

My Dear Friend

Your kind letter of the 2nd was received on the 15th and I was very glad to hear from you again. I take the first spare time I have had since our late battle to write you a short acct of what I saw of it.

Our brigade was out on picket duty from the 7th untill the afternoon of the 10th, when we received orders to withdraw our pickets, return to camp, and prepare to march. We did so and, next morning, our entire corps marched down to the river bank opposite Fredericksburgh and then awaited further orders. In the meantime, the 50th NY (an engineer regt) had been attempting to throw a pontoon bridge across at the old ferry, but the rebel infantry kept up such a fire from the houses, cellars, &c, through the city that they were unable to get the bridge across, and so Gen Burnside ordered our batteries to bombard the city, which was accordingly done and soon the brick buildings in all portions of the city were tumbling down and by noon, the city was afire in 7 different places, but our troops did not succeed in getting the bridge across untill towards night, but when they did finish it, the 7th Mich, 20th Mass, and other regts rushed over, and soon drove the rebels out of the place, and, that night, a division of Sumner's troops held the place.

The next day there was not much done except constant skirmishing by the pickets and occasionally a few shots fired from our heavy batteries for the purpose of feeling the enemy's position. But the day after that the great battle came off. It was commenced early on the morning of the 13th by Sumner's troops, who were sent up division after division to storm the place. The rebels were posted on a range of hills about 2 miles back from the river. They had thrown up a strong line of earth works upon these hills and planted cannon upon them, tier after tier as thick as they could work them; their light artillery upon the first hills, and heavy artillery upon the higher hills further back. The ground from these hills towards the river although undulating, gradually sloped down towards the city, and, as it was an open plain from the city out to the rebel works, of course the rebels could just sweep our men away by the hundreds. In front of the rebel batteries, they had a line of infantry posted in rifle pits, and their sharpshooters were concealed in great numbers all over this plain. Under such circumstances, we could expect but one result, which was that when our men advanced, they were drove back every time with great slaughter, from where our corps were stationed (on this side of the river), we could see our troops advance, see them mowed down by the rebel artillery, and although they would charge up bravely again and again, they would only rush upon their own destruction.

The rebels fired their artillery so rapidly that it seemed one continual roar and we could not distinguish the discharge of a single cannon, whilst the musketry kept up such a continual rattling, that it seemed more like the popping of immense numbers of fire crackers than anything else. Our troops had fought all day long, untill 3 P.M., without gaining any advantage at all, and they had all been engaged except our corps (which was the reserve), and now it came our turn.

Crossing the river and through the city upon the double quick, we formed our line of battle in the outskirts of the city, Humphrey's division upon the right, and our own Griffins upon the left, with Sykes' division as our reserve. Gen. Butterfield gave the order to charge and forward we went upon the run, without attempting to fire as the other troops had done, as by so doing we would only have lost time. The rebels sent the shot and shell amongst us thick and fast, causing great gaps in the ranks, worse on the right, however, than it was on the left, and the rebel infantry sent perfect showers of bullets to meet us, yet we kept steadily on untill we had drove the rebel infantry back to their entrenchments and we had gained possession of a ridge, only 40 rods from the main works of the enemy. From this ridge we poured our first fire, and then, as we knew it would be useless to attempt to storm the enemy's fortifications, we kept ourselves under cover of this ridge, and kept up a lively firing upon the enemy untill after dark, and then both sides stopped, as if by mutual agreement.

Our division remained in its position all night, and Humphrey's division went back to the city, and Sykes' division (regulars) took their place. The next morning, Sunday, as soon as it was day light, the rebels sent a few shot and shell over amongst us, as if apparently to try the range of their pieces, and then, unaccountably to us, they ceased firing, although (as we knew by this time), they could have played terrible havoc with our two divisions, if they had felt so disposed. Our regt was on the extreme left and my co., B, on the extreme left of the regt. Where we were the ridge ceased, and beyond it, to the left was a low field, whilst beyond that was another ridge running in the contrary direction from the one that protected us, and during the forenoon, the rebels sent a body of infantry around under cover of this ridge to the rear and upon our left, and the first intimation we had that they were there, they sent a shower of bullets over amongst us. We, however, turned our fire in that direction, and as our regt were armed with rather the best rifles, we succeeded after about an hours sharp firing, in driving them back and were not troubled by them any more that day.

Our two divisions remained in that position right under the rebel batteries all day long, without any troops being sent out to relieve us. In fact, they could not have come out to us without being all cut to pieces, and after the taste we had of crossing the plain the day previous, we did not care much about attempting to return in daylight, so we remained there all day long, expecting every minute that the rebel batteries would open upon us. However, they did not, and it is said that 3 rebel generals are to be court-martialed for it. About 12 that night, there was a brigade come out to do picket duty where we were and we returned to the city and slept that night upon the sidewalk. The next day, the 15th, everything was generally quiet about the city except the rebels would occasionally throw a shell over amongst us, probably for the purpose of keeping us awake. I had a good opportunity that day to observe the damage done to the city by the bombardment, and I saw entire blocks of brick stores on the main street that had been knocked down by our shot, whilst among many buildings, both houses and stores, had been burnt. Those that were left had been ransacked by our troops and most everything in

GENERALS HUMPHREYS'S AND PORTER'S DIVISIONS CROSSING
THE POTOMAC RIVER, AT BLACKFORD'S FORD
(THE PICTORIAL BATTLES OF THE CIVIL WAR, NEW YORK, 1895)

them either taken away or destroyed. That night it was determined by Gen. Burnside to
evacuate the place and our brigade was to be the rear guard, so about 12 o'clock, we went
out to the front and relieved the brigade on picket. In going out there, we passed about
½ mile more to the right than we had on Saturday afternoon, whilst making our charge,
and over the ground where the hardest fighting had taken place, and nearly all of the
dead lay strewn upon the ground yet. In one place we found where they lay as thick as if
a brigade had been ordered to lay down and had laid down right in their places. Supposing it to be the troops we were to relieve, I asked what brigade that was, when some one
said they were dead men, and upon examination, it proved to be so. I thought I had seen
some pretty bad sights since I had been in this war, but I never saw anything so horrible
as that before. As soon as we arrived out at the picket line, it commenced to rain. This,
of course, was very favorable to us as it concealed our movements from the view of the
enemy.

At 4 A.M., we fell back to the outskirts of the city and at 7, as all our troops had
crossed, we marched down to the bridge and our regt were the last ones to cross except
a few of the engineers, who were waiting to take up the bridge. After crossing the river
we marched back to our old camp, which we reached at 12M on the 16th, all of us pretty
well wet through, and completely tired out, and we were very glad indeed to get back to
the old camp, you may well believe.

The loss in our regt was 41 in killed and wounded. Capt. Mahan and Lieut. Hughes were both severely wounded. That was all the loss amongst the officers. The loss in our regt was small, however, compared to that in other regts, yet as we only had 250 men to go into battle with, we could not lose many. The loss on our side figures up a total of over 15,000, I believe, over half as many again as we lost at the great battle of Antietam, and more than double the loss of the western army at the bloody battle of Shiloh. Who is to blame for this, it is perhaps unnecessary to say, as it will probably be all known to the public one of these days. Yet in my humble opinion, our government at Washington is greatly to blame, for if they had intended to attack the rebels in that position, they should have sent us more men, and not have left an army of 100,000 alone to attack an army of 150,000 in an almost impregnable position, and we all know very well they have the men if they choose to send them on. When we were ordered to march, we certainly expected Gen. Banks' expedition was going to be sent up the James River, and then the forces on the Peninsula and in N. Carolina were to join it and Richmond threatened by this army, which, of course, would have compelled the rebel army here to fall back upon Richmond, without our having to fight this battle. Then the two armies of ours could have been united and with the assistance of our iron clad gunboats, the rebel capitol could have been taken. But, no, it seems Gen. Banks must be sent down south to capture some city that probably is not worth powder enough to blow it up with, and the rebel capitol, which is, in fact, the heart of the rebellion, is to be left untouched, and our great army scattered around, generally, wherever they can be of the least service. It seems to me, lately, that our rulers are going mad, and are trying to do their best to destroy the army.

But, I suppose it seems worse to me here, than it does to the people of the country north, yet I cannot help wishing that the people of the North and South could have seen that horrible massacre, for if they had, they would be willing to settle up the war upon any terms without our fighting another battle. The rebel loss is said to be 3,000, only one fifth as much as ours.

On the 17th, we sent out a party of men under a flag of truce to bury our dead. I have given you no account of the part taken in the battle by Gen. Franklin's troops, as they were 2 miles below us, and I suppose you have read all about it in the papers. I received the sermon of Dr. Duffield's, which you sent me and, indeed reading it today, it arrived on the 18th. I am much obliged to you for sending it and was very glad indeed to receive it. And now I must bring this long letter to a close, as I must have pretty well tired your patience by this time. Please give my regards to Dr. Duffield and friend Henry and any other enquiring Friends, and, hoping to hear from you again soon, I remain, as ever,

> Respectfully Your Friend,
> C.H. Salter

Camp Rosencranz
Christmas Night [1862]

Dear Mother

Christmas has passed without the usual excitement. I have not received quite as many presents as usual, only two—a bottle of catsup & a bottle of porter. That box did not come along in time for Christmas dinner, so we had army fare for a change. I send you a bill of fare, so you can see how we live. I have received Jerry's letter in regard to the box, written on the 19th, & have been t see Mr. Willard twice about it. His goods have not come on yet. I hope I shall get it for New Years.

Last night we had orders to march this morning with 8 days rations & 2 ambulances, so Dr. Fish sayed he & I would go, so we got every thing packed & all ready but we didn't go. This morning the order was countermanded. We were told to be ready to start at an hours' notice. We all expect we shall move in the morning. I expect there will be a right smart brush out there before long, then we shall see what the 4th Cavalry are made of. I am rather anxious to start, for the Secesh need whipping & they never will get it till the 4th Mich catches up with them. Our boys had another skirmish today while out guarding a forage train. They killed one of our men & we finished 7 or 8 of them & they seemed quite satisfied to leave us alone.

We have rumors of a battle at Gallatin & that our forces whipped the rebels but that the 19th Mich suffered severely. No telling how true it is yet, I suppose. The rebels were under Kirby Smith. I wish the river would rise so that we need not be dependant on the railroad for our supplies & that the gun boats could come up. It has rained 2 feet.

Now, write soon & tell me all about Christmas & New Year.
Jimmie

Christmas Day
1862
Bill of Fare
Hospital
4th Michigan Cavalry

Bread—hard (alias Government Pies)
    soft
    corn
    warm biscuit
Soups—beef
    bean
    vegetable
Meats—beef steak
    do boiled
    bacon fried

Vegetables—onions boiled
    beans boiled
Relishes—catsup
    pickles
    butter
Liquors—porter

James Vernor
Hospital Steward

4

Into the Maelstrom

"The combat deepens, on, ye braves,
Who rush to glory or the grave!
Wave, Michigan! All thy banners wave,
And charge with all thy chivalry!"

As Union forces battled through New Years Day, 1863, at Stones River, Tennessee, the Army of the Potomac awoke to the news of the announcement of the Emancipation Proclamation, freeing the slaves in the southern states. The second full year of the war would see casualties mount as Americans slaughtered each other at Chancellorsville, Vicksburg, Gettysburg, Chickamauga, and Chattanooga.

Camp of the 16th Regt Mich Infantry
Near Potomac Creek, Va. Jan. 4th 1863

My Dear Friend

Your kind and very interesting letter of the 27th was received on the 1st and therefore it was a New Year present for me and a very acceptable one it was, I assure you. Since I wrote you last we have had nothing of any great importance transpire in our Army of the Potomac. We occupy the same camp yet and every thing goes on in the same old way as before the battle, and traces of that affair have disappeared from amongst us, and we are only reminded of it by the decimated ranks of the regiments that were engaged, and the numerous graves that have increased so fearfully of late amongst us.

We are now busily engaged in drilling, doing picket and guard duty, &c, and during last week we had our muster for pay, and I had the job of making out the pay rolls for the company. On the 30th inst at 2 P.M. our division received sudden orders to get ready to march immediately, to take 4 days rations in our haversacks, leave our tents in camp, as well as the officer's baggage, but everything we needed was to be carried by ourselves, as no wagons were to be taken with us. Accordingly, we packed up, and fell in at 3, and taking our place in the line of the division at 4, we commenced our march. No one except Col. Barnes, who commanded the division and the colonels commanding brigades, knew where we were going and various were the conjectures as to the object of the expedition. A good many thinking that we were going out to intercept Stuart's cavalry, who were at that time making a raid up near Alexandria, and one officer very facetiously remarked that as the Negroes would all be free on the 1st, we were going out to drive them in. That is, if the rebels did not drive us in ourselves.

Soon after we started it commenced to rain, and was very cold but we kept on as well as we could and by 8 P.M., we had reached Sudley Church, which is 9 miles west of here, and is the place where the rebels captured a party of the 3rd Penn Cavalry a few days ago. We remained there three hours and then moved on 5 miles further and halted about 1 mile from Ellis's Ford on the Rappahannock. We then rested for the balance of the night, in an open field, but we could not sleep at all, as we were all wet and too cold to sleep. Early next morning we moved down to the river and as our skirmishers approached the ford they found a body of rebel cavalry there, doing picket duty, who fired upon our men and then fled. Our skirmishers wounded and captured two of them, and during the firing, a secesh lady, living in a house close by was, unfortunately, wounded by a stray shot, which was fired at rebel soldiers near the house. Our surgeon attended to her case, but she did not seem to mind it at all, but on the contrary said she was used to hearing bullets whistle and did not mind them at all, but would much rather she should be hit than to see one of the rebel soldiers hit, and our surgeon made up his mind that she was a pretty strong minded secesh woman.

The 1st and 2nd brigades of our division crossed the river and went west several miles on a reconnaissance to see what they could discover, but did not meet with any of the rebels and returned to the ford towards night. Our brigade remained at the ford, guarding it all day and we were not at all sorry that we did not go with the others, as we would have had to cross the river, as they did, in water three feet deep, in the last day of Dec., and it would have been very conducive to our health, I suppose. The object of the expedition was to capture a body of rebel infantry doing picket duty at Kelly's Ford, which is about 10 miles above where we were, and our division was to move up this side of the river and attack them, whilst Gen. Averill was to take his brigade of cavalry, cross the river and, coming up in the rear of the rebels, cut off their retreat. But, after we had started, Gen. Averill received orders to go in pursuit of Stuart, and so we received orders to return to camp on the 1st. But why it was that our commander did not attempt the capture of the rebels with our division of infantry, I cannot say, but it certainly looks to me like a poor piece of generalship.

We slept in the woods that night and next morning (the 1st), at 8 we started for camp and, after a very rapid march our brigade reached camp at 12M, having marched 14 miles in 4 hours. This we consider to be as good a march as any troops in the army can do and it shows why our brigade is called the "Light Brigade." We were pretty tired after we reached camp, and therefore we could not be said to have enjoyed our New Years very well. In fact, we had none of the luxuries of the season to assist us to enjoy the holiday, and we were so fatigued that we could not feel that it was a very happy day with us.

However, we had reason to be very thankful to the Almighty, to think we had passed safely through such a year as the previous one has been for our regt, as well as many others. And those of us that were left yet, do feel very grateful to think that, whilst so many of our comrades have fallen in battle, from disease and died from wounds received in battle, that there are 250 of us left yet, to serve and fight for our country, when it is needed.

Gen. Butterfield, our old favorite and former commander of this brigade, after having first been transferred to the command of the division, and then of the corps, has now been made a Major General and ordered to a command out west, and Gen. Meade, who commanded a brigade of the Penn Reserves last winter, and who, when he was a captain in the coast survey, was at one time stationed in Detroit, has been appointed to take command of our corps. Gen. Griffin now commands our division, and he is now the only general we have left in the division, and as he was absent at the time of the late expedition, the senior colonel, which is Col. Barnes of the 15th Mass. Regt., took command of the division; Col. Stockton being absent in Michigan, Col. Weeks of the 12th Regt. N.Y. had command of our brigade. There are so many of our generals absent from the army at the present time that I do not believe it is the intention to have any more battles with the rebels here for some time to come. And there is an impression throughout our entire army that we will remain inactive for the next two months, unless the rebels should advance to meet us, as there is a rumor at present that they are doing, for we have just heard that the rebel army is moving off towards Warrenton, and perhaps they may intend to make another raid into Maryland and in that case, we shall have to move from here very soon. But in that case, it will be the best thing that could happen to us for then the rebels will be obliged to meet us in the open field, and we can go into a battle then with a great deal more confidence than we could to attack such places as their position back of Fredericksburgh. I can scarcely believe the rumor, but yet, more startling events have occurred before this in this war.

We have just heard that the Monitor is sunk, but I hope it will prove to be not so. We have not yet received the particulars, nor the result, of the battle near Murfreesboro. I have looked for reports of Michigan Regts. engaged but as yet I can not find any. But yet I suppose the Ninth were there as you stated they were in Gen. Thomas corps. I hope before this time that you have heard that your son Henry is safe. At least it appears from what partial accounts we already have of the battle that it is a terrible affair, and we are anxiously waiting to hear of the result, and to hear whether our friends are safe or not. When next you write, please let me know if Henry is safe and if the Ninth were engaged in the battle or not.

I received the sermon you sent me, which was wrote by your son the minister, and was much interested in reading it. But not so much so, though as I was in the one you sent me of Dr. Duffields, the Fast Day sermon. The last one I have read over several times and it has done me a great deal of good, as I can see there pointed out to me God's ways and power, as concerns the present war, and it shows me and convinces me of my duty to the government, which, I must confess, that lately I had had a great many doubts about the Govt. and about their efficiency, and even honesty in conducting the war. But I think that, after all, if the people will sustain the Govt., and God will assist and aid us, we can yet reestablish our Glorious and beneficial old Union. In fact, the sermon is suited to the times, and after reading it over, I believe I can comprehend the subject, and understand my duty better than ever before. I am under great obligations to you for sending it.

Sergt. Platt of the 5th Regt must have been sent up to Washington or somewhere else up north to hospital, soon after the battle, therefore it would be useless to look for him here. The weather here for the last week has been quite pleasant, and whilst we remain in camp, we can enjoy it very well, but if we should have to march now, we should feel the cold weather nights very badly. We have just received the long expected Emancipation Proclamation of the President and now I suppose it will change the policy and plans of our government altogether. I hope it will change for the better.

Col. Stockton is now absent on a visit to Michigan and most of our generals can get leaves of absence whenever they want it, but as for the company officers and men, they cannot obtain a leave for even a single day. But then I suppose we are of no consequence. But I must bring this long letter to a close, as I have wrote all I have time too, and all I suppose that you have time to spend in reading. It is now Sunday evening, and we are expecting that very likely we shall receive marching orders tomorrow, therefore I must be making preparations accordingly. Please give my kind regards to Dr. Duffield and all enquiring friends. Also, remember me to Friend Henry when next you write. And hoping to hear from you again soon, I remain,

Respectfully and Truly Your Friend
C.H. Salter

P.S. Please excuse this blot as I spilt some water on the letter after writing it, and now can scarcely spare time to write it again. C.H.S.

Murfreesboro
Jan 7 1863

Dear Parents

I hope you are not getting alarmed about me but I could not get a letter through before & take the first chance to do so. I am out of paper & can't get any in this place, so I thought I would use up my old acct. book. My last letter was written on Christmas night. The next day (Friday), we had orders to march to the front, leaving all extras at Nashville. I was busy all day packing & started for Nashville after dark; camped in Nashville over night; in the morning, went to see Mr. Willard about box; found it had not come; left N[ashville] about noon, caught up with the regt after dark & went into camp in a very nice cedar grove.

We stayed in this camp all the next day (Sunday), short of provisions; killed a Secesh hog, found it very good eating. The next morning, we were ordered out on a scout; the regt went about 10 miles & found the enemy across a river in quite large force; thought we would not hurt them, so we about-faced & marched back again, ahead; (7 chickens) the result of the scout.

Tuesday we marched on to the front & encamped in another cedar grove. The farmers about here have plenty of cows. We can afford cream in our coffee now. (Wednesday). We marched this morning out on the right wing, found a good many stragglers coming back from the field; all said that the right wing was all cut to pieces. Our brigade was sent forward on the double quick, except 4 companies of our regt, who were left as reserves. Stayed all day until dark & thought it unsafe to stay longer, so we went back to our camp & sent out pickets in the direction we came from.

In the morning, (New Years Day), a messenger came to tell us that 3 or 4,000 rebel cavalry had been seen coming this way, so our cavalry & a regt of infantry was drawn up in line of battle & our cannon placed in position & all were waiting anxiously to hear the first gun fired. While we were waiting, an order came purporting to come from Rosencranz that the Army of the Cumberland was on the retreat & every thing moveable was to fall right in with the wagon train & make its way to Nashville. The order of course included us, so the ambulance fell right in & marched on. The regt followed. It was one of the most exciting scenes I ever saw. The excited teamsters kept their mules on the jump most of the way & the infantry, with anxious looks, trying to keep up with them. It was getting to be a regular stampede, when all at once, Bang Bang went 2 cannon & whiz, whiz went the shells over our heads. Then the panic began. The teamsters cut loose their mules & went a flying; the infantry ran back as if their necks were in danger & the cry arose, they are coming, they are coming. I stood in the front of my ambulance & asked them, who were coming; the rebels, the rebels, they said.

Sure enough, all at once, they came piling out of the woods, yelling like wild men. I asked the Dr. (Fish), if I should turn around & get out of this & he said, no, stay where you are, they won't touch us, we are non-combatants. We might have got out of it if he had let me alone. I will show you by this sketch.

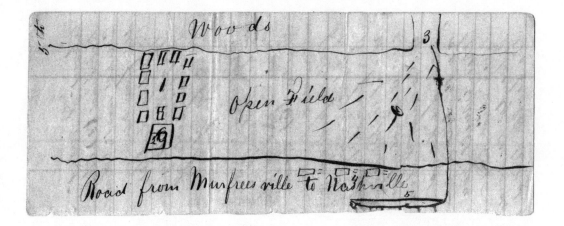

1. park of wagons
2. large house
3. road the rebels came from
4. our ambulances
5. post fence
6. secesh cavalry

Now, if when the rebels first came out at 3, we had turned about & went behind
(1), they could not touch us for our cavalry & the straggling infantry was inside of it &
fought them back but we didn't. The rebel cavalry came across the field (6) & surrounded
us. One fellow poked a pistol in my face & asked me if I surrendered. I told him, of
course I did. Well, he said, go to the rear, then. Well, you see, I did not like to go across
the field to go to (3), for fear some careless fellow might hit me by mistake with a bullet,
so I jumped down behind the post fence (5), intending to go around it & then cross the
field (see mark). But he rode up to the fence & poked his pistol at me & banged away. I
shant pretend to say how near he came to me, all I can say is he did not hit me. I asked
him very politely, what he was about & jumped back into the ambulance. The rebel told
me to drive across to (3), which I proceeded to do immediately. While we were going
across the field a bullet came through the ambulance & just grazed my cranium. Talk
of music, it is nothing compared with the whistle of bullets, but I can't see it when they
come so near.

When we got into the woods, they ordered us out of the ambulance & made us foot it
for 5 miles over one of the worst roads you ever saw. We stopped at a large white house &
our arms & etc were taken away from me. That is the last of my sword. Boo, Hoo. I feel
so bad. It was a regular nuisance anyhow, so I shant miss it much.

They formed us in line & marched us on about 10 miles more & stopped for the
night. Our captors were very kind & allowed us to ride part of the time behind them. On
this last march, one secesh took away my blanket & one exchanged over coats. It was sort
of one sided affair & it made me mad & I told him just what I thought of him in plain
words, if I was their prisoner.

The next morning, we resumed our march & got into Murfreesboro about noon & were taken to the court house & paroled. Dr. Fish got liberty for me to help him in caring for our wounded, of which there was a great many in the town. We went to work & have since then taken care of between 150 & 200. We worked night & day. We have reduced the number now to about 40, the rest have been sent home for exchange. They were sent by the rebels by way of Vicksburg.

On Sunday (Jan. 4th), the rebels evacuated the place. Their troops were drawn up in line of battle in front of our hospital all day, but left in the evening. Monday, the city was [as] still as a mouse all day. Tuesday, morning (6th), our troops came pouring in on every street. The 4th Ohio Cavalry were the first in the city.

I am still at work on our wounded because I had liberty to do so. I hope to be exchanged soon, for I don't think I am doing right in working after our army gets in here. That goes rather against my oath, but it's a work of necessity & can't be helped. The provost marshal says we will have to wait where we are until Genl Rosencranz issues an order relative to paroled prisoners. I hope he will issue it soon, for I want my exchange so that I can go to work on good earnest again. If I had known that they paroled hospital stewards, I never should have been taken. I think I should have skeddadled first. I don't like the idea of going to Camp Chase or some other place & waiting my exchange. It will be very tiresome to stay in one place so long, when I know how much good I could do in the field, but what can't be cured must be endured.

I saved my valise from the secesh & consequently all my clothes, which pleased me. You may be assured I have arranged to get a secesh relic or two. I got a double-barrelled shot gun & a delicate tooth pick in the shape of a Bowie knife. I have not received that box of good things yet but hope to pretty soon. You don't think things in it will spoil, do you? I hope not for we have been short of rations so long I want to have a feast.

For once, our regt is in camp about 1½ miles from here. I am going to try to go out to it to day. This place is not a very large or extremely nice place, but it will be remembered for some time on account of the large battle fought here.

But I must stop. I hope you were not anxious about me, but I would have written before but could not. I don't know wether you will be able to spell this out or not. I had to write it in a hurry.

> Good bye from your affect son, Jimmie
> Excuse all blunders
> From Jimmie

Camp of the 16th Regt Mich Infty
Near Potomac Creek, Va. Jan 11th 1863

My Dear Friend

Your kind letter of the 4th was received on the 7th and it seems it was wrote on the same day I wrote you a letter also. The piece it contained, "Brave, Kind and Happy," has been read and pondered over by me and it has suggested many new and, I hope, better thoughts. I shall hereafter use that simple prayer, every morn and night, and I think it will do me a great deal of good. I believe that since I have belonged to the army I have tried, as well as I know how to live the life of a Christian, and although not belonging to any church, as a member of it, I have tried to live up to the laws of God, as laid down in the ten commandments, as well as I could here in the army. And although I know very well that I have often failed to keep them, yet I believe I owe my preservation through all the hardships and dangers I have passed through to that and I have always been in the habit, before going into a battle, to pray to the Lord every moment I had time, and we always have heretofore in every battle I have been in, had plenty of time, as a large battle never takes place, or at least never has with our army, but that we have plenty of time to pray, if a person felt so disposed.

And even on the battlefield we often have time for prayer, as for instance, when we are lying down in line of battle, behind a ridge or hill, waiting for the enemy to charge, or waiting perhaps to charge ourselves. And I may perhaps be considered by some as super-stitious, but I have always thought and believed that I owed my preservation during the different battles I have been through, to the prayers I have been in the habit of offering up to God on those occasions.

I suppose that before this time you have heard from your son Henry and that he is safe, as I can find no account in the papers of any of the 9th Mich being killed or wound-ed. The N.Y. city papers contain the names of several of the 11th, & 13th Mich amongst the killed and wounded, but so far I have not seen the names of any belonging to other Mich regts. We are just now very anxious to hear from Gen. Sherman's army near Vicks-burg, as the last news we had from him, he was repulsed and rebel accounts represent that he has re-embarked aboard of his transports again. If his army is defeated, it will more than counterbalance the victory gained by Gen. Rosencranz army at Murfreesboro.

Our army remains comparatively quiet, watching the enemy across the river. It appears that the rebels have withdrawn a large portion of their force, several miles back from the river, probably for the greater facility of getting supplies by the R.R. On the 7th our army corps, the 5th, had a grand review before Gen. Burnside. But, as we now have no brass bands in our corps, it did not seem as pleasant an affair, as when we were reviewed a year ago, on Minor's Hill, by Gen McClellan. And the great difference in the numbers of the old regts makes it seem as if they were only skeletons of what they once were.

On the 8th, our regt went out on picket duty. Our picket line is about 4 miles west of our camp. Saturday it rained hard all day and was very cold, so we greatly missed the shelter of even our little tents. I am greatly obliged to you, for your kind offer to send me something from Detroit, but I do not need anything, but what I can procure here, or send to Washington for. But as to your offer to do anything you can in Detroit, I think you can do me a great favor, as I wish to obtain a commission in the regular army, and as I am not able to leave my regt long enough to see the proper authorities about it. Therefore I cannot obtain the comm. without some one to assist me. I have wrote to my Father about it, and he proposes to send a recommendation to Senators Chandler and Howard, as the commission can be procured through them, and the recommendation of some of the prominent citizens of Detroit would have a great deal of influence to procure the commission. And I have wrote to my Father, to have him see Mr. D.B. Duffield, about it. And I would like also to have you speak to your son about it, and try to have him use his influence to procure the commission. As I have been in the army now for nearly twenty-one months, or since the 19th April, 1861, and have taken my part in every battle that both the Mich 1st, three months Regt and my present Regt have been engaged in, I now wish to get a promotion, into the Regular Army of the United States. For if I could procure the same commission in the regulars which I hold here, it would be regarded as a considerable promotion, and to procure the commission of second lieut. in the U.S. Army, would really be a much better position than that of first lieut in the volunteers. And I have always had a desire to join the regular army, therefore, if you would speak to Mr. D.B. Duffield about the matter, you will confer a great favor to me.

I should think it would be a great deal better for Col. Duffield to accept the post on the Hudson River R.R. than to remain in the army, even if he had a Brig. Generals' commission, especially since he is disabled. I see that Gen. Terry has been ordered to Fortress Monroe. There is a rumor here that we are advance in the course of a day or so, though we have not received any reinforcements as yet and if we do advance across the river again with the small force we have here, I am very fearful of the result.

But I must now bring this letter to a close. Please give my kind regards to Mr. Duffield and all enquiring friends. Also remember me to Henry when next you write to him.

> I remain
> Respectfully and Truly Yours
> C.H. Salter

> Camp of the 16th Regt. Mich Infantry
> Near Potomac Creek Station, Va. Jan 18th 1863

My Dear Friend

Your kind letter of the 13th has just arrived and as we are now under marching orders, and I do not know when I shall have time to write again, I thought best to write today. Since I wrote you last, Sabbath preparations have very quietly been going on here, for another "Onward to Richmond" movement. All of our sick have been sent to Washington, or other places north, fresh ammunition has been dealt out to each regt, and the men have constantly been supplied with four days rations. We received orders to be ready to march this morning, but when the sun rose, we received another order giving us another 24 hours to remain in camp, so that now we expect to march tomorrow morning.

The Eighth Army Corps, which has been doing guard duty in Maryland, under command of Gen. Wool, has been sent down here to reinforce us and as I write, the first regt of that corps has just passed here, on the cars, having just come from Acquia Creek Landing. And probably, by tomorrow morning, the entire corps will be here. And probably before you receive this, you will have heard of another great battle having been fought, on the other side of the Rappahannock. I do not know what the plan of the attack upon the rebels is to be, but, I have confidence in General Burnside to believe that he will not send us into such a trap as we were sent into last time. I hear rumors that we are to cross the river, both above and below the rebel stronghold and attempt to outflank them. But of course, we cannot tell untill the time of attack arrives what the plan is to be.

We have read accounts in the northern papers of one division having been sent away from the rebel army opposite us and that they have gone to Alexandria, or Charleston, or to reinforce Bragg. But careful observation of their camp from a balloon, which is sent up on our side every day, does not show any diminution of that force at all. Although, if it was so, we should be very glad of it, as it would greatly enhance our chances of whipping them. Our army is in tip top spirits, and was never in better condition to fight than at present. But we regret having to leave our comfortable winter quarters, which we have built since the late battle, by raising our tents up on logs, as the next six weeks are the worst of the year, for cold and wet in this portion of the country. And, if we are continually engaged in an active campaign, we shall suffer considerable. We do not mind either the rain or the cold weather whilst on the march during the day time, but it is at night when we halt to bivouac out in the open air, that we suffer from exposure, and about all of our army dread that a great deal worse than they do the fighting. When our army moves, the men carry everything they have with them, and in consequence, when they have their knapsacks, musket, belts, canteen, and haversack with four days provisions to carry, they have a pretty heavy load. The officers have also to carry everything they want to use with them, but they can leave in camp, all they do not wish to carry.

I see by the papers that the rebel Forrest has been routed by General Sullivan so it seems we have one general out west who is capable of meeting, attacking, and routing the guerillas. I am very glad to hear that friend Henry is safe after the Murfreesboro battle. I suppose it must have seemed like a triumph for the old Ninth to enter the village after their banishment. I hope when the Major is promoted to the colonelcy that they will make Henry major, as I think it is nothing more than he deserves. But, it has been my experience here in the army to find that many deserving officers do not get the promotions they deserve, whilst others, who are known in their own regts to be entirely unfit for the positions they occupy, are often promoted yet higher, by reason of favoritism, or perhaps the influence they have with the powers that be. Major Barry left us last Friday, as he has obtained leave of absence to visit home, on account of sickness. Lieut. Titus, (of the company of sharpshooters which are attached to our regt), has resigned on account of ill health, and gone home also; and Lieut. Weber of Co. G has resigned for the same reason, and is shortly to leave. And this, together with the number of officers who are away sick or wounded leaves us only 17 officers here for duty.

The weather today is quite pleasant, and if there were any chaplain in our regt, we might have a very pleasant meeting in the open air. But we have not had any chaplain with us since we left Antietam, and in our brigade of six regts, we have only one chaplain and he belongs to the 20th Maine, a new regt. However, as we do not have any divine service, I busy myself with writing letters, especially as I expect, that for the balance of this winter, I shall have but very little time to write and am very certain I shall not have as good quarters to write in as we now have.

Gen. Griffin returned from Washington last Friday, and now has command of our division. Col Stockton has not returned yet, and the brigade is now under command of Col. Vincent of the 83rd Penn Regt., who is a very good officer, and is well liked by the entire brigade. It seems as if the war was only commencing with our last attack on Fredericksburgh, then reechoed by the western army at Murfreesboro and Vicksburg, and probably this week we shall have a battle on the other side of the river, which will be a fiercer struggle, and larger battle than any that has yet occurred during the war. But, I have not the least doubt we shall drive the rebels back to Richmond, without scarcely halting, though whether we can succeed in taking Richmond or not is another question.

We are in expectation of receiving assistance from the 7th Army Corps, which has been at Yorktown under command of Gen. Keyes. And to judge from the movements in N. Carolina, I think our forces there are going to create a diversion in our favor, as we have accounts that Gen. Foster is concentrating all his forces there and threatening Raleigh, and the rail road communication through that state. However, I have always found that it does not do to place too much dependence on these accounts of promised assistance, when the battles are about to take place.

I received a letter from my Father yesterday and he says, that he would see Senator Chandler before he left the state and probably secure his assistance to procure a commission in the regular army for me. Last week I sent in to General Hooker a request for two days leave of absence in order that I might go to Washington and see what I could do about it myself. But in consequence of the preparations for an advance, no passes could be granted for even one day, so I suppose if I wish to enter the regular army, it will have to be done by the influence of friends at home.

But I must bring this letter to a close, as I have not much news to write. Please give my kind regards to Dr. Duffield and any enquiring friends. I do not know when I shall be able to write again, but will do the best I can. Hoping to hear from you again soon

I Remain
Respectfully Your Friend
C.H. Salter

Murfreesboro
Jan 13th 1863

Dear Brother

I am still here you see & I can't tell when we will get away from here. There is 3 stewards in the same fix as me, all waiting for something to turn up but it don't. I am still taking care of the wounded here. I reported to the provost marshal & he told us we should have to stay where we are until we are relieved. I hope that will be soon, for I feel kinda risky staying here. Just imagine what a fix I would be in if the rebels should get me again before I am exchanged. I suppose we will be sent to Nashville or Louisville to be exchanged. I hope they will hurry up, for I want to be with the regt again. I went out to the regt the other day & had a talk with Col. Minty about it. He said that I might come back & go to work again & run my own risk of being caught again & rather recommended me to do so, but I told him I did not like to break my oath & preferred being exchanged first. He said that would be some time yet as they didn't exchange any more prisoners but I think that's all gammon, for he is the only one I ever heard say so & I rather think he is mistaken. I hope so any how.

Ed Owen did not get that promotion to quartermaster after all. He is acting sergeant major & I expect will get a lieutenant's commission soon. This is a splendid day. I am sitting by the open window writing this. The sun shines & it is as warm as can be. I suppose it is quite different in Detroit. I expect the sleighs are cutting around as usual. Do you have any club sleigh rides out to Wilson's this winter & how is it about those club dancing parties[?] Have you got up as many as usual this winter[?] I wish I could go to 1 or 2 of them with you, but as I can't I suppose you dance for me once in a while, don't you. If you don't, you must as I shall forget how. I think I told you George Clark had broke his arm, didn't I[?] It is getting along very nicely. He will be able to begin to use it in a few days. Col. Minty has been acting Brigadier; our brigadier is off on furlough. He makes a splendid one, the men all say. I should think he would.

But I must stop for this ends the paper. Remember me to all my friends from

Your Paroled Brother
Jimmie

Murfreesboro, Tenn.
Jan 15th 1863

Dear Mother

I received your letter written on the day after Christmas yesterday morning & perhaps you think it didn't look good to see some of the family once more. I tell you those pictures did look good. They are first rate ones to. They look as natural as life. When I opened the letter, every one wanted to know where I got the perfumery.

I think you must be well off to write on perfumed paper, if you ones can, we ones can't. That's all I can say about it. I think you fared pretty well for Christmas presents. I think of the two I rather prefer them to my New Years one. You must have had a very pleasant time in the afternoon. I should have liked to have stepped in & taken supper with [you] but for certain reasons could not do so. I will try to be there next time, that is, if Uncle (Sam) has no objections & I hope he won't. That box has not arrived yet. I suppose Mr. Willard has got it through but he is at Nashville & I ain't, so I can't get it quite yet. I hope the contents will not spoil; do you think it will[?] I expected Mr. Willard would come on to night or in the morning. The first train of cars was to run through to night but the rain, which every Union man has been wishing for has come at last & washed the bridges all away that our men have been repairing. At least, that is the report & I guess it is true, for it has rained hard all day yesterday, last night & today & no signs of its holding up.

In this country a very little rain goes a great ways, for the soil is such that the rain don't soak in very fast & so it runs off & away it goes in the river. I hope now that it has started, it will keep on until it has rained the river high enough for the gun boats to play a part in the war. Genl Rosecranz gave the secesh a specimen of what he could do & if the gun boats can give us a hand, he will give them a lesson they won't forget in some time, I Reckon. The rebels bother us a considerable by getting around behind us & cutting off our supply trains. We had to live very economically to keep from getting out of grub for a while, but have got plenty now for the present use & that's all a soldier looks out for. But it is no fun to live 6 or 7 days on 2 days rations as some of us did. I lived 4 on 2 days rations & thought that was pretty tough, but the Boys didn't complain much, for they were so busy they had no time to think about it. The rebels wore longer faces on Sunday (Jan 6th), than our boys did when the grub was all out.

I received 3 papers from home 2 or 3 days ago. I suppose they were sent by Jerry or Father. I read them all through from beginning to end. I don't have any thing to do now but loaf. That's the beauty of a parole. I hope Genl R will bestir himself & exchange us or something else for I don't like this idle way of living & want to quit it as soon as possible.

You want to know what is the state of my wardrobe. Every single thing except 2 collars is dirty & I can't find a wash woman to get them washed. Every stocking is toeless & part of them heelless. The fact is I can't pluck up enough courage to commence to darn them. I wish you had them all for about 2 or 3 hours. I think they would look a little the better for it, but what can't be cured must be endured. I suppose if I can't get shet of the job, somehow I shall have to do it myself, or go without stockings. Which shall it be. I forgot to mention that there is a fine large hole in the toe of my left boot. I feel worse about that than any thing else. There is no shoe maker here yet or I should have it fixed in a hurry.

But I must stop this or I shall have you all thinking that I am a pretty hard looking fellow, but I don't think so myself & don't want others to think so. Give my love to all the folks & reserve some for yourself.

> From
> Jimmie

I can't tell when this letter will go out, now the bridges are gone, but I think it [will] go as quick as yours did. It took yours 19 days to come here. Jimmie

Camp of the 16th Regt Mich Infantry
Near Potomac Creek Va Feb 3rd 1863

My Dear Friend

Your kind letter of the 25th was received on the 30th inst, and I am greatly obliged to you for your kindness in speaking to your son Bethune about assisting me to get a position in the regular army, and although he thinks he cannot be of much assistance to me, yet I am just as much obliged to him, for his willingness to do all in his power.

When I wrote you last, we were under marching orders, and on the 20th inst, at 2 p.m., our division fell in, and marching west, we started to reach the river at one of the fords above here. The roads were in a bad condition before we started, and on that day the rain commenced again, and the storm continued for about 48 hours. The roads were so bad that the troops ahead of us could not get on very fast and blocked up the road so that we could only make 3 miles that day, and then bivouacked in the woods for the night. The rain poured down all night and, as we had left the tents all behind, we received the full benefit of the water. The next morning, we started again, and by this time the roads were so bad, that the artillery could not be got through by the horses, and the Infantry had to take hold and assist to drag the cannon and caissons. We worked hard all day, but could only succeed in getting about six miles further that day, and we bivouacked in the woods again that night, and by the next morning the roads were so very bad that it was impossible for the artillery to get along, and our wagons could not get out to us with provisions, and we had to go to work building corduroy roads to save us from starvation, and to let the artillery get back to camp. Our regt had a certain portion of the road given to them to build. The road ran through a large plantation, and, as we had no axes, we had to use the fence rails to build the road. Arriving opposite the house, the regt marched over to the fence and each one taking a rail, marched over to the road again to lay them down, and as they picked up the rails it made about the quickest disappearance of a fence that most any one ever saw, and as the regt marched off with the rails, the darkies came out of the house and it seemed as if they would go crazy with laughing at the strange sight. We were kept busy for two days in building roads, and then on the 24th returned to camp without having even crossed the river, though we had done a plenty of hard work, and were completely tired.

But we were satisfied and I think our generals are satisfied also that no active campaign can be carried on in Virginia before the last of March or first of April. Virginia is, in fact, the worst country in all the U.S. for carrying on an active campaign in the wet months during the winter, because when the rains first commence, the ground becomes very soft and it continues so untill the rainy season is over, and the heavy army wagons and artillery cannot travel, unless they have corduroy roads built for them. If we had to depend upon nothing but our wagon trains to bring us supplies from Acquia Creek, we should be scant off for rations, this winter, but fortunately, we have the railroad here, and on that the cars can bring us all the supplies needed.

Since we have been back in our old camp, we have been busy in remodeling our camp, and rebuilding our huts, and now we have the camp in pretty good shape. We have log huts built, using the canvas tents for roofs, and fire places in each hut, so that we are at least protected from the weather when we are not on duty, and each company street is graded, and everything that we could do to make our camp neat and comfortable has been done. We are now for the first time since we have been in the war living in winter quarters, and of course, we are not very anxious to leave them and engage in active operations again. On the 27th and 28th, we had a severe snow storm and the snow lay from 6 to 8 inches deep, but the next day, the weather became warm again, and soon there was nothing left us but the mud again.

We have had a complete change of generals throughout our entire army. Gen. Meade now commands our centre division, Gen Sykes our corps, and Gen. Griffin our division. Gen. Butterfield has been appointed chief of Gen Hooker's staff. This is the first instance I have known of a Major General being a staff officer. The Army of the Potomac is to be entirely reorganized, with new generals, and many of the regiments are to be consolidated, and it is hoped that in the course of time the army will be in a little better shape than it is now. The paymasters have lately been down here paying off the troops a portion of what they owe them and in consequence the men are in a little better spirits than they were.

On the 28th, I received a box of provisions, sent to me by my Father. The box contained butter, dried beef, dried fruit, &c, and it came just in the right time, as we shall very likely remain here long enough to use it up. I shall be very glad to write in my next letter to my Father to request him to call and see you, when he comes to the city, as he probably will be very glad to call upon you, knowing as he does, the interest you take in my behalf. I was very sorry to hear that you had been sick. I should think that Mr. Henry would scarcely thank Gen. Thomas for appointing him A.A. Inspector General, as from what I have seen here of the duties of that office, I know it to be hard work.

I shall be greatly obliged to you for writing to Mrs. J.M. Howard, and probably if she will mention my name, as recommended by you, it will do a great deal of good, when my request is sent in. I have not heard from my Father lately and therefore, do not know what steps he has taken in the matter, but I am in expectation of a letter from him soon. I find that it is impossible for me to obtain leave of absence for any time at all as yet. So I cannot do anything myself. But I am in hopes, that, sometime between this and spring I shall be able to get away for a few days, and have a little time to attend to my own affairs. I feel sometimes as if I was tired of soldiering and would like to be home rather than endure all the hardships we have to. But then I feel that whilst the war lasts, it is my duty to remain and do all I can to put down the rebellion, and when the war is over, the hardships of the soldiers are over also, and then the position of an officer in the regular army will be one that is worth having and, in my opinion, a man can do as much good, as an officer in the army, even if it is in time of peace, as in a good many other positions. Col. Stockton has lately arrived from Michigan and is now in command of the brigade. I will now bring this letter to a close as I have probably wrote all that can be interesting to you. Please give my kind regards to Dr. Duffield and any other enquiring friends.

> Hoping to hear from you again soon,
> I Remain
> Respectfully and Truly Yours
> C.H. Salter

Medical Purveyor's Office
Murfreesboro, Tenn.
Feb 7th 1863

Dear Father

Your letter of Jan 14th came to hand 2 or 3 days since. I am not exchanged yet nor sent to Camp Chase as you can see by the heading of this. If I had been, you would have heard of it before this. If they had sent me there, I should have applied for a furlough but I don't expect to [be sent there]. I think I shall be exchanged here or at Nashville & I hope it will be pretty soon.

This is one of the most pleasant days I have seen since I have been in the service. It is as warm as can be; it seems just like a spring day & I don't know, but it is. Our brigade has gone out on a scout. It went 4 days ago & sent in yesterday for more rations. Dr. Fish is out with them. I believe I wrote that he was Division Surgeon in one of my letters. He held that position about one day; he is now Brigade Surgeon. Dr. Bacon is back to the regt. He & Doc Armstrong runs the machine now.

Tell Charlie that I thought of Detroit more last night than I ever did before at one time since I left home. I wished that I could have popped into Aunty's about 10 o'clock. I think they would have been somewhat surprised. But for reasons to numerous to be mentioned, I could not come. If you see George Maurice, I wish you would tell him he had better answer that last letter or I shall have to come & give him a lecture on the subject.

Give my love to all the folks & write soon.
From Jimmie

Medical Purveyor's Office
Murfreesboro, Tenn.
Feb 8th 1863

Dear Mother

I think I will answer your letter this afternoon & then I shall have answered all but Libbie's. When they all come in a heap, I can't tell hardly which to answer first. You spoke in your letter of Dr. Fish getting clear. You know that they can't hold surgeons & he has done a great deal for me. You spoke of me being out of money; I have about $4.00 left, yet there is not any chance to spend money in this place. I am not in want of anything & we expect to be paid off next week (or rather this week)—the paymaster is on the road now. He is only going to pay up to the 31 of October. That won't be much, will it. You know I arranged it so that Jerry could draw $20.00 per month in Detroit. I don't know how they will arrange it here so that he can but I will tell the paymaster about it & perhaps he will give me a draft on the paymaster in Detroit for it so that Jerry can draw it there.

That said box (you are not tired of hearing that are you) has not arrived yet. I see by one of the Detroit papers that Mr. Willard has been here once & gone back to Nashville. I suppose his goods had not arrived at that time & I did not see him any how. But there is hope as long as there is life, so I live in hopes.

> Give my love to all the folks & write soon to
> Your Affect Son
> Jimmie
> You can send this copy of Dr. Fish's letter the rounds.
> Jimmie

> Head Quarters 4th Mich Cavalry
> Camp Stanly near Murfreesboro
> Tennessee Jan 27th 1863

James Vernor, the Bearer of this is Hospital Steward of the 4th Regiment of Michigan Cavalry. During the progress of the battle near Murfreesboro on the 1st inst, he was captured by the enemy attending an ambulance. He might have escaped but remained at the post of duty exposing himself thereby to great personal danger.

He was taken into Murfreesboro where I found him & succeeded in getting permission for him to assist me in caring for our poor wounded men who were prisoners. During the progress of the battle, & until our troops occupied Murfreesboro, Mr. Vernor rendered me valuable assistance in dressing wounds & providing for the wants of the wounded U.S. soldiers. I hardly know how I could have got on at all without him.

Although not formally paroled, he was required to take an oath that he would do nothing to aid the enemies of the (so called) Southern Confederacy until duly exchanged. Up to this time, Mr. Vernor has been in the hospital department in Murfreesboro, working faithfully for the good of our soldiers under his permit granted by the Rebel authorities to me. He is about to leave with other paroled prisoners. I commend to him to the kind attention & good offices of all Loyal Citizens & Especially ask the officers & soldiers of the U.S. Army who may meet him to show him every kindness as he is a worthy young man & true & loyal soldier.

> Geo W. Fish
> Surgeon 4th Mich. Cavalry
> (copy)

Camp of the 16th Regt Mich Infantry
Near Potomac Creek, Va. Feb 8th 1863

Rev. Mrs. Duffield.
My Dear Friend

As Capt. Elliott of our regt has obtained a leave of absence for 15 days, and is going to make a visit home, I take the opportunity to send a note to you by him. Capt. E[lliott] you probably were acquainted with before we left Detroit, and you also, no doubt, recollect that it was in his company that I came out with. This is the first time that Capt. E has been absent from the regt. since we have been in service, and therefore no one can doubt that he deserves a leave of absence.

Since I wrote you last nothing of importance has taken place here. We have remained in camp as usual. The weather has been very disagreeable, for it has either rained or snowed every day, and the roads are in a worse condition than ever I have seen before, in fact, the ground everywhere is so bad that it is impossible for artillery, or loaded wagons, to move about at all, and we know full well that this state of affairs is sure to last untill about the 1st of April, if not longer even than that, and therefore you need not expect to see active operations carried on here in Virginia before that time, and in fact, it cannot be the intention of our government to attempt much in this quarter. But as near as I can judge, it seems that our army here is to be broken up, as the 9th Army Corps is now leaving here and going back to N. Carolina, or S. Carolina, where they came from last August, and will, I suppose, participate in the battles and movements that are daily expected to take place there.

And there is great probability that other portions of our army will also be sent to other points, as we cannot do anything here, and our government can hardly afford to let this large army lie idle for the next two months; though what portions of our army are to leave, and what to stay, I do not know. We are expecting soon to hear of another hard battle being fought at Vicksburg and, as Gen. Grant's army is to participate in this attempt, we are very much in hopes that it will be successful. By the reports in the papers, I should judge that Gen. Rosencranz army was likely to have another combat with the Rebels, but perhaps the Rebels are only threatening Rosencranz in order to prevent him from sending any troops to assist in the attempt to take Vicksburg.

We had an exciting account of a naval battle being fought at Charleston the other day. But, I guess we shall soon have an account of a great deal larger one there, both by the army and navy. It seems that our government are putting forth every exertion possible to get iron clad vessels sufficient to do whatever they undertake in a very short time. And it seems to be the prevailing idea throughout our army that this war will be ended before this next summer is over, either by our forces conquering the Rebels, or else the government acknowledging their independence, as it seems hardly possible that the war should last more than six months longer at the most, without something taking place that will put a stop to it. I have heard that the most reliable news about our army is that two army corps are to be sent to the Carolinas, two more to be sent out west and the balance is to remain near Washington, and will form the Army of the Potomac, though somewhat reduced in size from the original one, and the movements now going on would seem to indicate that is to be the plan for the future, but whether our corps will remain here or be sent somewhere else, I do not know, but I suppose that in less than two weeks there will not be a single regiment where our army is now encamped. Therefore, my next letter will probably be wrote from some other camping ground than this.

But I must bring this letter to a close, as it is nearly time for Capt. Elliott to leave. Please remember me to Henry when next you write, and give my respects to Dr. Duffield and any other enquiring friends.

This Respectfully Yours as ever
C.H. Salter

Camp of the 16th Regt Mich Infantry
Near Potomac Creek, Va. Feb 21st '63

My Dear Friend

Your kind letters of the 7th and 15th insts both arrived in due time. I am very glad to hear from you and greatly obliged to you for your kindness in writing to me when you are so busy, and have so little time to write.

I take the first opportunity I have had to write to you. Since I wrote to you last no great events have taken place, with us. Our brigade went out on picket for four days last week. The picket line is about four miles west of our camp. We found the roads to be in very bad condition, both in going out and returning. The weather has been very stormy. We have had several snow storms, and rain about every other day, so that the ground is kept wet, and the roads so bad, that we cannot make any forward movements at all. We have been very busy lately in putting our camp in good order. We have made a brush fence all around it, and set shade trees out all over the camp, and have trimmed it up, about as neatly as a camp could be. But in the meantime, we have not done any drilling and some of the officers are inclined to think that our Lieut. Col. Welch, who is now in command of the Regt, can superintend such work, better than he can a battalion drill, at least since he has had command of the Regt., he has avoided battalion drill very carefully.

Last Monday, Messrs. Parsons and Phelps of Detroit, were here and, after inspecting our camp, they pronounced it the prettiest and neatest of any they had seen anywhere in the army.

I am very thankful to you for your trouble in writing to Mrs. Howard, and I presume that Senator Howard is right, and that it is about impossible to procure a commission in the Regular Army at present. However, when this war is ended, or when the time of the three years' regiments is up, then the government will have to raise a large standing army, and I shall probably have an opportunity to enter the Regular Army, at that time.

I am very glad to hear that Henry has received the promotion to the Lieut. Colonelcy of his Regt, as I think that he is deserving of it, if anyone in the Regt is.

We have received an order that Beauregard issued to the inhabitants of Charleston and Savannah, wherein he warns all noncombatants to retire from both cities, calls upon all able bodied men from the mountains to the sea to rush to arms to defend those places, so that it appears, he expects one or both places to be attacked by our forces down there very soon, and I presume the next battle we hear of will take place down there.

Our army here is not idle, for we are busy in throwing up entrenchments on every good position near our camps and especially along the railroad, there is quite a good sized fort being erected on a hill, close across the Potomac Creek. These preparations are probably being made with a view to protecting our railway communications for supplies, so that when we advance from here, a small force will be sufficient to guard the railway from any sudden attacks made by the enemy in our rear. We did think a few days ago when the 9th Army Corps was being moved from here, that our army was going to be broken up, and sent to various portions of the country, to reinforce other armies. But although the 2nd Corps has been sent up to Alexandria, we see no signs of any other corps leaving us and we have six corps left in our army yet. The conscription bill lately passed by our Congress seems to give great satisfaction to our army. The soldiers, in general, are greatly pleased to think that the government is now bound to bring out men enough to crush the rebellion, whether they are willing to enlist or not. There will not be much pity for those drafted men here in the old regiments. I hear that they have lately made a draft in Michigan, and that we are to have a squad of the drafted men are to be sent down to our regt.*

Col. Stockton is now absent on sick leave and the brigade is now under the command of Col. Weeks of the 12th N.Y. Regt. We expect Capt. Elliott will be back here next Monday or Tuesday as also Lieut. Jacklin, who went with him. Capt. Fuller of my company is, at present, absent on a furlough also, and perhaps I may be able to get a leave of absence some time this spring, and make a short visit home. Lieut. Hough of Co. E, of our Regt, formerly Orderly Sergeant of my old company, who was wounded in the last battle of Bull Run, and has been in hospital at Alexandria, has just returned to the Regt. He was in the same hospital with Sergt. Pratt. He says that the Sergt will not get over his wound for two months to come yet.

But I must now bring this long letter to a close as I have but little news to write. Remember me to Henry when next you write to him. Give my kind regards to Dr. Duffield. Hoping to hear from you again whenever convenient,

> I Remain,
> Respectfully Your Friend
> C.H. Salter

---

*When President Lincoln called for 300,000 militia to serve for nine months in August 1862, he ordered the governors to draft from the militia to fill the quotas. Draft riots occurred in Wisconsin and Indiana and threats of riots in Pennsylvania. The draft was postponed.

Barracks No. 1
Nashville, Tenn.
March 2nd 1863

Dear Jerry

I have received an answer from Gen'l Rosecranz & he says my parole is clearly not binding & orders me to rejoin my regt immediately. I shall go out on the cars in the morning; direct letters here, after to the regt via Nashville. I will leave orders at the barracks for my letters to be sent to me if any come.

Dr. Bacon came in yesterday & went out this morning. He seems to think there will be a fight in front soon, but if the roads don't dry up, I think it is doubtful. Armstrong is expecting his commission soon, [as] the papers have gone to the Governor. I suppose you know Ed Owen has got a lieutenants command. Our Lt. Col. & 5 or 6 other officers have resigned & went home yesterday.

Yours in Haste
Jimmie

Camp Minty
Near Murfreesboro
March 6th 1863

Dear Mother

I have just opened that package sent through Mr. Campin. He sent it to me from Nashville through one of his clerks named Mr. Drummond. Imagine my astonishment, if you can, when Geo. Clark came down to my tent & told me there was a man from Detroit up in his tent with a package for me. Why, I never dreamt of such a thing. You ought to have seen me make tracks for George's tent. You would have thought something was up. I reckon you don't have any idea what an effect a man from Detroit has walking into camp, especially among us fellows from Detroit. I tell you, Mother, those stockings came just in time to save my credit. You ought to have seen me last night, examining my stock & making scientific calculations which would be the easiest repaired. But those awful holes defied even my skill to mend & so I packed them all carefully away in my valise once more.

Tell Jerry I am very much obliged to him for those stamps, but shall be unable to remember him to Lt. Fife at present, as he has gone home on leave of absence. He was not very well when he left Nashville. I may meet him again in my travels though you did not tell me who sent the paper & envelopes. Whoever it was, you must thank them for me. They came just in the nick of time, for I was entirely out.

The regt has been partly paid off & expects the rest soon. I shall get about $150.00 when they are paid off, if I ain't mistaken. I am glad you liked Dr. Fish's letter. You must

save that & also that copy I sent home of the one I wrote to Gen'l Rosecrans. I see by
your letter you have been trying to move again; what is the reason & where did you want
to move to; up on High Street, <u>Eh</u>. I suppose you think there isn't much news in this.
The fact is, the news out here is mighty scarce. The regt has gone out on another of those
scouts, will probably be gone about 6 days. There has been a great change in the regt
since I left it, a great many promotions have taken place & the regt is very much altered.

Remember me to the Briscoes & to Mr. & Mrs. Armitage & write soon to

Your Affec Son
Jimmie

Camp of the 16th Regt Mich Infantry
Near Potomac Creek, Va. March 7th 1863

My Dear Friend

Your kind letter of the 26th inst was received on the 4th inst and I was very glad to hear from you once more as indeed I always am. By the state of affairs here, since my last letter I can only write as usual, "all is quiet on the Rappahannock." We have made no movements and all we have seen of the enemy was a few days ago, a force of rebel cavalry made a dash at our pickets, but were drove back, after a slight skirmish. Their object was to get at and destroy the bridge across the Potomac Creek, but they found so many Yankees in the way that they had to give it up for the present. The bridge is a wooden one about 200 yds long, and 96 feet high. It has been built since we arrived here last November and could be very easily destroyed by the rebels if they could get at it.

We have lately thrown up two small forts on a hill which overlooks the bridge and all the surrounding country. The first fort is right over the bridge, and about ⅛ of a mile back is another one yet higher, which commands the first, besides which there are several rifles pits thrown up in convenient places, so that a small force can garrison, and hold the place against a large force of the enemy. When our army advances, this place will be an important position to hold, as if the enemy could destroy the bridge, they would effectively cut off our communications.

The weather has been about as wet as usual during the last two weeks and the roads are as yet impassable for loaded army wagons and artillery. On the 22nd, we had a snow storm that gave us about fourteen inches of snow on the ground, but it did not last long, as in three or four days it was all melted and then muddier than ever before.

I suppose that the people of the North are waiting anxiously to see the Army of the Potomac advance and attack the rebel army, but their expectations are not very likely to be realized, for whilst they are looking for that, we are looking and waiting for the rebels to attack us. As of course with the taking away of the 2nd and 9th Army Corps from our army, our army is weakened so that it only numbers ¾ of what it did before that and lately the rebels have been rushing troops up to Fredericksburgh, and, from information in possession of our Generals, it appears that they are only waiting for the roads to become passable, when they intend to attack us.

Well, that is just what will suit our army. We would so much rather have them come over here and attack us, than to have to cross the river and attack them again. However, whether we attack them or they us, we expect to have a terrible hard battle next time, and we are in hopes that the government may send us more reinforcements before it does take place.

The conscription bill passed lately by Congress takes up most of the talk of the soldiers, and probably I do not need to tell you that it pleases them greatly. A rumor, through the Michigan regiments, that there was to be some troops picked from the Mich. Regts to be sent home to enforce the draft there, set them all to wishing that they would be amongst the fortunate ones, if fortunate it could be called, for it is a sad thing after all, to drag men away from their homes to place them amongst the horrors of war. And yet it is no worse for them than it is for us who have volunteered. I sometimes question within myself whether we are not all doing wrong to be fighting as we are, but then the cause in which we are engaged is such a holy one that more than in it seems to me it must be right, after all. But it will take a wiser man than I to decide the question. However, my experience here has been such that it will make me, I hope, a wiser and better man than I was before, and I think a great many others also, who were as I was—thoughtless and careless untill they came to the war, and here learnt how frail is human life, and how soon we may be called into eternity at any moment, and also learnt what small consequence, apparently, the life of a human being is. The worst trouble with us here, or with the soldiers who have religious feelings, is the scarcity of chaplains. We have now in our brigade only one chaplain who belongs to the 20th Maine, a new regt that came out last fall. All the chaplains of the old regiments have left and gone home some time ago, and although the vacancies are open, none appear to present themselves, to fill them. I suppose, however, that in other brigades there are more than in ours. In our brigade, the chaplain has about as much as he can attend in the hospitals, and attending burials, &c, without leaving him much time to see to the spiritual wants of the well men.

Capt. Elliott has not returned to the regt yet, and also two other captains who left here about the same time and as no other officers can have furloughs untill they do come back, the prospect of any of us getting leaves of absence this spring is pretty poor. Gen. Griffin says he will have them tried by a military board to see if their prolonged stay is legal, as the Gen. thinks that there is no authority in Mich. to give them extensions on their leave. It is very unjust in them to keep all the rest of the officers waiting as they have to say the least.

My Father does not write very encouragingly about the prospects of getting into the regular army. In fact, I think it is as Mrs. Howard wrote you about it, and that it is useless to try to obtain a commission in the regular army at present. However, I thought it would do no harm to try, at least.

I guess it is about as hard to obtain furloughs where Henry is as it is here. When next you write, please remember me to him. As it is here now, if these officers who are now away on furlough, should return right away, it would be three months before my turn came to go, even if there should not be any order issued before that time to stop furloughs, so that my chance for visiting home is pretty poor. However, if I am unable to visit home, I shall not complain as that would be arraigning Providence. But I shall try to be as contented here as possible.

And now I must bring this letter to a close. Please give my kind regards to Dr. Duffield and all enquiring friends. And, hoping to hear from you again soon, I remain, as ever,

Respectfully Your Friend
C.H. Salter

Camp of the 16th Regt Mich Infantry
Near Potomac Creek, Va. March 20th 1863

My Dear Friend

Your kind and interesting letter of the 20th was received yesterday, and I am greatly obliged to you for taking so much pains to write to me, yet I think you are mistaken in thinking you owed me two letters as I believe you have answered every one I have wrote and with more promptness than any of my others correspondents, who are but very few, however.

Since my last letter of the 7th, we have remained in camp, except four days last week when we were out on picket duty again. We were posted on the usual line, about 4 miles west of our camp.

The weather has been pretty much the same as we have had for the last three months, plenty of rain with occasionally a snow storm. Today it is quite cold and has snowed hard all day long. The snow is now about six inches deep. I should suppose the weather here is fully as severe as it is in Michigan, although I cannot tell. It was much warmer and pleasanter here a year ago, than this present month has been, and the season is much more backward than it was last year at this time. Therefore, we don't expect to commence active operations here as early as we did last year.

There is now a rumor that we shall advance to attack the enemy, about the last of this month. Certain it is, we shall have to advance then or else wait untill our army is filled up by means of the conscription act. As there are so many of our regt whose time is up in May, that after that, our army can only remain on the defensive untill we have at least 100,000 more sent to us. If we do cross the river now, we expect to have to fight the hardest battle that has yet taken place during the war, as the rebels have every position where there is a possibility of our coming, strongly fortified.

On the 17th, Gen. Averill crossed the Rappahannock at Kellys' Ford (about 15 miles) above this place, and had quite a battle with the rebel cavalry, driving them back four miles, untill they reached their earthworks. Our forces took 80 prisoners, and brought off the wounded of both sides. The fighting was done entirely with the saber, no shots being fired on our side and but very few on the part of the rebels. The principal object of the expedition was to ascertain the position of the rebel entrenchments. And it was very successfully done.

Those officers of our regt on furlough who overstayed their time have all returned now, and are being court-martialed for it. They were detailed by Col. Smith of Detroit to remain and take charge of some drafted men, who were to be brought on to Mich. But, our Generals here say that Col. Smith has no authority to detain them.

I do not know what will be done with them. I read an account in the Detroit Advertiser of the riot there.* It is very disgraceful for the city government that they should not

---

*On March 6, 1862, a mob attempted to "bring to justice" a light-skinned African-American named William Faulkner, who was jailed for an alleged crime against two young girls, one white, one black. Unsuccessful in this, they attacked black townspeople and destroyed, looted, and set fire to at least fifteen of their homes and businesses.

be able to preserve better order than they do. If there had been a company from one of the old regts there, I think they would have scattered the mob in a very few minutes.

The latest news we have from Vicksburg and Port Hudson are not very encouraging as it appears Gen. Banks has been repulsed from Port Hudson, and our forces in front of Vicksburg have not done as well as they expected to do. Yet, we hope they may soon capture that rebel stronghold.

It seems to be harder to obtain furloughs where Henry is than it is here, for since the return of those officers, two more have gone, and if they continue to grant furloughs for five weeks longer, I shall obtain my leave of absence for 15 days, although I have not much hope that they will continue them so long as that.

I am obliged to you for those papers you sent. They contain much valuable reading. I do not much regret not being able to obtain a comm. in the regulars, as it would not be any better than the position I have here, during the war, and if I serve as long as this war lasts, I think that will be enough for me. And I am of the opinion that my health will not last during the war, if it lasts much longer, although I sincerely hope it will. It requires a person of pretty strong constitution to stand all the exposure we are subject to. I have now climbed up from a private to be a first lieutenant and I would like to get another promotion before I leave the army. And if I remain here a few months longer, it is very probable I will receive it.

But, I must now bring this letter to a close as I have no more news to write. Hoping that this will find you well. Please give my kind regards to Dr. Duffield and write whenever convenient.

> I Remain
> Respectfully Your Friend
> C.H. Salter

Camp Minty
March 26th 1863

Dear Charlie

I take up my pen in hand to inform you I am well & hope this may find you enjoy-ing the same blessing (I believe that is the proper way to start it). Yours of the 13th came duly to hand. I have not received any since. Papers come oftener than they used to. I am very sorry to hear you have been the victim of false reports once more, but as for me I would willingly become the victim if by that means I could get up among civilized folks once more. I think I would enjoy a few more of those club parties, but duty before plea-sure & if that is the case, I think I will stay in the army for the next 28 months or until the end of the war if not sooner discharged (no prospects of that at present).

Bye the bye, I hear that they are starting hospitals in the different states for soldiers who have been sick for 3 months. If that is the case, why can't I get a place in one of them in Detroit. I should like that first rate. They must want stewards & if so, why don't I run just as good a chance as any one. Just enquire, if you please. I feel somewhat interested in the matter.

I hope that business will get better in your office so that you will continue to work there for that is a good place. You can't be drafted from there, can you. What is going to be done about that Conscription Act. Are they going to send some of <u>you ones</u> down here to help <u>we ones</u> fight the rebels. I hope so for I would like to see some of the young men of Detroit show their patriotism. If they won't do it voluntarily, they must be made to.

I went over to the 9th Michigan last Sunday. I had no idea that I knew so many in it. I found Capt. Wiggins, the engraver; Lieut. Charlie Thomas, a capital school scholar—do you recollect him; & Jimmie Hyde, from Marshall. They have a splendid place for a camp, the same ground they were on last year, when they were captured. They have got it all decorated with cedar trees. They are on escort duty to Gen'l Thomas. There was a rumor yesterday that Bragg sent in to Gen'l Rosecrans to surrender the place but I don't believe the story. I think Bragg is retreating & is merely pushing in our pickets for effect & as for a surrender, I don't think Rosey will do it without a fight.

But I must stop. Give my love to all the folks & write soon to Jim
Be sure & enquire about that hospital for me & let me know about it.

Jim

Camp Minty
Near Murfreesboro
April 1, 1863

Dear Mother

How do you like my picture [?] I think it is a first rate one. I thought you would think perhaps that 6 months would make quite a change in a fellow down here & I would just show you what a great mistake you made. I had this picture taken by a traveling artist. His tent is about ½ mile from here. Armstrong & I went over yesterday & had them

JAMES VERNOR
(BURTON HISTORICAL COLLECTION, DETROIT PUBLIC LIBRARY)

taken. I suppose you have heard before this that Armstrong is Asst. Surgeon now. I think he had his picture [taken] entirely on account of the straps, but as for me nothing but my Phiz was the cause (good cause, wasn't it).

I received a letter from Fanny yesterday & one from Hattie about a week ago. Papers come quite regularly. Now I get some most everyday. Who sends them. Who ever it is, sends a pin with each. I am very much obliged to whoever it is. April has come at last & with it pleasant weather. Citizens around here say that cold weather is about gone. Yesterday was an awful cold day, it put me in mind of northern weather.

I wish you could see our camp to day. The boys have set out cedar trees in front of their tents & it makes the camp look splendid. They took the idea from the 9th Mich. Infantry.

Ed Owen came out on dress parade the other night with his new suit on. It was sent to him. Stevenson made them. The regt is in fine trim now, all ready for a forward movement, but we don't get orders to move. The rebs made a dash on us night before last. The regt turned out at 2 o'clock in the night with a cheer, but they didn't come as far as we expected them to. They stopped about ½ mile from us & ran off again. The boys went to bed again as if nothing had happened. The rebs won't catch the 4th Mich asleep, no use trying. We are the farthest out in this direction.

Good Bye
From Jimmie

Camp of the 16th Regt Mich Vol Infantry
Near Potomac Creek, Va. April 20th 1863

My Dear Friend

As expected, I left Detroit Thursday evening, upon the boat for Cleveland and, pro-
ceeding by the way of Pittsburgh, Harrisburgh and Baltimore, reached Washington on
Saturday morning, without having been detained on the route at all. However, we had to
remain there untill the next morning, when we got aboard of the mail boat, and steamed
down the Potomac, for Acquia Creek Landing, arriving at camp that noon.

The President and Secretary of War came down upon the boat with us and were met
at the landing by Gen. Hooker and staff. I do not know what they came down here for,
unless it was to get some of our good fare (viz. hard bread and salt meat), of which we
have such a plenty.

I found that our army had received marching orders, and would have left their camps
before I came down but for the continued bad weather which prevented them. We have
orders to take eight days provisions with us, and all the blankets and shelter tents we
want to use, and both officers and men are to carry everything they have themselves, as
no wagons are to go with us. But officers' valises are to be left with the wagons at camp;
our army ovens have been sent down to Acquia Creek Landing; and, we are again living
on hard bread. The sick of the army are all sent to the hospitals at Acquia Creek, and
every preparation made that possible could be to be in readiness for marching. I do not
know what we are to do, for even if we drive the rebels back to Richmond, we cannot
lay siege to that place, at present, as if we do, we shall be there in May, when the time
of about one half of our army is up, and when they have us, we shall only have an army
sufficient to defend Washington without acting upon the offensive at all. But, I suppose,
that the intention of our government is to use those troops, and do all that can be done
with them before their time expires.

They have had a good deal more rain here than I saw whilst up north, and today it
has rained hard all day. Our tent leaks and the water runs right through. It seems all the
more uncomfortable to me after having just been home than it did before. My time was
so very short that I could not even call upon all of my friends there in Detroit, and if I
could have had another week, I should have been much better satisfied to return than I
am now. I was very sorry I had not more time to call upon Dr. Duffield and yourself.

Lieut. Rice returned to the regt with me. They were all very glad to see us back, especially those that were waiting for our return before they could go. But, I do not expect
that there will be any more furloughs granted for some time to come, as our marching
orders always put a stop to that. There was some changes in our regt during my absence—Capt. Mahan of Co. L resigned on account of sickness. He has the consumption
and can not expect to live long. Capt. McLaughlin of Co. C, who was formerly 1st Lieut.
of Co. B, has been dismissed the service for fighting with a private. And Col. Stockton
has preferred charges against Lieut. Col. Welch, and he is to be court-martialed also. If
they keep on dismissing at the rate they have been doing, I shall soon have a captain's

position vacant for me, although I would prefer not having it to having one of them dismissed in that manner.

I see by today's paper that the rebels under Van Dorn were expected to attack Nashville, and that there is a probability of their having another battle there. At Washington, N.C., the rebels are still besieging our forces there, but our operations here will probably soon cause them to leave that place and come up this way. Our cavalry have been several days on an expedition in the rear of the rebels, and the last we heard of them they were at Gordonsville. They sent in a squad of prisoners, and have been doing the rebels a great deal of mischief. Perhaps we may follow them in a day or two and drive the rebels back to Richmond, if we do nothing more.

There was some fear that the rebels would make an attack upon Suffolk, but now our forces there are so strong that they can hold it against any force the rebels have to bring against it. Our forces in South Carolina do not appear to be doing anything at present, and the probability is that it will be a long time before they attack it again.

When I arrived at camp and enquired for my letters I received yours of the 6th inst, and was glad to read it, although I had seen you since it was wrote. When next you write to Henry, remember me to him and tell him not to be discouraged, because the Major's position was given to another, but try again, and he may finally get something better. And now I must bring this to a close as I have not much news to write. Please give my regards to Rev. Dr. Duffield, also your son, Dr. Duffield. And write whenever convenient.

> I Remain
> Respectfully, Your Friend
> Charles H. Salter

Camp Minty
Near Murfreesboro
May 8th 1863

Dear Mother

Your very welcome letter & ditto box arrived 2 or 3 days ago. Every thing was in the best kind of order. It came through rather quicker than the other one.

The smoke beef & butter are splendid. We don't see such down here very often. The catsup I have not opened & those stockings are just a fit. I don't know how you made them so, but then if [I] recollect right you are better by gross work than if you work by rule & I suppose that accounts for it.

I should have answered your letter the very day I received it but I have been very busy for the last week. The other steward (Mr. Wilson) has been quite sick & so I had most of the work to do. I have had to make out the weekly & monthly reports of sick & wounded & send them to the surgeon general & it has kept me quite busy. But they have gone now, & I shall have more time to myself. I hope to make only two reports now & they are not very hard work. Mr. Willard is stopping with Capt. Rhodes of the 1st E&M. they are about 3 miles from here. I rode over & eat dinner with him & the captain & brought my box back. He is coming over here in a day or two. He has got a slight twinge of rheumatism. He says sleeping in tents don't agree with him. He would not make a [good] soldier, I think. I wonder how he would stand a scout. I think I will invite him to go out with me on the next one, just to show him the beauty of the country. That's all. I guess he would see it before he got back. He is just learning to ride. He says he don't see why we all like to ride horseback so well. He prefers the ambulance, yet he will get over that soon. A good horse is the best thing in the world to ride on. I think so, anyhow.

Lieut. McKenzie's time must be most out, he has not got back yet. Did he come up & take dinner with you. I hope so for he could give you all the news in this part of the country much better than my pen. Mr. Houseu is expected back this afternoon. I have sent the ambulance down to the depot for him. Armstrong started home on furlough for 10 days on Monday. Have you heard from him. He sayed he might go to Detroit, but it depended on circumstances. I hope he did. Mother, did you know ¼ of my 3 years was gone. Why, just look at it. Only ¾ more & I shall be home again enjoying myself. Not that I don't enjoy this kind of life, but I think I have a slight preference to civilized life after all.

We have had very disagreeable weather for 3 or 4 days past; it rained all the time & was real cold. We were not at all prepared for it. We had sent our stoves all away. This change is not the best kind of thing for sick men but I must stop. Good bye from

Your Son
Jimmie

Camp of the 16th Regt Mich Vol. Infantry
Near Potomac Creek, Va. May 16th 1863

My Dear Friend

I have not heard from you since my last letter of the 20th. But, presuming you would be glad to hear from our army after the late battles, I thought best to write to you today. Our corps left camp on the 27th last and, marching up the river to Kellys' Ford, crossed on pontoon bridges then marched towards Fredericksburgh, arriving at the Rapidan, we waded across in 4 feet of water, and captured a rebel company doing picket duty there. We arrived at Chancelorville on the 30th. Next day our division went on a reconnaissance towards Fredericksburgh. We had gone about 4 miles when we heard firing in our rear. The rebels had attacked the balance of our corps at Chancelorville. Gen. Griffin had us about face and we hurried back to the assistance of our comrades. But before we reached the place, the 2nd Army Corps arrived and they were holding the enemy in check. We had some hard fighting that afternoon, but nothing was gained by either side.

That night the 3rd, 11th, & 12th Corps arrived and we prepared for the battle that was to come off on the morrow. Our corps was given position on the extreme left and formed line from the river, up to near Chancelorville, and as soon as daylight [came] each regt went to work putting up breast works of logs and earth, as we expected the enemy to attack us there. But they went up to our right and attacked the 11th Corps first. This corps is composed mostly of 9 months volunteers, who enlisted last summer, and they had not been in any battle before, as they were with Gen. Sigel during the last battle of Fredericksburgh. And they did not attempt to hold their position, but broke into confusion, and fell back probably about a mile, and then the veteran 3rd Army Corps was sent up, and they rushed up on the double quick, and engaging the enemy, drove them back untill they became engaged with the main body.

The 2nd and 12th came up, and the battle became general. A portion of the 11th Corps was rallied again, and fought well, but the most of them could not be brought up again. Gen. Sykes' division of regulars from our corps was sent to the assistance of the 2nd Corps, and our division moved to the right untill we were upon the left of the 2nd Corps to support them. The battle was kept up all day long, and then after sunset the moon shone very brilliant, making it about as light as day. And the battle then raged even more fiercely than it had during the day. It was the most terrible battle I have yet witnessed. The rebels and our men both fought with much more determination and fierceness than ever before in any of our battles. But at midnight it ceased and our corps was sent up to the right where the fighting had been, and the 11th Corps sent to occupy the breastworks we had built.

Our regt was given position behind some breastworks the rebels had commenced, but left at our approach. We were on the extreme front line. In front of us, at a distance of from 20 to 50 yards in various places, was a thick wood and it was in that wood that most of the fighting took place. It commenced about 7 A.M., the rebels attacking us. They advanced sometimes out of the wood, and would attempt to break our lines, but would get drove back every time, when we would in turn pursue them into the wood untill we were

UNION FORCES BURYING THEIR DEAD ON THE BATTLEFIELD, IN FRONT
OF STONEWALL JACKSON'S BATTERIES, AT FREDERICKSBURG, VIRGINIA.
(THE PICTORIAL BATTLES OF THE CIVIL WAR, NEW YORK, 1895)

drove back. At one time, the enemy charged out of the wood right in front of our regt.
We waited untill they were pretty close, and then we commenced firing and our artillery
fired right over our heads with grapeshot into the rebels, and soon as they could, they got
out of the way.

At another time they massed a large force about ¼ mile to our left and thought they
would take some artillery we had there. They came out of the woods, hurrahing and apparently in fine spirits, but as soon as they were fairly out of the wood, 60 pieces of artillery opened fire upon them with grape and canister, and our musketry all along the line
poured a rapid fire into them. The rebels paused a moment, and then took to their heels.
But before they got out of the range of our batteries, they had left large numbers lying
dead and wounded upon the ground. After that, they did not attempt to make another
charge, and nothing was done that afternoon but skirmishing.

That night and the next day, the rebels were so quiet that we suspected they were
retreating, and the 2nd Brigade of our division was sent in to charge them and ascertain
what they were doing. The 4th Mich Regt was deployed in front of the brigade as skirmishers and they advanced over the field and into the wood in splendid style, and soon
the roar of musketry told us well enough that the rebels were there yet. The brigade went
right up to their breastworks and fired over them at the rebels, but found them too strong
and fell back to our lines. That night I took my company out on picket in front of the

regt, and as it was a bright moonlight night, we could see pretty well, and we had a good deal of skirmishing with the enemy's pickets, and, at times, the bullets whistled around us pretty lively. But, towards morning, we were relieved by a company from the 4th, and that day, Tuesday, passed away quietly untill in the afternoon a hard rainstorm came upon us. The rain poured down faster than any storm we have had here this spring, making the roads very bad; and Gen Hooker gave orders that the army should fall back across the river. Our division was to cover the retreat, and all night long they were leaving us, and marching down to the river and across. Our division fell in at 3 A.M., then retreated slowly down to the river and waited untill all the rest were across. Then we crossed and the 1st Michigan took up the pontoon bridges. We then marched back to our old camp in the midst of a hard rain. We arrived at 3 P.M. on the 6th, after a march of about 25 miles that day.

We had been gone from camp nearly 10 days, had marched over 100 miles, forded 3 streams from 3 to 4 feet deep, carried eight days provisions, our arms, and all the clothing we required upon our backs, and done our share of the fighting, and had very little sleep so that we were pretty well tired out. We found that since we had been gone, the officers tents had all been sent away and we had to put up the little shelter tents, same as the men use. But after all we were in good spirits, not discouraged as we were after the battle in December last, for we were satisfied we had done everything we could do under the circumstances. The rebels had a much larger force there than we expected to meet, and, as they were between us and Sedgewick's corps at Fredericksburgh, there being a distance of only 1 mile between, they could send troops from point to point with great facility, and after Sedgewick was drove from the heights of Fredericksburgh, it was our best policy to fall back across the river, as we could not hope to retake them again.

The officers' report on our loss I have not yet seen, but it is estimated at about 13,000, of whom 2,000 are supposed to be prisoners. We lost Gen. Berry, commanding a division in the 3rd Corps, and Gen. Whipple, commanding a division in the 2nd Corps, besides Lieut. Col. Sherlock of the 5th Michigan, and many other distinguished officers. The rebels had about 13,000 killed & wounded, and we took over 5,000 prisoners from them. They lost two generals killed, one of whom was the famous Stonewall Jackson, shot by some of his own men. They were pretty badly used up, and if we could have held the heights at Fredericksburgh, we would have destroyed their army. But, of course, it is easy enough, after the battle is over to see where the mistake was. But, at the time, we all supposed the fighting was all to be at Chancelorville. And after the heights were taken, the 1st Corps was sent from there up the river to assist us, and thus weakened our force there, and they arrived where we were too late to be of any assistance.

But, I must now bring this letter to a close, as it is time for the mail to leave. Please give my kind regards to Rev. Dr. Duffield, Dr. Duffield, and all enquiring friends. Also remember me to Henry when next you write. Hoping to hear from you soon,

> I Remain,
> Respectfully, Your Obdt. Svt.
> C.H. Salter

Camp Park
Near Murfreesboro
May 20, 1863

Dear Father

Yours of the 9th, written in Albany arrived here some days since. I suppose you have got home again by this time. You must have had a pleasant time of it, even if you did find Old Albany greatly changed. I was very glad to hear that Aunty was getting better & hope she will continue to recover.

Mother & Mattie are enjoying themselves out to Big Rapids by this time, I suppose. I wish you could have gone with them & then I would want to be there to go hunting with you & fishing too, for I enjoy that some. We have a mess of fresh fish here occasionally, but we have to catch them if we want them. Nobody sells them here, so you see we don't go just for the pleasure of catching them alone but more for that of eating them & they have a curious way of catching them. Here you take a stick & wade into the river & poke the stick under the rocks & when you scare one out, watch it & see where it goes & then follow it & put your hands into the place it goes & pull Mr. Fish out. Always wear gloves when you fish in this way for fear of fins.

I am going fishing this afternoon with a seine. I don't know what sort of luck I shall have. I hope it will be first rate. We fish in Stones River. It is about ½ mile from camp & there is lots of fish in it.

I have been out on picket twice lately. Yesterday, I had all the strawberries I wanted & plenty of milk. We stood about 4 miles from camp. It is about 6 miles from town. We did not see a reb, but saw a few rebel sheep of which we captured four. We are to have roast mutton for dinner. I wish you could eat dinner with us but I suppose you will have a better one where you are. But when we get mutton, potatoes, bread/soft, milk & butter, we think we are having a pretty good dinner. But as it is [al]most time [to] eat said dinner, I will bring this to a close by sending much love to all the folks.

From
Your Affec Son
Jimmie

Camp Park
Near Murfreesboro
May 20, 1863

Dear Mother

Your welcome letter of the 8th came safely to hand with the pants 5 days ago. The pants were a fine fit. Armstrong was home only 5 days. That was too short a time for me. It would hardly pay for going but he said he was anxious to get back long before his time was out when he heard the news of Hooker's fight. He said he expected to hear from that army every day that it was fighting, but no such news came. There was a rumor that our brigade was going to the Potomac, but it has not been confirmed & I think it very doubtful. I hope we won't for this is a very fine country in the summer time. I went out on picket yesterday & 3 days ago just for the fun of the thing & to pass away the time. I lived on the fat of the land, of course. The first time we had all the fresh fish we could eat & yesterday we had <u>strawberries & cream</u>. Oh No! I guess soldiers don't live much. I warrant you have not seen a strawberry yet. If you want to live, you must come down here. It won't be long now before the peaches & apples & blackberries will be ripe. I can live on such things with plenty of milk & to make a sure thing of the milk, I stole a cow off a reb & have her tied up behind our tent. We have bread & milk for dinner just when we want it & you can judge how often that is, can't you!

You seem to think it is a very dangerous thing to go out scouting, but I can assure you it is not for when we go we are sure to make the rebels run, that is if we find any, for we always take them by surprise. We have only had 2 or 3 men shot on scouts yet & then there is so much sport about it & you get a first rate chance to see the country besides & that is worth the trouble it costs so you must never feel anxious when you hear that I am out on a scout. But just think what a nice time I must be having.

I had a letter from Father last week. I suppose he is home by this time. He said he was going to N.Y. the next day.

I suppose you will get this letter at Big Rapids. What did Hattie do when you walked into the room. I would just like to have been there & seen her.

I opened that can of catsup a few days ago & it was splendid. It put me in mind of home as much as any thing I have seen since I have been out. But I must stop & go to dinner, so Good Bye.

From
Your Son
Jimmie

P.S. we had roast mutton & bread & milk for dinner. I feel much better. Jim

Camp of the 3rd Brigade, 1st Division, 5th Corps
Near Falmouth, Va. May 24th 1863

My Dear Friend

Your kind letter of the 16th inst arrived Friday, and I was glad to hear from you once more. It appears that your letter was wrote about the time that my last letter was, but I do not expect that you can, or that you have the time to write always when you receive letters, therefore I did not wait for an answer, but wrote to you as soon as I could after the battle, and so I will always do, whenever I have anything important to write about.

Since my last letter, our brigade has moved camp. It was becoming very dusty in our old camp along the railroad, and, as camps had been very thick around us all winter and spring, it was unhealthy, so they picked out for our present camp a large green field, about 2 miles from our old camp and half way between it and Falmouth. The ground is high, and the camp is the pleasant one we have had in nearly a year. We have a small brook on each side of the camp, and as there are no other troops camped nearer than ½ mile from us, we hope to keep clean and healthy during the warm weather whilst we remain here.

It was to us like leaving the city and going into the country to pass the summer months, so great is the change in the appearance of our old home and the new. We are also situated but a short distance from the picket line, so that it will not be much of a walk, when we have to go out for picket duty. I suppose you have heard that our colonel and, since last September, commander of the brigade, Col. Stockton, has resigned, and is, I presume by this time, on his way home. The reason of that was that he has been seeking for the position of Brig. Gen., ever since he first assumed command of the brigade. But for some reason, probably best known to the government, he has been unable to get the promotion. And now, he has the offer of the position of Brig. Gen., providing he raises a brigade, and he has gone to undertake it. Before he left, the officers of our regt bought a splendid sword and gilt belt to present him with as a token of our esteem. The presentation took place at dress parade last Friday evening, after which Col. Stockton bid farewell to all the officers of the brigade who were assembled for that purpose. And then he left us, probably for the last time, as his brigade is to go to Tennessee. The sword and belt cost $140, and is as nice a one as any Brig. Gen. would wish to have.

Col. Vincent of the 83rd Penn Regt now commands our brigade, which is reduced to four regts now, as the 12th & 17th N.Y. Regts, whose two years time lately expired, have gone home, and we have now the 44th N.Y., 20th Maine, 83rd Penn and our own regt left, numbering in all about 1,500 men, or about one and a half full regts. At present, about all of the 2 years regts and 9 months regts have left us, in consequence of which our army is much reduced in numbers and for that reason, I do not think that any more active operations or offensive movements will be undertaken untill our army is reinforced sufficiently to bring it up to its old standard in point of numbers. And as that will take quite two or three months, there is every prospect that in that time, the rebels will cross over, and try to drive us back to Washington, or to destroy our army. But, we are ready for them at any time they choose to come, and, in fact, we would prefer that they should attack us than that we should have to attack them, as the party acting on the defensive always has the advantage. Our army is in good spirits, although I cannot say that we are eager for another advance, as we have no idea of making one for months to come, so we do not think much of advancing.

But, we have as well recovered from the battles, as we could after the loss of so many of our forces. The official returns of the killed and wounded place the figures at over 11,000, and this does not include any of those the rebels took prisoners or the missing, and I think the proper estimate of our loss is about 18,000. The rebel loss was also very severe, and as during most of the fighting, they were the attacking party they suffered even more than we did. Their loss was especially heavy in storming and retaking the heights of Fredericksburgh, as there they were exposed to the fire of our artillery in a fearful manner, and we have every reason to believe that their loss was [a] full 25,000.

We learn from deserters that they had, before the battle, 120,000 men, and, as they have been reinforced by 2 divisions from the backwater, since this force must be full as large, now, as it was before the battle, whilst I know that our army does not now number more than 80,000. Therefore, we cannot think of attacking them under present circumstances. Our wounded who fell into the hands of the rebels were badly treated during the battle. As at Chancelorville, they were gathered together and placed in rear of the rebel batteries, where many of the shot and shell from our batteries fell amongst them, killing some and wounding many others, although, of course, we did not know at the time what was being done to them. I saw, when the ambulances came over with the wounded, one poor fellow belonging to the regulars of our corps, who had one leg taken off by a rebel cannon shell, then taken prisoner, and placed by the rebels behind one of their batteries where one of our shell struck him and took off the other. He was nearly dead when I saw him.

Sunday morning, as soon as the rebels gave up their attack upon us, they set fire to the woods in front of us, where most of the fighting had been done. And there must have been many wounded men besides the dead lying there, though we do not know whether they removed the wounded or not, as the wood was composed of dry underbrush, besides the trees, the fire burnt rapidly through the entire length of woods in front of our army. And, we could not advance through the wood untill the fire ceased, which was not untill the next afternoon, and it was whilst that fire was raging through the woods that the rebels sent a portion of their force to retake Fredericksburgh. And thus they obtained a considerable advantage over us.

We hear good news, so far, from Gen. Grant's army, and hope he will succeed in taking Vicksburg and getting possession of the Mississippi. By the way, you spoke of my Mother. Henry was partly right, for my own Mother died when I was only two years old. But, I have a stepmother, who has always treated me very kindly indeed. From the time my Mother died untill I was six years old, I was taken care of by my Grandfather and Grandmother, my Mother's parents, [in] Albion, N.Y. State, and then my Father married again in Detroit, and sent for me to come, since which time I resided with my Father in

Detroit, in business there untill, in 1860, he moved out to the country, and I remained in Detroit, in business there untill the war broke out.

But I must now bring my letters to a close. Please give my respects to Rev. Dr. Duffield and your son, the doctor, and any other enquiring friends. Write whenever convenient, if you please, but do not allow your letters to me to inconvenience you when you are busy in the least.

> I Remain
> Respectfully Yours
> C.H. Salter

Camp Park
Near Murfreesboro
May 22nd 1863

Dear Brother

Your very welcome letter came to hand 3 or 4 days since & as I have just returned from one of the hardest scouts I ever have seen. You must not expect any thing more than the particulars & I hope you will be as much entertained with them as I was but I doubt it some.

We received orders to be ready to march with one days rations in haversack at 8 P.M., on dress parade yesterday. Three rousing cheers was the reply to the order & at 8 precisely we were formed in line on the Salem Pike, in the following order: 4th Regulars; 7th Penn; 4th Mich; 3 & 4 Ind; & 39 Ind (Mounted Infantry). The line was formed & we started forward at ½ past 8; went about 8 miles & turned to the left on a dirt road or rather a cow path. It was the worst one I ever went over. Any how, we followed this road for about 8 miles when we turned into the woods—that is the last we saw of roads until the morning. All we had to do now was to follow the horse ahead of us & keep a sharp eye on the ground & keep our horses from stumbling, which was decidedly hard work in the dark. Part of the time we went on the gallop & the rest on a walk. There was in the neighborhood of 25 men unhorsed in the woods on account of branches & stones. Only 2 or 3 of them were badly hurt & one horse got his neck broke after traveling 10 or 15 miles through these woods.

We came to a halt & were told what we came out for; namely, to break up a rebel camp at Middleton, which was about 5 miles from where we were halted. As soon as the column closed up, we moved forward. The 4th Regulars took the right flank, the 7th Penn. went directly forward towards Middleton. The rest, led by the 4th Michigan took the left. When we came within 3 miles of the camp, we were ordered to charge & then the fun began. But you can't appreciate that, I suppose. Imagine 1,500 or 2,000 cavalry going through the streets of Detroit on the keen run & every one anxious to go a little faster.

But to proceed to the end of the charge, we dashed in to their camps just as they were sounding reveille. It was rather unexpected, for they had not any idea of visitors quite so early but, notwithstanding all that, they turned out & made the best show (of their heels), they know how.

We captured between 80 & 100 prisoners & about 200 horses & all their camp equipage. We set fire to their saddles, tents, blankets, arms &c, &c, & burnt them up. We had one man wounded but he will probably recover, wounded slightly in the left lung. His name is Edward Racine of Co. H. he is a number one soldier, I tell you. He was halted by 3 or 4 of the rebs & called upon to surrender, but he said he could not see it in that light but would be very happy to have them throw down their arms & go with him. They answered him with a volley, wounding him. He fired one shot & fell off from his horse. That shot was fatal for one of the rebs, for it killed him on the spot. I jumped off & bound up his wound & had him put in a carriage & sent to Murfreesboro with a Lieut. who was wounded of the 4th Regulars. The rebel regiments in this place were the 1st & 4th Alabama Cavalry. We got the regimental colors. Geo Clark captured them. He is sergeant major now. He had to wade, of course, in blood & thunder, &c up to his knees to get them. Anyhow, he got them & brought [them] into camp in triumph. If you see Dave Edwards, or any of the boys, tell him of it. Our regt formed the rear guard coming back & had to beat off the rebels several times before they would let us alone. There was 12 or 15 wounded in the brigade but only one from our regt. We arrived in camp at noon to day. We did not leave the saddle 20 minutes all told since the time we left camp until we entered it again.

I expect to make one good night sleep of it to night, you may rest assured of that. I have been in swimming this afternoon in Stone's River, would you like to go in with me the next time. If so let me know. The water is quite warm & it is splendid bottom when you get down to it.

But I must stop. Excuse all mistakes for I am most awful tired. Give my best respects to all my friends & write soon to

Your Brother

James Vernor

Charlie, if you can, draw your pay on the pay roll enclosed. I should advise you to do so, but be careful they don't pay you in Confederate Scrip.

If a reporter should want to make a few extracts from this, I have no objections. Col. Minty led the brigade & the flag is to be sent to the Gov. in a few days.

Camp 16th Regt Mich Vol Infantry
Near Ellis's Ford, Va. June 7th 1863

My Dear Friend

Your kind letter of the 24th inst was received on the 30th, but I have not been able to get time to write untill today. However, I had wrote a letter to you on the same day you wrote to me. Since then, we have been kept busy as we could be all the while. We had expected to remain in that camp, where we were then, but on the 28th, we received orders to march, and our brigade marched up the river, and we were scattered between Banks' Ford and U.S. Ford, to do picket duty. Our regt was camped near Ballard's Dam, about ½ way between the two fords and our pickets were stationed along the bank of the river; the rebel pickets on the opposite bank, at the distance of about 30 rods. The pickets did not fire at each other at all, nor even load their muskets but were on quite friendly terms. They would talk across the river, and sometimes the men would swim over and have a little talk with each other. We exchanged papers whenever we had any to exchange, and the latest news we had, we read in the Richmond papers. It was the 4th Virginia, rebel cavalry, that were opposite us, and we saw many northern men amongst them. One man was from the western part of Michigan, and another from Philadelphia. I asked them how they came to be in the rebel army. They said they were working in Virginia, and went into it for the fun of it. But they did not think there was so much fun in it now, as they had imagined, yet they did not appear to be at all anxious to leave the rebel army.

We remained there doing picket duty untill the 4th inst, when we were relieved by a brigade of regulars from Sykes' division, and we packed up and marched 10 miles up the river that day, and next day 3 miles farther and arrived at our present camp. We are now about ¼ mile from the river, near Ellis's Ford, where our regt is doing picket duty. We see the rebel pickets on the opposite bank, and are on as good terms with them, as with those at Ballard's Dam. Our brigade is all camped within 3 miles of our regt, and doing picket duty along the river. The balance of our division is at Kelly's Ford and other places farther up the river.

We are nearly two days march from Falmouth, and we do not receive papers here, as we did at our old camp on the R.R., so it seems as if we were shut out from all news entirely. We hear that the army is moving, that they have crossed the river and taken the heights back of Fredericksburgh again, and a great many other stories, but we do not <u>know</u> anything about what has been done there. As for ourselves, we have received orders to be ready to march. We have now everything packed up and are expecting every minute to receive orders to strike tents, and to march, but, we cannot tell where we are going. Yet we are in expectation of having more fighting to do very soon, though whether the rebels are to attack us or we attack them, is a matter of doubt. It is thought by many that the rebels have gone up to Warrenton, and that we shall have to fight them again, on the bloody ground of Manassas, which seems to be their favorite place. But I hope we shall not have another fight there.

If we march now, I shall have to ride in an ambulance, or get a horse to ride, as I have been sick for the last two days, and am not scarcely able to march now. But, I shall be well enough to march in a couple days more, I expect. We have not heard any news from Vicksburg since the 2nd inst, as all the papers we get now, we get by mail. We expect that the rebels are preparing to attack us, or else have sent a portion of their forces to attack Grant, and if so, he will have to hurry up in taking Vicksburg, or he will have a strong force in his rear to fight also. But, whilst all our armies are busily engaged most everywhere in fighting, we cannot understand why Gen. Rosencranz remains idle. It seems as if he should attack Bragg in order to prevent him from sending too many rein-forcements to Johnston, and, it is certain, that he is sending a portion of his troops away. Gen. Rosencranz has an army, which is now larger than even our Army of the Potomac, and has a much smaller force opposed to him, than we have to fight, and it seems as if he had ought to be doing something. We hope Gen. Grant will be successful in taking Vicksburg, and, if he is not, it will be a severe reverse for us. We look for it as being the greatest victory gained yet during the war, if it is taken together with the rebel army in it.

I do not think I shall come across that young man you spoke about, Thos. W. Morton, as the 28th N.Y. is not in our corps, nor do I know where the regt is. I wish that I could come across him, as it would perhaps be the means of doing him some good. The weather here for the last two days has been quite cool and pleasant. We have several showers of rain also. Our present camp is in a pleasant grove where we are sheltered from the rays of the sun on warm days, and we could make a very pleasant camp of it, if we were allowed to remain here.

But, I must now bring this letter to a close. Please give my regards to Rev. Dr. Duf-field, to Dr. Duffield and remember me to Henry, when you write to him. Hoping to hear from you again soon.

> I Remain, as Ever
> Respectfully Your Friend
> C.H. Salter

Camp Park
Jun 19th 1863

Charlie

Yours of the 9th came to hand in due season. I wish I could make this as interesting but news is scarce. The only piece of news that I can tell you is that we have been out on another scout to Lebanon. We found the rebels thicker than we expected & consequently, we came home again & just in time for if we had stayed ½ hour longer, we should have been surrounded & then we would have had a chance to show the fighting qualities of the 1st Brigade. But we had Col. Minty to lead us & the consequence was just as our rear guard passed Baird's Mills, they saw the rebels come out of the woods on both sides of the pike. But they were too late, for when they had us surrounded, we were not there. The rebels had 3 to our 1 besides several pieces of artillery. But we have orders to march tomorrow morning & I expect it will be to the same place & then, says I, rebs look out for yourselves, for we are to take a larger force this time & if they do [the] surrounding [then] two can play at the same game & if they should find themselves surrounded when they are scattered about, they would find their foot in the wrong shoe, which would not be so pleasant again. We will see how that will turn out. I expect when we get there, we will find they have ran away.

The next scout will probably last 6 days. The last was only 2 days & nights. We sat in the saddle 44 hours, with the exception of about ½ hour on the first afternoon. Of course, I was not sleepy, Oh! No! but I found myself nodding quite often. I can tell especially in the night time.

Col. Minty had an interview with a fine young lady in an undress uniform about 11 o'clock P.M., when we were coming back from Lebanon. She took us for rebels & she called the colonel & told him that there was a lot of yanks over on a side road & if he would send some men over there by a certain road, he could catch the whole lot. The colonel talked with her some time & then he told her who he was & ordered her under arrest, but let her go again. That same lot of men over on the side road was the 4th Mich. Now imagine the consequences if she had told the rebels instead of the colonel. We might be taking a second trip through Dixie perhaps.

But I must stop. Remember me to all & write soon

To
Jimmie

16th Mich Regt
Aldie, Va. June 25th 1863

My Dear Friend

I have not received any letter from you since my last letter on the 7th. But, we have not received any mail at all since the 13th, as we have been on the march all the while, and I expect that when the mail does reach us, I shall have quite a numbers of letters.

Our regt left Ellis Ford on the morning of the 14th, joined the brigade at Kelly's Ford, and we marched that day to a small station on the R.R., about 3 or 4 miles north of Warrenton Junction, where we found our entire corps assembled. We had tramped 22 miles that day, rested on the ground that night; next morning, fell in and marched to Manassas Junction, a distance of 12 miles, and rested there one day. Then on the 17th, we fell in at daylight, marched to Centreville, then west to Gun Springs, a distance of 20 miles. On these marches we suffered more than we have on any march before, as the weather was very warm, the roads exceedingly dusty, and very little water to be found upon the way. But, we rested at Gun Springs the next day, and a thunder storm came up, which laid the dust [down] and cooled the air. On the 19th, we came to this place, which is situated in a gap in the Bull Run Mts. We bivouacked in a large field where our cavalry had a battle with the rebels but two days before. Our corps came here following our cavalry corps, to support them, and the cavalry are camped between this place and Middleburg.

On the 21st, at 1 A.M., our division received orders to fall in, in fighting order, and we left here at 2 A.M., reached Middleburg about 6 and saw the enemy about 1 mile beyond. Our brigade was the advance of the division, and our regt the advance of the brigade. There was a brigade of cavalry and a battery of artillery with us. The country through there is very hilly, the road from Aldie to Upperville being nothing but hills and ravines all the way, whilst all the fences through there are built of stone, so that it is very easy to get positions for defence. The rebel force consisted of 8 regts [of] cavalry and a battery of artillery, as we found out from prisoners we captured. They had a strong position on a high range of hills, and had cavalrymen dismounted and posted behind the stone walls as skirmishers. Our brigade formed line of battle, our regt in the center nearest the road, and our sharpshooters were sent out as skirmishers, our battery brought up, and the battle commenced. Our skirmishers soon drove back the rebel skirmishers, and our artillery exploded a rebel caisson filled with shell, and then we charged upon them, driving the rebels from their position, and our regt captured a splendid cannon from the rebel battery. The rebels, however, only fell back to another hill, and the battle continued same as before.

But our brigade pressed hard upon them and by 3 P.M., we had drove them 6 miles after a good deal of hard fighting, and hard work, and we had them on the full retreat, when our cavalry charged upon them, and drove them through Upperville and into the Blue Ridge at Ashby's Gap, and our victory was complete. We made 150 prisoners, killed 20 rebels and wounded a great many, besides killing over a hundred of their horses. We captured 2 cannon, 3 caissons full of ammunition, besides large quantities of small arms. The loss upon our side was very small. In our regt, we had 1 man killed; Capt. Mott, and 8 men wounded. The Capt. was very badly wounded and we do not expect he will live. He was sent to Washington the next day, since which we have not heard of him. The loss in the other regts engaged was not as much as in ours, as we were always in the advance and in the thickest of the fight. One of our men killed a rebel captain who was a candidate for election to the rebel congress, as was shown by papers found upon him. We also mortally wounded another captain, whom we left in a house by the roadside, for the secesh ladies to take care of. We bivouacked that night upon the field from which we had last drove the rebels, and next morning fell in and marched back to Middleburg and rested there untill near night, when we returned to camp, satisfied that we had whipped the rebel Gen. Stuart at last.

The rebel prisoners said that they were not used to fighting with infantry, and that all the cavalry in our army could not have drove them from their position. But they could not stand before infantry, and they said that they were watching all the while for a chance to charge upon our cavalry, but our infantry was always in the way.

Camp near Frederick, Md June 29th 6 A.M.

Your kind letter of the 15th inst was received yesterday evening, and as I had not time to send or finish this letter at Aldie, I write a few more lines this morning. We left Aldie at 6 A.M. on the 26th, marched north through Leesburgh, crossed the Potomac at Edwards Ferry upon pontoon bridges, and halted at 8 P.M., 5 miles this side of the river, after marching 23 miles that day. We started again next morning and marched this way, crossing the Monocacy River in 3 feet [of] water. We halted at night at our present bivouac, 3 miles from Frederick city. We now have orders to march at 8 this morning, and expect we are going to meet the rebels. We do not have much news about them here, as we do not see any papers. But, I suppose, our generals know where the rebels are and know what they are doing. But we never know everywhere we are going. All the orders we have are to be ready to march, and the generals lead us to where they want us. You know about as much about what we are doing by reading the papers, as we do ourselves.

I am sorry to hear that your health is so poor and hope you will not push yourself to too much trouble in writing letters to myself or other soldiers, for that matter, as we often have much more time to write than you do. But I must now close. Give my love to Mr. Duffield. We have to strike tents now.

Truly Yours
C.H. Salter

Head Qrs. 4th Mich. Cav.
Camp in the Field
July 1st 1863

Dear Mother

I suppose you have heard ere this that the Army of the Cumberland was on the move. Well this is the 8th day we have been out & we have been busy, I can assure you. It has rained every day except yesterday since we started. I was somewhat dissapointed yesterday. The Governor & several others came to see us & [I] looked in vain for Ben, for I heard he was coming down with them, but Major Greg says he could not get reddy on time to come.

We have done some very hard fighting since we started. Besides several small skirmishes, on Saturday, the 27th, we had the hardest fight the 4th Mich. Cavalry was ever in. We were ordered to take the enemy entrenchments by Col. Minty. We turned into the woods to the right & marched 3 or 4 miles into them, when we reached the left end of their entrenchments. We then charged into their works & drove them back, but they reformed & came at us, but we were too good for them & they had to give way; but they did it slowly. It was the sharpest firing our regt was ever in. We drove the rebs out of the woods, almost onto the pike when they received reinforcements & formed in lines 3 ranks deep & were just making ready to charge upon us when Col. Minty charged down the pike with 3 regts, driving them out of their position & in the end surrounding them & taking the whole crowd, colonel & all.

Their Major asked what regt it was that drove them out of the woods & when we told him it was the 4th Mich, he said he thought his regt (51st Alabama), were good on skirmishing but could not come near us on it. We had 5 of our men wounded & several horses. Mine was slightly wounded in the front leg. Charlie Hudson was acting adjutant & was wounded through the right shoulder. We are in camp about 5 miles from Manchester & I am going to send this back by some of the trains to Murfreesboro. I will give you an account of our marches when we get to Chattanooga or some other place where we are to stop for some time, I suppose. The Bugle has just sounded the General, which means to pack up & be ready to start, so I must bring this to a close. Give my love to all.

Good bye
Jimmie

Bivouac 16th Mich Regt July 12th 1863 8 a.m.

My Dear Friend

Your kind letter of the 27th was received on the 8th, and I take the first opportunity I have of answering it. My last was wrote at Frederick. We marched for that place on the morning of June 9th, going north to Walkerville, Liberty, Middleberg, Westminster, Littleston, Hanover, Cherrytown, and arriving at the battlefield near Gettysburg on the morning of July 2nd, after the hardest [march] that our army, or our corps, had had since Popes' campaign. Our corps was the last to arrive, as such was the order of march, and we, with the 6th Corps, were placed in reserve near the line of battle. There was not much fighting that morning, although the 1st & 11th Corps had a hard battle with the enemy the day previous. The battle commenced by the rebels attacking our forces about noon, and at 2 p.m., the enemy was discovered attempting to send a large force to turn our left, and our corps, commanded by Major General Sykes, was ordered to repulse them. Our division, commanded by Gen. Barnes, was the first. We moved on the run, about two miles to the left (all the while exposed to the fire of the enemy's artillery), and came to a large hill, or range of hills, which the enemy were at the same time attempting to gain. We arrived first, formed line and advanced over the hill and as we arrived on top, saw a long line of rebels coming over and down a range of hills opposite us.

If we had been 5 minutes late, the enemy would have gained the ridge we were on and turned our left flank, and it would have been very hard to drive them from it. As we advanced over the hill, the firing commenced, both sides advancing untill down in the hollow, when our brigades succeeded in driving back the rebels, to take refuge behind the rocks, and the ridge opposite us, although about 200 rebels broke through the line of the 20th Maine, on our left. But they closed up again, and thus leaving the rebels in their rear, they made them all prisoners. The brigade had lost so many in this close hand to hand fight, that we were unable to pursue the enemy after we drove them back. But, we done the same as they did, took refuge behind the rocks and ridge of our hill and kept up musket firing untill dark.

The 1st Brigade, to which the 1st Mich. belongs had about the same fortune we had in driving back the enemy. But the 2nd Brigade, to which the 4th Mich. belongs, did not succeed so well. The rebels attacked them with a large force, and drove them back about ⅛ mile. The 4th Mich., 62nd Penn., and 32nd Mass. Regts., lost their colors, and about ½ of their officers and men. The rebels bayoneted all they could get hold of. A rebel officer had seized the colors of the 4th and Col. Jeffreys was defending it with his sword. He was bayoneted by the rebels, as also the color bearers, and many others, who were also trying to recover the colors. However, the 2nd Division, (the regulars), soon came up to support our division and assisted us to hold our ground, and the 2nd Brigade to recover theirs. The 3rd Division (the Penn. Reserves, who joined our corps at Frederick), went to our left and had a desperate hand to hand conflict with the rebels there, but succeeded in driving them back and taking many prisoners also.

In the meantime, the battle was raging along a line of about 4 miles in extent, with about the same result everywhere, and when night came on, our entire line had drove the enemy from 1 to 2 miles all along. The rebel corps, with which we were engaged, was Longstreet's and with our brigade, was a Texan brigade of Hood's division. The rebel officers whom we took prisoners said that they had been with Lee's army ever since the war broke out, and their brigade had never been repulsed in any charge they had made before. We told them the reason was simple enough. They had never encountered our corps on the battlefield or seen the maltese crosses on our battle flags in a fight, or else they would know better than to think of charging upon us. But, it was the hardest work we ever done to drive them back, and the most desperate fighting I ever saw, for where we were there was scarcely any artillery engaged on that day, the fighting was all done by infantry, although we have been engaged in other battles where we have had more men cut down by artillery, but we never had such a terrible close bayonet fight before. It seemed as if every man, on both sides, was actuated by the intensest hate, and determined to kill as many of the enemy as possible and excited up to an enthusiasm far exceeding that on any battlefield before that we have been engaged in. I know I felt so myself, although I never did before.

The loss in our regt was 21 killed and 34 wounded. Amongst the killed was Lieuts. Brown from Hillsdale, Jewett from Saginaw, and Borden from Ionia. Amongst the wounded, Lieuts. Borgman and Cameron. The latter had just been promoted to Lieut. from Orderly Sergt., and was wounded in the side besides having his left arm taken off. That night, we slept upon the hill and next morning we were moved about 1 mile to the right, and our division supported some batteries and on that day occurred the grand artillery fight. But we did not lose scarcely any men in our division. Our position was a good one where we were not much exposed, each regt built up a stone wall to protect us in case the rebels should make an attack with infantry, and we remained there also during the 4th, and that night the rebels commenced retreating.

On the morning of the 5th, we advanced 2 miles over the battlefield, and over all that space the dead bodies of both men and horses were strewn very thickly, both our own and the rebels, although the rebels had many more dead than we had. The appearance of the battlefield was awful to look upon, as all such large battlefields are after the battle, with the dead lying in all places, mangled and mutilated in every manner. We buried all of our own dead, and marked the graves in such a manner as to designate who they were. But we had no time to bury the rebel dead, nor the horses, as a portion of our army was already in pursuit of the rebels and we had to go also. We fell in towards night and marched south towards Emmittsburg. The road was so crowded with troops that we could only go 6 miles by midnight, when we halted to bivouac for the night. The next day the road was filled with other corps who had to go ahead of us. But on the morning of the 7th, [we] fell in at 4 A.M., marched south through Creagerstown, and then halting at night, within 5 miles of Frederick. The next morning we marched to Middletown, and during all the time since the battle untill we arrived at this place, it had rained continually, and the ground was very wet and muddy, both in the roads and fields through which we marched and at night we had to lay upon the wet ground, without tents, and for four days there was scarcely one of us, who had any dry clothing on us. But since then, the weather has been very warm and dry.

On the 10th, we marched up on South Mountain and bivouacked in the mountains, and next morning marched on the Williamsport road, crossing the Antietam at Delamore's Mills. We then formed line of battle and sent out skirmishers expecting to have a battle with the enemy, but nothing but firing with the enemy's skirmishers occurred, and towards night, we advanced in line of battle for 3 miles and halted at 7 P.M. in our present bivouac, which the rebels left only 3 hours before we arrived, and this morning, we are waiting for orders. I do not know what Gen. Meade is trying to do, nor what the rebels are doing, but from what I see, I should judge we are trying to surround and destroy their army if possible and we expect soon to have another great battle with them. Our troops are in good spirits, and will fight well, although we are all very much in need of clothing, as since we left Falmouth, and have been on the march all the while, we have been unable to draw or issue any clothing, and most of the men are getting to be very ragged. But, I suppose we will have plenty of clothing as soon as we get through with this little job.

By the way, there was a report in the papers that I was killed, which arose in this way. In the place where I was in line, there were a great many killed or wounded and I was struck in the cheek by a piece of rock, which knocked me down, and made my cheek bleed, and some of them that saw it, and afterwards went to the rear, reported that I was killed. But they did not get rid of me quite so easy as that after all.

The 24th Mich. are reported as losing 348 men, but out of that there is only 30 killed, both officers and men. They had very much the same set of fighting that the 4th Mich. had, and the 4th had more men killed, and full as many wounded and hardly any prisoners, as they are too old soldiers to allow themselves to be taken prisoners. The 24th Mich. had over 600 men to go into the fight with, whilst the 4th had not quite 300, and our regt only 200, so that the 24th could lose many more men and not suffer any more in proportion. Lieut. Humphreyville, [of] Co. K in the 24th who was killed, was an uncle of mine. He was my stepmother's brother.

All the papers that I have seen yet seem to lay the blame of our former defeats on our former generals, and give the credit of the victory of Gettysburg to Gen. Meade. But our army knows this to be not the true state of affairs, for we will fight better in Pennsylvania or Maryland than we will in Virginia, for in the present case we are defending our own soil, and in Virginia, we feel that we that we are invading the rebel soil, and so with the rebels. They fight better in Virginia, than they do up here. And I contend that it was the Army of the Potomac that won the battle, and not Gen. Meade, and that we would have done just as well, or better, under McClellan, Hooker, or any other general. We are not fighting for generals, but for our country, and I hope that northern people some day will give the credit of our fighting to the soldiers, and not to make such gods of the generals, past or present, as they do.

But I must close this already too long letter. The bugle is just sounding for our brigade to fall in. Give my best regards to Rev. Dr. Duffield, Dr. S.P. Duffield, Mr. Pitts, and remember me to Henry when next you write.

> Respectfully, Your Friend
> C.H. Salter

Bivouac 16th Regt Mich Vol Infty
Near Warrenton, Va. July 29th 1863
10 P.M.

My Dear Friend

Your kind letter of 16th inst arrived yesterday, and I answer as soon as possible that you must excuse pencil writing as ink is not in our regt except at the Adjts. office. Since I wrote to you last, we have been continually on the move. First the rebels crossed the Potomac on the night of the 13th, and on the 15th, we commenced our march, going east over S.[outh] Mountain again, to Middleton, then south to Berlin, where the pontoon bridges were laid, and our corps was the first to cross into Virginia again, on the 17th. Then marching south along the eastern base of the Blue Ridge, we arrived at Manassas Gap, on the morning of [the] 23rd.

Hill's rebel corps held the western entrance to the Gap. The 3rd Corps, and our own entered and after marching 10 miles over hills and through ravines, we met the enemy. I was sent with my company, with the skirmishers of the brigade, upon the extreme right and we had to climb up over some of the largest and steepest hills I ever saw. But we had a splendid view of the main forces down in the Gap. We advanced along with them, and the rebel skirmishers fell back as we advanced, and just as it was becoming dark, we reached the highest peak on the western side, and our main force had drove the rebels entirely out of the Gap. Then we had a splendid view of the Shenandoah Valley, with the river winding through it, the villages, the farm houses and everything, as far as the Alleghanies. We remained on the mountain that night. Next morning, we saw a division of our forces advance as far as Front Royal. But the rebels had all gone south, except a brigade of Stuart's cavalry, who, of course, run as our forces approached. And the entire rebel army had gone so far south, that we had to give up all hopes of cutting them off.

Our forces found over 200 badly wounded rebels in Front Royal, whom the rebels had left, being unable to take them with them. And besides, this many slightly wounded had gone off with the rest, and, as we returned through the Gap, we found over 100 bodies of rebels, who had been killed or wounded and afterward bayoneted by our men, who have not forgiven the rebels for their atrocities at Gettysburg and other places, and, I am afraid they never will, as the majority of the 3rd & 5th Corps declare they will bayonet every rebel they can get at, on the battlefield. There were also over 200 prisoners taken by us in this skirmish. None of the skirmishers of our brigade were shot, although many hurt themselves by falling upon the rocks—(I for one).

We returned part way through the Gap that night (the 24th), and next morning commenced our march for this place, arriving here on the 27th. Our present camp is about 4 miles S.E. of Warrenton on the Bealeton Road. The 6th Corps are at Warrenton, the 1st at Bealeton, on the R.R., and the balance of our army are camped between us, on the R.R. We are very busy drawing clothing &c, to issue to the men, as we have not had time to attend to that business, before, since leaving our camps near Falmouth, and, the men (and officers too for that matter), were becoming shamefully ragged.

I do not know how Lt. Borgman could have said he saw me fall, as I only had a scratch on the cheek, and a slight bruise on the right arm, and I never was even reported amongst the wounded. I was standing up and looking at Lieut. B. and saw him go back to the rear. But I did not even know he was wounded untill after dark. Lt. Jewett and Lt. Brown were both killed within 3 feet of me, and perhaps some one might have told Lt. Borgman I was killed. I much regret the loss of my uncle, Lt. Humphreyville of the 24th Mich., at Gettysburg. He was only five years older than myself, and we were great friends. He was my stepmother's only brother. I cannot say that I am greatly pleased at the result of the battle of Gettysburg, although, it is vastly better than a defeat, yet if it <u>had been better managed</u>, we should have lost <u>thousands less</u> than we did. Gen. Reynolds done very wrong in advancing so far as he did and bringing on a fight before the balance of our army could get up. It was his ambition that caused him to do it, as he thought that he could whip the rebels before Gen. Meade came up. But, poor man, he paid his own life for it amongst the rest. And I think that if either Gen. McClellan or Gen. Hooker had been in command, matters would have been a little better managed. But, of course, the general cannot do everything, the great responsibility depends upon the mass of the army, if each man does his duty or not. But, after losing so many dear friends and brave men in one battle, I cannot help feeling hard about it, and complaining.

Gen. Meade's object in sending us through Manassas Gap was to cut off the rear guard of the rebels, A.P. Hill's corps, but we were unable to march through the heat over the hills and mountains fast enough to get through in time, and so it failed for that reason.

I acknowledge God's mercy in sparing my life through so many hard battles and try to devote myself to his service, although I know I fail often in so doing, under the peculiar temptations we are subject to here, especially in rousing a person's temper, or anger, in camp or on the march, and all such like temptations, which it seems, we are subject to much more than when at home. But I try my best to do my duty faithfully, to my country and to the men under my charge, and have kept up, and had charge of my company, many times on the march, when really sick, and I would have dropped out of the regt., but for the bad example it would set.

I must now bring this to a close. It is becoming late, and we may have to march again tomorrow morning. Please give my regards to Rev. Dr. Duffield, to your son Dr. Duffield, and any enquiring friends. Also remember me to Henry when next you write. I wish they would send a portion of that western army here to help us, now that they have the war about ended in the southwest.

> Hoping to hear from you again soon, I remain,
> Respectfully Your Friend
> C.H. Salter

Camp Weber
Near McMinville
August 6th 1863

Dear Mother

This is the first time in most 2 months we have been still long enough to give a fellow a chance to write in place & I take this opportunity to let you know my whereabouts. I have answered all my letters up to date, so rest quite easy for more. The last letter I had from Detroit was from George. I look for one every night but am always disappointed lately. If I don't get one to night I shall think the mail department is out of kilter.

We left Manchester on the afternoon of the 31st & arrived here on the 2nd of this month. At 3 o'clock on the 4th, we started out on a scout. The intention was to go to Sparta (about 26 miles from here), & get there at just day break, dash in & take their camp. The rebel General Forrest, with his whole cavalry force & some infantry & artillery were in camp. Then we arrived at a little place called Rock Island at 11 o'clock at night. We found the enemy's pickets about 2 miles beyond this place. The capture of these pickets was the key to the whole movement & this was entrusted to the 3rd Indiana & by some mismanagement, they did not fully surround the pickets & consequently those not captured put spurs to their horses & gave the alarm in the camp of Forrest. If the enemy were asleep, we were strong enough, but after they were awake it would have made the issue of a battle very doubtful & Col. Minty is not the man to run any such risks. Consequently, we turned around & marched back to camp which we reached at noon yesterday. The boys were rather disappointed at not seeing a fight & wish that the colonel had let them take the pickets. I don't think quite so many would have been left to run in to camp & give the alarm.

The mountains about here are full of rebels. 400 have came in & given themselves up, saying that they are tired of fighting & are anxious for the war to come to an end. The Tennessee soldiers, especially the Tennessee soldiers will not amount to much in a fight. They keep deserting as fast as they get a chance, which we give them every time we go out on a scout.

Ed Owen came back to day. He says he left you all well & that you would have sent letters by him but you had just written. I have not received them yet but shall watch for them every night. Has Jerry received my letter with the money in it? How does them shirts get along? Send them as soon as possible. Give my love to all & write as often as possible.

To your affect. Son
Jimmie

Camp of 16th Regt Mich Vol Inft
Beverly Ford, Va. Aug 16th 1863

My Dear Friend

Your kind letter of the 9th was received yesterday, and I am very glad indeed to hear from you, from Dr. Duffield, and from Henry once more. As you perceive by [the] heading of this letter, we have moved again since I wrote last. On the 3rd and 4th insts, we moved from our camp near Warrenton, to our present camp, which is situated upon the bank of the Rappahannock, at Beverly Ford, about 9 miles above the railroad.

We have been kept busy in doing picket duty, and in throwing up entrenchments on this north side of the river. We have built earthworks for all the batteries we have in our corps, besides throwing up long lines of rifle pits for the use of the infantry. These preparations are all for defense, and now we are every day expecting to have use for them, as the rebels have found out that our army is not as large as they thought it was at Gettysburg, and they are concentrating their army up the way, and preparing to attack us. There is no doubt of this. It has been ascertained by our scouts and spies to a certainty.

Our army at Gettysburg numbered but 45,000 men in all of the 7 corps comprising the Army of the Potomac. The rebels crossed the Potomac with 70,000 men, and are supposed to have lost 35,000 men. Since their return here, they have received considerable reinforcements from Richmond, from near Suffolk, and other places, whilst our army has not received a single regt to reinforce it. On the contrary, we have had quite a number of troops sent away. This last week a brigade of regulars from the 2nd Division of our corps were sent to N.Y. City to duty there, another brigade of regulars will also leave us this present week. This, with our losses at Gettysburg, has reduced our army so much, that it would be madness for us to attempt to act on the offensive, when we know the enemy has a much larger force than we have, and choice of position also.

At present, we are under marching orders [and] expect to leave our camps very soon. The general opinion throughout our army is that we must fall back to Centreville, or the defenses near Washington and remain there untill our army is filled up again, before we can do anything towards crushing the rebellion or taking Richmond.

This army is looking anxiously to see the draft carried out in the northern states, and to see the men coming down to fill up the broken ranks of our old regiments, for full well we know, there is no other way of obtaining men left to us now. We have received a few conscripts from the eastern states here already, but they do not come in numbers large enough to amount to much. By the way, it seems to me that Michigan is behind the rest of the states in enforcing the draft and supplying their old regiments with men.*

---

*Governor Blair wanted the state to fill its quotas through enlistments first and gave the state ample chance to do that before instituting the draft. He gave them until December 30, 1862. The draft in January 1863 resulted in 1,278 men drafted in twenty counties, which seems low and indicates that more of the quota had been met. Another draft in October 1863 yielded an additional 6,383 men under Lincoln's latest call for more troops.

I wish I knew the name of that invalid officer you mentioned in your letter, as he said he had fought by the side of the 16th. I should probably know him, or at least the regt to which he belongs. 4 officers from our regt have entered that corps, viz, Capts. Myers and Martin, and Lieuts. Chandler and Hough. And more that are wounded will also join. The Invalid Corps is an excellent thing for officers and men that have been wounded, or are unfit for duty in the field.*

The weather for the past two weeks has been excessively warm, and it has been about as much as we could endure here in camp. I do not know what we should do if we were on the march. Last Wednesday night, we had a hard thunder storm. I never saw so much rain come down in a few hours, as we had that night. The ground all through our camp became flooded with water 4 to 6 inches deep. I had built up a bunk before that, so that I kept out of the water. But those who had no bunks raised were flooded out of their tents and such scenes as there was in camp that night, were not often seen, even by us in our camping out.

Col. Welch is yet absent from the regt on sick leave, and Major Elliott has command of the regt. Major E. has but lately received his commission as Major. You will recollect he came out as Capt of the co. I came out with. I have now been sent to that Co. (E), to command it and I shall now very likely remain in it, as long as I remain in the service with this regt. as I prefer it to any other co. in the regt. The few days rest we have had here has done us all a great deal of good, although it was in very warm weather, and we have had a good deal of work to do. A party of 100 men from each regt in our brigade have been at work upon the R.R., repairing it for the last 8 days, and have just returned to camp.

I hope your trip to Maine may result for the benefit of your health. But I am afraid that you interest yourself so much for the soldiers that you are very apt to overwork yourself, in trying to do so much for them as you do. I am very glad that Rev. Dr. Duffield sometimes finds something in my letters to interest him, as I usually try to give all the news from our army.

But I must now close. Please give my best regards to Rev. Dr. Duffield, to Dr. S.P. Duffield, and hoping to hear from you again soon

I Remain
Respectfully Your Friend
C.H. Salter

P.S. Please remember me to Henry when next you write. I have just seen Col. Throop of the 1st Mich. He is well, and in good spirits. C.H.S.

---

*In April 1863, the U.S. War Department created an Invalid Corps consisting of officers and men who had been or were in the army and were now disabled. They formed two battalions, one for those who could bear arms and the other for those more severely handicapped and fit for hospital service only.

Monday Aug 25 1863
Smith's + [Cross] Roads, Tenn.

Dear Mother

This is the first chance I have had to send a letter through since we started. The mail starts from here in an hour. We have been marching most of the time since we left McMinville, over the mountains.

Well, as I expected, we started at midnight & had a hard march to Sparta. We marched all day & reached Sparta at about 4 o'clock. We charged into the rebels & drove them, capturing 17. They took a new position however, & held us until dark, wounding 16 in our brigade. But just at dark, we made another charge at them & scattered them for good, for that is the last we saw of them. We camped on the battlefield over night. We started at 8 o'clock the next morning for the mountains. When we got to the foot of it, we halted for dinner. We fed here & carried green corn up the mountain for feed at night & morning. It was decidedly the worst road to take teams over ever traveled, but with patience & perseverance we reached the top of the mountain after 7 hours of hard work. Just as we got to the top & were thinking of camping for the night, we ran against the rebel picket & of course, we had to chase them a few miles but we did stop on the top of the mountain all night. For all the pickets, the next morning we went down, down, down & finally got down to the level again at a place called Pikesville.

We stayed there one day & started up, up, up again over another mountain, the top of which we reached at 10 o'clock P.M. & went into camp. The next morning, we started down again at day light & reached this place at 10 A.M., where we stayed all that day & the next. [The] day before yesterday, we started out & moved 6 miles up this (Tennessee) Valley, where we have been until this morning, when we started back again & have just reached this place again. We expect to go out on another scout again this evening. This is one of the hottest kinds of a rebel hole but there is lots of Union folks in this vicinity, where we can get potatoes, &c & consequently, we can manage to live, for if we had to depend on the rations sent to us over the mountains, we would fare rather hard, I reckon. But we can live on corn & potatoes in a pinch, besides we confiscate all the wheat & have that ground for us by the mills here, so we have plenty of biscuits & once in a while a little butter—taking all things into consideration, we fare pretty well for soldiers.

I suppose you have heard of our fight at Sparta. Before this we fought the rebs at a very great disadvantage. They were posted in a mill across a little creek & we had to come in open sight to shoot them & so they got a fine sight at us. We had all of our men wounded at this place. We had 4 in one regiment. Col. Minty came very near being killed here. He went out in an open field to give orders & the first he knew, a volley from a party of rebs that were concealed in the edge of the woods were firing at him & his escort, wounding a Lieut. who was riding by his side. You can imagine how long the rebs were allowed to stay there. Our boys soon cleared that place out, I can assure you.

But I must stop. Give my love to all & write often to

Jimmie

Cumberland Church
Sept. 9 1863

Dear Mother

Those shirts have arrived & are just the things. Every body wants to know where I got them & if I have not got one to spare. I could have got $3.00 a piece for them but I could not see it in that light. They suited me a little too well to part with them. You must not be afraid of my leaving off my under shirts, for it is so cold here in the night, that we need all the clothes on we can get. My under shirts are in good condition, if I recollect right. As for my stockings, I have two pair left, I think. It is [al]most a month since I saw my valise.

We left the Cross Roads day before yesterday & came to this place, which is 6 miles down the Tennessee Valley, towards Chattanooga. We were camped here about 2 weeks ago, I think. I wrote home from there then. We expect to move forward to day. We will cross the river (Tennessee) & probably move down towards Chattanooga. Burnside & Rosecrans are both across the river. We are on the extreme left of Rosecrans' Army & our pickets meet Burnsides'. We hear that they are fighting at Chattanooga. I don't think that the rebel army here is going to do much fighting. They are deserting very fast. They come & give themselves up to the pickets all along the line. One captain & 14 men gave themselves up to our pickets last night.

I suppose Ike is home by this time, isn't he. How does he look? Does he look like all the rest of the Old Salts or do he look natural as ever? Can he tell big stories? I warrant you he can. I suppose he & George are having a fine time together. Well perhaps it will be my turn one of these days, for there is an old saying that "every dog has his day." We are having very fine weather here. NO rain of any account. The worst thing is the dust, for when we move, we are enveloped in a cloud of it. It puts me in mind of our march through Kentucky last fall. We will <u>never</u> have another such a march as that was. Then we actually suffered for water.

Now we have the best kind of water & plenty of it besides all the vegetables &c, &c, we can eat. We are living in clover now, to what we was last fall. Has Jerry got those rebel papers I sent him yet? But in order to get this in to the mail, I shall have to stop, so write often to your son

Jimmie

P.S. I have got about tired of franking letters. Jim

Chattanooga, Tenn.
Sept 23 1863

To Charlie
Dear Brother

I have a few minutes to spare this morning before we go to the front & I will use it to let you know that I am still alive & kicking. This will be the 6th day of the fight & so far we have been driven back about 9 miles. We are expecting reinforcements every hour. This will probably be the worst day in the 6. We have got as far back as we can go & hold our line on this side of the Tennessee River. The infantry have been digging all night in the rifle pits. Rosecrans has been all around the lines & thinks he can hold the place. Our horses are faring very hard as we can get no corn on this side of the river.

Our brigade was the first one engaged & held the whole rebel army at check for most of the first morning & just got out of the gap where they were fighting on time to save themselves. We were flanked on both sides before we gave up the position.

Our brigade lost between 150 & 200 killed, wounded & missing. So was the report, but it is cut down a great deal since. The loss in our regiment are 2 killed, 7 wounded & 1 missing. I was to Stevenson on the first day of the fight but returned the next day. Has Ed Owen got home yet? I left him at Stevenson on his way home. George Clark came very near being captured on the first day. He was 2 miles from the regiment when they began falling back & before he knew it, the rebs were between him & his regt, so he took it cross lots & through the woods until he reached the regt.

The ball has opened. There goes the first gun this morning, so I will stop & get this into the mail before we are ordered to move out.

Love to all
Jimmie

Camp Starvation
Maysville, Ala.
Oct 20 1863

Dear Mother

This is the first chance I have had for a long while to let you know that I was alive & kicking, but there is a mail going from this place in the morning & I take the opportunity to let you know that for all their endeavors to starve us, we are still alive thanks to the well filled smoke house of the good Union citizens of Tenn. & Alabama, which we emptied for them without asking many questions.

We have, as I suppose you know, been chasing the raiders all over the country for 18 days & during that 18 days, we have received 6 days rations & in consequence, have had to forage on the citizens for food or starve. Of these 2 evils, the boys chose the least, so it has been every man for himself among the citizens. This foraging has been carried on to such an extent that it has finally ended in making a perfect set of thieves of the cavalry, for there are just enough bad men in it to spoil the whole lot. There has been several arrested for stealing money & clothing from the citizens & if this foraging is continued for 10 days more, the cavalry command will be perfectly demoralized. It is bad enough already & taking away Col. Minty did not make our brigade feel any better. I hope he will come back again soon, as well off or not, better than when he left us. If he brings back a star, nobody will feel bad a bit.

But I must stop, for my light is almost out. Love to all. Write often to

Your Affectionate Son
Jimmie

P.S. we have just received a new supply of rations. Bully. JV

Bivouac 16th Regt M.V.I.
Near Warrenton, Va. Oct 22nd 1863

My Dear Friend

Your kind letter of the 4th inst was received on the 10th, but as our army has been on the move ever since then, I have not had time to write untill today.

On Oct 9th, it was ascertained that the rebels were advancing upon us, and that night our corps packed up, and next morning fell in at 2 A.M., marched to near Raccoon Ford, lay in line of battle all day, and then returned to camp to bivouac that night, as it was found that the enemy was massing his troops at Madison Court House. Next morning, the 11th, we started off before daylight, marched to the Rappahannock, crossed and bivouacked in our old camp near Beverly Ford. The rebels made their appearance upon the opposite side, and next morning, the 2nd & 6th Corps and our own deployed in line of battle. Our regt, out in front as skirmishers, and the 6th Corps upon our left, we advanced upon the rebels who had a position upon a ridge near Brandy Station. They held their ground and skirmished with us untill our line was within a half mile of their position, and then they broke & run with our cavalry after them. We followed after, and halted in line, near Culpeper, built up large numbers of camp fires, and, about midnight, we very quietly fell in, and marched back across the Rappahannock, and then to Warrenton Junction, where we halted at night, after having marched about 30 miles.

Next day, (the 14th), we marched as far as Manassas Junction, when we heard firing in our rear. The rebels had attacked the 2nd Corps, our rear guard at Briscoe Station, and we double quicked back there to assist them, arrived at the battle field about sunset, and found that the 2nd Corps had already taken 1,000 prisoners and 5 cannon. And after our appearance, the rebels fell back and we continued our march, crossing Bull Run creek. We halted at midnight, after having marched about 25 miles. Next morning we fell in and marched to Fairfax, and took up our position about 1 mile west of the village. Our line extended from Bull Run to our position. Our siege guns were mounted on the works at Centreville, and we were in hopes the rebels would attack us so that we could give them a good whipping. But they did not, and we had a heavy rain storm on the 16th, then, at night, fell in and moved to Centreville, in the midst of a hard rain. We had half dozen little streams to wade across, but we arrived at our destination about midnight, and lay there the next day, then on the morning of the 18th, we moved back to Fairfax, as the rebels were expected that way, but the rebs declined to attack us in that position, and on the 19th, we commenced our pursuit of them.

We marched that day to the old Bull Run battle ground, and halted to bivouac for the night. I went over the ground that our brigade had fought over, and found it pretty well covered with human bones and many skeletons entire, also found the remains of Capt. Ransom, and Lt. Chittick, and the color bearer, a young man named _____, [blank in original] of our regt. They were recognized by the clothing, which still remained upon them. Darkness came on whilst I was looking over the field, and I could not prosecute my search any farther.

Next morning, we fell in at 2 A.M. and moved to our present bivouac, which is about 4 miles north of Warrenton. Our corps is now in reserve, all the other corps are in advance of us. We expect that we are to hold the line of the Rappahannock, the same we had last August & Sept. before advancing. It is a much better line than the Rapidan, as it is not so easy for the enemy to outflank us, as they did this last time. But we never would have had to fall back from that position if our government had not sent off the 11th & 12th Army Corps to reinforce Rosecranz after his defeat. Now that Rosecranz has been re-inforced by 30,000 men from our army, and 40,000 from Gen. Grant's army, he has the largest army any general has had yet during the war, and he ought to advance and crush Bragg's army and cut off the rebels from all the southern or gulf states. I would prefer to see Gen. Grant in command of that army as, I believe, he is the best gen[eral]. But we must wait and see what Gen. Rosecranz will do.

I am very glad that Henry passed through the battle with only a slight injury. Since I wrote you last, I have heard nothing from my expected commission, save what you wrote me. Yet I know the reason why I do not receive it and so I am patient to wait. It was recommended by Major Elliott, but was not sent, I presume, because it was not recom-mended by Col. Welch, who commands the regt (when he is here), but who has not been with us since July 17th, having been sick now for about 6 weeks, so that we have not in reality anyone to command us, and the interests of both men & officers of our regt have been sadly neglected. This being the reason of my not having received the commission before this, I am content to wait awhile longer, hoping it will all yet be right.

I can sympathize now with you in having the rheumatism, as the exposure of the last two weeks has brought it on me, and if it continues, I shall try to go to hospital at Washington to recruit. But I expect it will pass away when we get in camp and get fixed up comfortable again. The nights here are pretty cold now to be sleeping out doors, as we have been doing for some time. We shall try to fix up our present camp to make it as comfortable as possible, if we do not move tomorrow.

You must excuse poor writing in this letter, as it is wrote under difficulties. I will try to do better next time. Please give my kind regards to Rev. Mr. Duffield and your son the Doctor. Hoping to hear from you again soon, I remain,

Respectfully Your friend
C.H. Salter

Camp 16th Regt Mich Vol Inft

Near Warrenton Junction, Va. Nov 6th 1863

My Dear Friend

You very kind letter of the 1st has just been received, and I am very glad to hear from you, and your friends at home. Your letters are always most welcome, for they are almost always the most interesting of any that I receive. I am glad to hear that friend Henry is well, and enjoying himself as well as circumstances will permit. I have no doubt that he must have improved in chimney building, since he has been in the army, as indeed all of us have. As for myself, I think I have learnt a great deal about such work here, and also about cooking and many other things of which I was quite ignorant before coming into the army. I wish that you could have seen that tent, or rather hut that I had at Culpeper. I think it would have surprised most any of my friends to see what a nice place I built up, with the poor facilities for such work there. But now, I suppose, some rebel is living in it, and enjoying the fruits of my labor as their army is supposed to be in that vicinity now.

My last letter was wrote when we in camp about 4 miles on the other side of Warrenton, I believe. On the 24th, our corps moved to Auburn, a little village near the scene of the battle on the 14th. We remained there untill the 30th, when we moved to our present camp near Warrenton Junction. The 3rd Corps is camped here with us, or near us. Since we have been here, we have put up our tents so that we are living very comfortable (for soldiers). We have built beds with poles, and covered with "Virginia feathers" (cedar boughs). We have plenty of blankets to keep us warm, and each man, officers as well as privates, is allowed one loaf of soft bread each day, and even that is quite a treat to us, as indeed it is to all soldiers that are in the southern conthievaracy, and that little touch of rheumatism I had has disappeared, and I do not think I shall be troubled with it again, but I think you attached most too much importance to what I said about it, for nearly all of our old soldiers, who have been here in Virginia are troubled more or less with it.

I am obliged to your son, the Doctor, for his advice upon the subject, and if I am troubled with it again, I will go to Washington some time this winter, when we are in winter quarters and I can be spared from the regt, as well as not, but not untill then will I leave the regt if I can help it.

Our army is now under marching orders, and we expect to move again in a day or two, as every preparation has been made for another advance movement, although it is very doubtful about what is our destination. It is quite certain that we shall advance to the Rappahannock, but whether we shall cross or not is perhaps unknown to anyone but our commander, Gen. Meade. Many think that we will move down to Fredericksburgh, and winter there, as we would have a better line of communication open for our supplies than we have on the line of this railroad. But, in another week, probably, we shall know where we are going, and speculation on that subject will be at an end.

You mention in your letter the case of my promotion and speak of writing to my colonel about it. But I do not think that is necessary, as the facts of the case are there. Our Lt. Col., (we have no colonel), has been absent sick most of the time since last August or July, it was, I believe he left us. Major Elliott commanded the regt after he left, and in August, Major E recommended me to Adjt Gen Robertson and, of course, through him, to Gov. Blair, for a captain's commission. The commission was not sent, as it is their rule not to send any commissions except upon the recommendation of the colonel or lt. col. commanding the regt, whether he is present or absent, and as Lt. Col. Welch has been absent since, myself and several other officers and sergeants expecting promotion, have had to wait, not knowing, in fact, whether we are to get promoted or not. I have been, since last April, the senior lieutenant in the regt. and no promotions have been made in our regt since then, which is not the case, I suppose with hardly any volunteer regt in the service. Our Lt. Colonel's name is N.E. Welch. His residence is Ann Arbor, but he is in Detroit a great deal, when in Michigan. Perhaps he would attend to the matter if you should drop him a line upon the subject, although I am expecting he will be here before a great while, and then I can see him myself. I have been urged by some of my friends here to apply for a higher position in some of the colored regiments now forming, but I tell them that I prefer being a captain (if I can get it) in the old 16th, to having any office short of a colonelcy in a new regiment, either white or black.

I am obliged to you for the piece you sent me, "The Young Man's Prayer" and have studied the piece and find it very interesting, and hope to improve by it. It has done me more good than anything else I have read in a long while. I am sorry to hear that Rev. Mr. Duffield thinks we are to have a cold winter, as it affects us soldiers most particularly, but the Lord knows what is best for us and perhaps we may pass over this winter better than last. I am pleased to see your son, the Doctor, doing so well and hope that he will have health to enjoy the benefit of his discoveries.

And now I must close, hoping you will write again as soon as convenient.

> I Remain,
> Respectfully Your Friend
> C.H. Salter

> Camp 16th Regt Mich Vol Infty
> Near Kelly's Ford, Va. Nov 22nd 1863

My Dear Friend

Your very kind and interesting letter of the 15th has arrived, and I am greatly obliged to you for writing so good and consoling a letter as that is, and as today is the Sabbath day, and no meeting is to be held in our camp (for want of a chaplain), I read over your letter, and think of it for better than a sermon for me today. "Alls Well" is a beautiful hymn, and "Jesus has a home for me" is very touching in its vivid truth and earnestness, as it appears to the soldiers mind and heart, most particularly.

I am glad to hear of Henrys prospect of happiness. I hope he will succeed in obtaining a leave of absence for at least 60 days, and that he may be happy through life with the partner he has chosen. I think under the circumstances, he will have no difficulty in getting an extension of the Secretary of War, as there is a Lieut. in our regt who has been absent for the same purpose, for nearly three months now, and he had no difficulty in procuring some 2 or 3 extensions.

I wrote my last letter and mailed it to you on the evening of the 6th. I said then we were expecting to have a fight soon, but I did not think it would come as soon as it did. We packed up the next morning before daylight and marched down to within 2 miles of Rappahannock Station, where we joined the 6th Corps, and formed line of battle, the 6th upon the right of the R.R. and our corps upon the left. Our skirmish line drove back that of the rebels untill they took refuge in the forts near the R.R. bridge. The rebel artillery kept up a lively fire upon us, but our artillery, coming up, engaged them, and then our skirmishers charged upon the forts, but captured them all and that too before the main body of our troops could get up. After that, they captured many more on the river bank, and charged upon a pontoon bridge on which the rebels were crossing, and captured the bridge and prevented any more rebels from crossing, so that all of them on the north side of the river were captured. And we had prisoners from 10 different rebel regts and out of two brigades, only about 600 escaped. It was the most perfect and glorious little victory that has been gained by us yet during the war. And farther down the river, at Kelly's Ford, the 3rd Corps had attacked the rebels stationed there, and had very much the same sort of a battle we had, driving the rebels before them, and capturing many prisoners, so that we were victorious all along the river, and gained 2,300 prisoners, with all their arms, 11 pieces of artillery, about a dozen stand of colors, and taken 2 forts and a pontoon bridge by storm.

We bivouacked there that night, and next morning our corps marched down to Kelly's Ford, crossed and went about 3 miles towards Culpeper, then halted, and bivouacked, and the next afternoon our division was detached from the corps, and marched back across the river, and then we were kept busy doing picket duty from Bealcton to the river, at a point about 3 miles south of Kelly's Ford. The railroad is repaired now, so that the trains are running to Culpeper again, and that is once more the depot of supplies for the Army of the Potomac, so that the rebels have not gained much by trying to drive us back.

Gen. Meade's head quarters are now in Culpeper and our army does picket duty along the north bank of the Rapidan, same as before we fell back last month. Our corps is under marching orders, and we expect that soon we will be sent to camp near the Rapidan and perhaps we shall cross it, and the army advance to Gordonsville. Although it is very uncertain about our going over across the Rapidan this winter, it seems to us as if we would have too long a line of communication to keep up. But we shall soon see what we are to do.

I am under great obligations to you for writing to Lt. Col. Welch in regard to my promotion, and I hope it will hurry him up. He is expected to rejoin the regt again very soon, and probable he will bring the commission with him. At least that is expected here in the regt, and then I will ascertain the reason for the long delay.

Major Elliott, who had been in Washington sick for the last two months, rejoined the regt on the 14th inst. He has nearly recovered from the injury received from a falling timber at Beverly Ford, but is not quite fit for duty yet. I received two papers from you other day for which I am greatly obliged. I sent you the Richmond Sentinel of the 5th. I found it in a deserted rebel camp, and though it was very dirty, thought you would like to see the paper as a curiosity in these times.

But I must close, hoping to hear from you again, as soon as convenient. I remain,

Respectfully Your Friend
C.H. Salter

P.S. give my regards to Rev. Dr. Duffield, to S.P. Duffield, and remember me to Henry if you please.

2nd Cavalry Division Hospital
Huntsville, Ala.
November 28 1863

Dear Mother

I have just came from supper & think I would like to have a little chat with you. I have answered all the letters I have received & am waiting for more.

You see by the heading of this that we have moved our division hospital to Huntsville. We got here night before last & have got the hospital in running order already & 27 patients in it. We can only accommodate 40 or so. You see that it is almost full so soon, but the reason of that is that we brought most of them along with us from Maysville.

Our hospital is right opposite the Court House & next door to the water Works, which, by the by, is a very fine one. Our spring furnishes the whole town with water. The water works is on the top of a hill & from under this hill a stream of water runs about 50 feet in width, which is drawn up on top of the hill & distributed to the people. Pure water is about the only blessing they have, for provisions are extremely scarce. The people are almost in a starving condition. This is not the <u>poor</u> families only, but the rich are just as bad off as the poor, for money is worse than useless. It will buy nothing & it takes up room.

To show you how hard up the families are in this place, I will tell you of an interview between Col. Sykes (commanding post) & the wife & mother of C.C. Clay, who is now at Richmond in the Confederate Senate (he was formerly United States Senator from Alabama). These two women came into the Col's office & fell down on their knees & begged him to give them something to keep them from starving. They had lived for some time on our biscuit & a cup of milk each day but now that had now given out and starvation stared them in the face & with tears in their eyes, they begged the Col. to help them, if it were a possible thing. They had not a stick of wood or a pound of coal in the house & had suffered for the want of them. Now, if you don't call this a pretty hard case, I am much mistaken. For a <u>Senator's</u> wife, I call that <u>rather</u> hard fare.

The Col told them that he would issue them rations for which they would be expected to pay at the end of the war & would have wood & coal procured for them, which he did before night & this forlorn family was once more in a livable condition. A great share of the people here are living on army rations.

Our regiment went out about 10 days ago. We have not heard from it yet. It is supposed to have gone towards Chattanooga, but that is only a rumor. We received very encouraging news from the front yesterday; rebel sympathizers look rather blue; citizens here think that the war is coming to an end but we all know that has been the opinion ever since the war commenced. When it comes to an end you will all know it by seeing me home. So for the present

Adeaux
Jim
Write soon

"Fort Vincent" Rappahannock Station, Va.
Dec 12th 1863

My Dear Friend

Your very kind letter of the 22nd & 30th inst was received on the 6th, and now I take the first opportunity I have had to write to you. I am greatly obliged to you for writing me so kind, good and interesting a letter, and to repay you, I will try to give you all the news of interest from our army.

Since my last letter when we were in camp near Kelly's Ford, we received orders to march on the 24th, and packed up and started at daylight, but it rained very hard that morning, and the ground was becoming unfit for marching, so after we had gone 3 miles, Gen. Meade sent us orders to return to camp and remain there 2 days longer. Then we started again on the 26th, "Thanksgiving Day." Our corps marched to Gold Mine Ford, (on the Rapidan), and the 3rd Division (Penn. Reserves), of our corps waded across the stream in 3 feet water. Then the pontoon bridge was laid, and the balance of our corps crossed, followed by the 1st Corps. We marched to Chancellorsville, and bivouacked for the night. Then next morning [we] started on again, going in the direction of Spotsylvania Court House. We had marched about 8 miles, our corps in advance, then our ordnance train, (without any guard), then the 1st Corps following us, when suddenly a brigade of rebel cavalry dashed in upon the train, shooting down the drivers, mules, &c, that made attempt to escape, and captured about 15 wagons with their drivers and mules, and set fire to the wagons. Our regt was ordered back together with a portion of the 62nd Pa. We ran all the way, but the rebels ran before we could get up to them, and we only killed one rebel officer, who at the time, was trying to destroy one of our ambulances. The rebels had gone, but we could not approach the wagons, as they were burning, and the shells in them were exploding, 5 or 6, sometimes at once, so we had to let them burn. After that, our regt was detailed as train guard for all the trains belonging to our corps, and that same day, marched back to Ely's Ford, where the corps trains were lying, and after that we were engaged in escorting trains out to the corps, with supplies and return, and guarding the trains when lying still untill on the morning of the 2nd inst., we received orders to return to our old camp, as the army was all coming back again, and we came back with the train to Kelly's ford.

Then next morning, [we] came up to this place, where a brigade of the 1st Corps had been stationed. They left the place to rejoin their corps, and we were given this station for our brigade to guard. 3 regts are on the north bank of the river, where they have two forts, rifle pits, &c. It is the battle field of 7th Nov, when the 6th Corps and our own stormed and took the forts, rifle pits, pontoon bridge, &c. But our regt has the post of honor. We are on the south bank of the river. Here we have one fort (the largest of the three at this place), which is situated on a hill overlooking the R.R. bridge that spans the river at this point, and also commands a fine view of all the surrounding country for 3 or 4 miles. 9 companies are camped on the side hill just outside the fort, and the other 2 companies are camped on another hill about 80 rods up the river. This hill is also fortified, having earthworks thrown up for a battery, and rifle pits, for infantry. Our fort is named in honor of Gen. Vincent, who as colonel of the 83rd Pa., commanded our brigade last spring and summer untill mortally wounded at Gettysburg, and lived just long enough after that to receive a commission as Brig. Gen. from the President's own hand, as a reward for conspicuous bravery on that occasion.

Our regt's head quarters are inside of the fort. Also, a section of a battery is to be placed in it, though it has not as yet arrived. We have to guard these works here, and also the R.R. bridge, and two pontoon bridges, besides a portion of the R.R. tracks. The balance of our corps is stationed along the R.R., from Centreville to this place, and one brigade at Beverly Ford, where we camped last August. The 4th Mich are at Bealeton Station, the great depot for supplies for our army. The balance of our army occupy their old camps, off towards the Rapidan. The 1st Corps is camped in our old camps from Kelly's Ford towards the Rapidan, the 2nd Corps is near Germania and Culpeper fords, whilst the 3rd and 6th Corps are near Culpeper, where Gen Meade has his head quarters.

Our army has now apparently gone into winter quarters, to the great joy of all the soldiers, and we shall remain in our present position for the next three months, if nothing unusual occurs to disturb us. We have been hard at work since we have been here, to build up warm quarters. Our regt has all got logs to build up the sides of the tents with, and, as stone is very plenty here, we have all good fire places to keep us warm. I was busy with building mine 3 days, but succeeded in getting one that does not smoke, except at the top of the chimney. In fact, I have now the best one I have had since I have been in the army, and I am very thankful for it. I would like to see Henry's chimney at Chattanooga, and to challenge him to a trial of chimney building. I prefer my fire place to a stove for use here in camp, although I have not built a log house as some have. As I have a good tent, all to myself, that I think will answer my purpose for a house this winter.

I read in some of the papers rumors that Gen. Meade is to be removed for not advancing any farther on this last movement. But we do not believe it at all here, as we know that Lee's army was in such good position, our loss would have been very heavy if we attempted to drive him from it, and our wounded would suffer terribly with cold before they could be got to Washington. As it was, some of our men on picket, out in front, froze to death on account of getting wet, and not having any fires to warm by. In fact, Gen Meade ordered us back to our camps simply as a measure of humanity, and our entire army thinks he done just right, and we thank him for it.

The weather here in winter is considerable colder than where Grant's army is fighting, and operations here cannot now be carried on as well as there. And it was the 11th & 12th Corps, from our army, under our Gen Hooker, that stormed and carried those precipices, and our army felt a thrill of joy when we heard what our old comrades had done, it seems to us that they belong to our army still, and that our army done the hardest part of the work there.

Col. Welch returned to our regt during this last movement. He spoke of receiving a letter from you recommending my promotion, and said that he had not time to reply to it before leaving Detroit, but would do so as soon as we became settled in camp, and, although he did not bring my commission along, he would send for it soon, and now he sends to Adj. Gen. Robertson for it. His letter is going by same mail as this, and if the Adj. Gen. is prompt in sending it, I shall get it this month and be mustered on the rolls for November & December as captain. I am under great obligations to you for your great kindness in writing to Col. Welch, for I know that it hurried him up, and if you had not wrote he would not have attended to it so soon. Adj. Gen. Robertson was in our camp for a few minutes, just before we started on our last advance, said he should have the pleasure of telling you he saw me &c. I did not say anything to him about my commission, but trusted all that to Col. Welch. I told him to tell you I was well &c. By the way, if you happen to see him, please ask him for me to be kind enough to send my commission as soon as possible, as I should like to have it before this month is out, otherwise, I yet remain a lieutenant during these 2 months, if not mustered as captain before Jan 1st.

But I must now close, with respects to Rev. Dr. Duffield, Dr. S.P. Duffield, and hopes that Henry has arrived home, and is happy in the society of relatives and friends.

Respectfully, Your Friend
C.H. Salter

2nd Cavalry Div. Hospital
Calhoun House Huntsville
Dec 18th 1863

Dear Mother

We have just finished moving our hospital over here & it has kept me pretty busy for the last 2 or 3 days but we are settled at last & are comfortable in this <u>big</u> house. It is so large that it takes about a cord of wood a day to keep us warm, but who cares for the expense as long as you don't have to pay for it. I have for my room the dining room. It is about 15 by 25 feet & is painted green. It has 2 windows, 3 doors & a fire place. Now can you imagine me in that room? I expect not. I wish you could see this house & garden. The house has 14 rooms in it (mine is one of the smallest) & the garden, OH such a garden. It would take full half a day to go through all the walls & it is all just as pretty now as it is in summer. The hedge & trees are all just as green as they would be in summer. I wish I was a good hand to draw. I would like to send you a plan of this house & garden, just to show you what sort of a place I am living in.

We have 30 sick in the hospital now. We received a lot of sanitary goods to day from the U. S. Sanitary Commission—at Bridgeport, which will come very acceptable just now as we are out of most everything in that line & stand in need of them very much. This will be the first lot of sanitary goods I have ever had any thing to do with. We have never drawn any in the regiment. Hospitals is the only place for them any how, for we don't keep our sick in the regiments, but send them to the hospital as soon as they are taken sick. They get better care in hospitals & then they are not on our hands if we have to move, which is an item, I can tell you.

Enclosed you will find a Christmas present for Father. It is a true Alabama pipe, real Secesh too. But I must stop, so I will wish you all a Merry Christmas & a Happy New Year. Excuse haste & a poor pen. This is the last letter I am going to write until I receive one from some body or other.

Your Affec Son
Jim

"Fort Vincent" Rappahannock Station, Va.
December 21st 1863

My Dear Friend

Your kind letter of the 13th inst I received on the 19th and am very glad indeed to hear from you and to know you were enjoying good health, and hope you may not be troubled with rheumatism this winter as you anticipate. I wrote you a letter on the 12th inst, which you have probably received ere this, and know where we are, and how situated.

But our camp is not trimmed with evergreens, for the reason we are in an open, bleak country, and have no cedars and but very few pines in our vicinity, so that I have no Virginia feathers to place upon my bed. But I have something better and that is a good hair mattress sent up from Washington. The weather has been very cold, for this southern climate, and we do not have wood here, to burn in our fire places. I have been so busy, I have not yet had time to build a log cabin, as many of our regt have done, but I am in hopes of being able to do it some time this week. We had a very severe rain storm this last week, and our pontoon bridges had to taken up, and the river rose very rapidly, bringing down with it large numbers of trees, drift wood &c, threatening to carry away the R.R. bridge. But we kept a number of men at work attending to it, and it stood bravely.

I am sorry to hear that Henry has not succeeded in getting his leave of absence, and I think if he does not get it very soon, I will be in Detroit before him, and not only myself, but also the regt, as we have concluded to accept the offer of the Government to reenlist for another three years and go home to reorganize and recruit. This offer applies to all soldiers that have been in the service 2 years, and are willing to reenlist. They receive $402 U.S. bounty, and the bounties now offered by the state and counties. But, soldiers who have not been in the service two years cannot reenlist under this act, and as our regt received a number of recruits last winter, they will have to remain here. We only received notice of this order last Saturday, and this Monday morning, about all the old veterans of the regt signed the enlistment papers. In my company, I have 32 old men, or rather those that are old in the service. Of these, 31 are willing to reenlist, leaving only one black sheep in the flock, and I have beside these 12 men who have only been in service a year or so, and consequently cannot enlist at present, and about every company in the regt has gone the same way, so that if the Government keeps this promise, we shall go home, probably in less than 30 days.

The regt is all in fine spirits, in thinking of the prospect and we hope to be the first regt that goes home for that purpose. My company, you probably remember, was raised in Detroit and I think I could do very well to open a recruiting office in Detroit, and with 31 old veterans to start with, I think I could soon raise a full company, for every man would do all he could to bring in recruits.

In regard to my promotion, I wrote you about that in my last, it is arranged satisfactorily. Now, Col. Welch expects the commission will be here before the 1st Jan., and our adjutant left this morning to go home on a leave of absence, and he promised to see that it was hurried up. Therefore, I have no doubt it will be along in due season. Adjt. Genl. Robertson gave you the main reason why my promotion was not made sooner, but now we hope soon to have a full regt and that we will have no more trouble about these promotions. I said that all but one of my company are willing to reenlist, and now he too has come to me and signed the enlistment papers, so that every one of my old veterans have reenlisted for the war, or for three years, and that after they have been in the service already two years and a half, and but very few of them have even made a short visit home during that time. I think that is a glorious example they have set for these young men at home who can enlist, but will not and of the 12 men of mine that are not old soldiers enough to enlist, every one of them would enlist if they were allowed the privilege of so doing.

We are as busy as bees, all working to get the privilege of reorganizing our regt, and there is not much of quiet about our camp, so that I am allowed no time scarcely to think of anything but business, yet I try to remember the good instructions I have had, and the good advice you have always sent me. I am greatly obliged for the tracts you sent in your last. They are very interesting. I have read them and gave them to some of my men whom I knew would like to have them, and would read them also.

Our regt will probably have to pass Christmas and New Years Day in this camp, as usual, as it is not likely we will get started in less than two weeks. And, as usual, those days will pass away the same as any other, without anything extra for us. But we do not mind it now. I sincerely hope Henry will get home before Christmas, and have the pleasure of spending the holidays at home.

But I must now close. Give my regards and best wishes to Rev. Dr. Duffield for a merry and happy Christmas, and also the same to any enquiring friends. And with my best wishes that it may prove a merry Christmas and happy New Years to yourself, I remain,

Respectfully Your Friend
Charles H. Salter

Please wish Henry a merry Christmas and a happy New Years for me. C.H.S.

2nd Cav. Div. Hospital
Huntsville, Ala
December 24th 1863
9 o'clock

Dear Mother

Christmas Eve & here I am way down in Alabama & just at this very time. You, I suppose, are enjoying your Christmas tree. I am very sorry & I must confess somewhat disappointed at not being there to help you enjoy yourselves.

This, I suppose will astonish you, but it is a fact nevertheless, for I expected to get a furlough & surprise you a few days before Christmas. But, in consequence of my being detailed in this hospital & both surgeons being absent on furloughs, I stood no chance, so you must make up for it by letting me know all about the tree & etc. when you write again.

I am all alone here now. Our division moved away this morning & no telling when I shall see them again. It all depends on our being able to turn the hospital over to the infantry that are coming in here tomorrow or [the] next day. If we succeed in turning it over, the dr. & myself will rejoin our command (so reads our orders), at the earliest possible moment.

We have now about 70 sick in the hospital & it just keeps me busy from morning till night but it is only once in a while we have to work very hard, so I guess I can stand it. Have you received my last letter & how did Father like his pipe? That is the kind every one smokes in this country (myself excepted). I for my part prefer the corn cob one. It is much cheaper & you can always get a new one if one burns out. If Father don't like that one, I will send him a corn cob one by mail. I could not find a wooden stem to it so he will have to use a reed one for the present.

Our boys were very much disappointed in being obliged to move from here before Christmas, as they had invitations to parties on that day, by the citizens. But they got over it before they left town, for they went off in high spirits. Where they went to, no one knows yet. But as I am getting sleepy & by this time you have got most of the things off the tree, I will thank you all for my presents and retire.

Good Night Mother
Jimmie

P.S. The mail has just arrived with six papers from home for me. Yours & Hatties' letters came last night. Also one from Willie. Love to all. Jim

5

Darkest Hour

"Fellow soldiers in life, let them slumber in death
Side by side, as becomes the reposing braves—
That sword which they loved still unbroken in its sheath,
And themselves unsubdued in their graves."

The third year of the war would be the bloodiest, if there can be such a thing, of America's national nightmare. Both armies had already taken a terrible beating, yet the aggregate numbers of the armies were nearly the same in 1864 as at the beginning of 1863, with the Confederacy actually having slightly more men in the ranks than before. The year would see the battles of Atlanta, Kennesaw Mountain, Franklin, and Nashville in the west and the Wilderness, Cold Harbor, Petersburg, and the Crater in the east. Across both theaters of war, General William T. Sherman would march to the sea. Ulysses Grant would become a lieutenant general and commander-in-chief and Lincoln would be reelected as president.

In Michigan, recruitment and enlistment were ongoing and getting harder to accomplish. Officers from several state regiments were in the state recruiting for their respective units; unlike other Northern States, Michigan sent replacement soldiers to the existing units, instead of creating new ones.

So it was with the 7th Michigan Volunteer Infantry, whose surviving members were home in late December 1863 and furloughed for 30 days, the prize for reenlisting as a unit. They had seen their share of combat, beginning with Ball's Bluff in August 1861. The 7th gained an enviable reputation at Fredericksburg when it volunteered to cross the Rappahannock River, under fire, in pontoon boats, to clear the way for the engineers.

In early February 1864, with the added promise of an enlistment bonus, John Presley raised his right hand and swore to serve for three years in U.S. service. John, the second son and third child of William and Martha, was born in 1845 in Stockbridge, Michigan, a largely farming community in Ingham County. He almost immediately bought a diary.

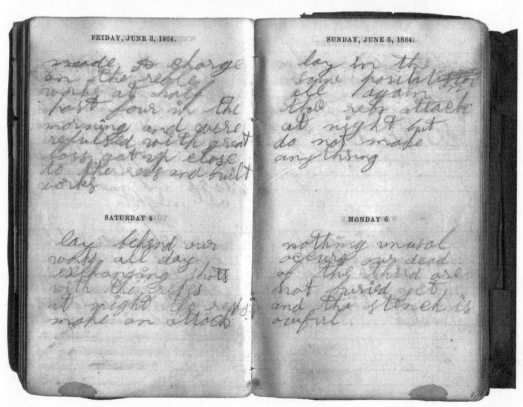

FRIDAY, JUNE 3, 1864.

made to charge
on the rebel
works at half
past four in the
morning and were
repulsed with great
loss, got up close
to the rebs and built
works

SATURDAY 4

lay behind our
works all day
exchanging shots
with the rebs
at night the rebs
make an attack

SUNDAY, JUNE 5, 1864.

lay in the
same position
all day, no
the rebs attack
at night but
do not make
anything

MONDAY 6

nothing unusal
occurs our dead
of the third are
not buried yet
and the stench is
awful

JOHN PRESLEY DIARY

My name is John Presley. I belong to the Seventh Mich. Infantry, Co. B. If I am found dead will some kind friend please send this to Mrs. Martha J. Presley, Stockbridge, Ingham Co. Michigan.

——————— February ———————

THURSDAY 11—enlisted for three years in the United States Service.

FRIDAY 12—started for Jackson and staid overnight at Mr. Jacobs.

SATURDAY 13—went to Jackson and was examined and mustered into the service and was sent to the barracks.

MONDAY 15—got a guard up to the prison with me and went through it.

SUNDAY 21—went to the prison to metting [meeting].

TUESDAY 23—Drew our uniforms.

WEDNESDAY 24—started for Grand Rapids; went as far as Kalamazoo and staid overnight.

THURSDAY 25—started for the rapids in lumber wagons; had a pretty hard ride of it; got to the rapids nine oclock at night and then marched to the camp two miles from the city.

——————— March ———————

WEDNESDAY 2—was not paid seventy three dollars bounty.

THURSDAY 3—started for Dixie; went as far as Detroit; there changed cars for Toledo; got there about twelve oclock at night; there changed for Cleveland.

FRIDAY 4—arrived in Cleveland at nine in the morning; staid there in the cars until noon, then started for pitsburg.

SATURDAY 5—arrived in pitsburg one oclock in the morning; found supper waiting but did not have time to eat it; changed cars for Baltimore.

SUNDAY 6—arrived in Baltimore about daylight; there eat breakfast, then started for Washington; got there about one oclock in the afternoon; stayed there overnight.

MONDAY 7—in the morning, went up to the capitol house and went through it; at ten oclock started for alesedronia [Alexandria]; arrived there about noon; got dinner, then went and got our guns, cartridge boxes and tents.

TUESDAY 8—got aboard the cars and went to Brandy Station where we arrived about two oclock in the afternoon; then we got off and marched to the regiment about three miles.

THURSDAY 10—went and got logs for our shanty; had to go five miles after them where the rebs had built them.

FRIDAY 11—built our shanty.

SUNDAY 13—had company inspection.

MONDAY 14—went out on general inspection; got put on fatigue duty for thirty days for having an oil cloth on my cap.

FRIDAY 18—the wind blows so hard that it almost blows our shanty over and the sand flies so we can hardly see; this afternoon was ordered to pack up and be ready to march at a moments warning as Stewardt [J.E.B. Stuart] was marching on raid.

SATURDAY 19—was taken with the mumps.

SUNDAY 20—it is pretty cold here now.

MONDAY 21—got excused from duty on account of having the mumps; last night the water froze in our canteens.

TUESDAY 22—cold and stormy with snow.

WEDNESDAY 23—waked up this morning and found ourselves nearly snowed under; the snow is about a foot deep on the level.

FRIDAY 25—returned to duty.

Camp 16th Mich Vet Vol Infty
Near Bealeton, Va. March 20th 1864

My Dear Friend

Your kind letter of Feb 27th was received some time ago, and I should have wrote you long before this, but that I had but just wrote on the 1st inst, and since then have been so busy, I have neglected to write. But today being Sabbath, I have plenty of spare time and will improve it by writing you a letter.

We are yet in the same camp we located in when we first came here last month, and have been busy in making a nice camp of it. We have log houses for quarters for the entire regt, [and] have a brush fence encircling the entire camp. The streets are all nicely graded, and we have built up as good a camp as any we have ever had yet. Besides keeping ourselves busy in drilling the new recruits, doing our usual share of picket duty, &c. Our Col. Welch and a lieut. have gone home to see what they can do in the way of getting recruits for the regt. Yesterday, Lieut. Wallace of the 5th Cavalry, and Lt. Hull of the 6th Cavalry, called upon us. They were just on their way back to camp after returning from their great cavalry raid, when they came so near to Richmond, and did not take it, and we have been under arms for the last two days as an attack is expected by Stuart's cavalry somewhere along the line of the railroad, but as yet he has not made his appearance, and we are beginning to think it is all a scare anyhow.

Gen. Grant is expected here soon to take command of our army in person, and we expect to have an active campaign, and a desperate one, too, very soon. Gen. Grant has now a more difficult task before him than any he has ever before undertaken. Here he has to meet the best general, and the best and largest army the rebels have got, and in the worst section of country in the U.S. to operate in, yet we have great confidence in Gen. Grant and hope he will be successful here. But many think that he has been sent here for the purpose of giving him a chance to destroy his reputation as a good general, in this same army that has ruined so many generals before this. They think that Gen. Grant was becoming too popular for the politicians and they, in consequence, take this method to ruin him. But whatever it may be, one thing is certain, that the Army of the Potomac has got to suffer and struggle on in the same manner we have been doing for the last three years, but we are willing to try it again once more, whilst we pray that this summers' campaign may end it, and allow us to have some rest from the fatigues of life in the field. It is the opinion of everyone in our army that the great struggle and the hardest fighting will take place this summer here in Virginia, and that if we are victorious, the rebels will have to leave the state, and if not, then we will be further off, (apparently), from conquering them than ever before.

The weather here has been very pleasant this month for March weather, and at our division head quarters they had a ball on the 16th inst, at which many ladies and gentlemen from Washington were present. They had a large frame work covered with canvass for their ball room. It was very nicely trimmed up inside and, I suppose, they had a very pleasant time there, but cannot say, for as I did not approve of having balls here in the army, I did not go to it, although the ball room was but 50 rods from my tent.

Today has been Sabbath, but as we have no chaplain in our regt, we have to pass it over very much in the same manner we do every other day, but we send down to Brandy Station, where the Christian Commission* have an office and get religious papers, books and tracts, which we distribute amongst the men every Sunday morning. Today I have been reading religious papers, amongst which are "The Evangelist" of New York, "North Christian Advocate" of Auburn, N.Y., "The Parish Visitor," "The Tract Journal" and "Christian Banner." The Christian Commission furnish us very liberally with all the books and papers we want. We distributed 50 Testaments in our regt today, furnished by them, and I believe they are doing a great deal of good.

But now I must close. Please remember me to Rev. Dr. Duffield and hoping you may find it convenient to write soon, I remain,

Respectfully your friend
Capt. Charles H. Salter
16th Mich Vet Vol Infty
Washington, D.C.

Camp 16th Mich Vet Vols.
Near Bealeton, Va. April 1st 1864

My Dear Friend

Your kind and interesting letter of the 26th inst arrived yesterday and I am very glad indeed to hear from you once more, and greatly obliged for your kindness in writing such a good long letter as this, and also for the kind advice it contains.

Since I wrote last, we have remained in the same camp, and nothing unusual has occurred in our army, except the consolidation of the army into three corps. Our corps will remain as the 5th Corps, but receives the addition of two divisions of troops. Our division, (the 1st), will be consolidated into two brigades, whilst the 2nd Division, the regulars, will consolidate into one brigade and come into our division. The 3rd Division, the Penn Reserves, will be the 4th Division of our new corps, as their time will be up this next May and then they will leave us with our first 3 divisions. Gen. Warren is to command our corps and Generals Sedgewick and Hancock the other two corps. Gen. Sykes, who has been in command of our corps is relieved from command, and is now out of our army at present.

---

*On November 16, 1861, volunteers from the YMCA established the United States Christian Commission to minister to the spiritual needs of the soldiers. The entirely volunteer organization raised $3 million in cash and even more in needed supplies. They distributed Christian tracts, Bibles, and pamphlets to the soldiers; operated portable libraries; and wrote home for the sick and wounded.

The 9th Corps, Gen. Burnside commanding, was to rendezvous at Annapolis for some expedition, but Gen Grant has ordered them to join our army as soon as they are assembled together, and it is expected the 11th and 12th Army Corps will soon be back here from the western army, and then we shall have our old "Army of the Potomac" all together once more. Gen. Hooker will also, probably come back with the 11th & 12th Corps, and under the generalship of Lt. Gen. Grant. I hope we shall be able to finish the hard fighting of the war this year. If you feel easier now that Gen. Halleck is out, and Grant is commander in chief, you can hardly form an idea how much the army appreciates the change. Halleck was to us, (like a stone around a mans neck, in the water), a dead weight, and it seemed as if he was cause of all our misfortunes, and our army all felt that they would not care who was placed in command, if they were only relieved of him, and Gen. Grant, probably, gives better satisfaction than any other general could at the present time, both to the army and the country in general. We feel that the dark days of the "Army of the Potomac" are about over now, and that in future we are to accomplish works that will entitle us to the name given us by McClellan, of the "Grand Army," and know that in this years' campaign, we are to assume the most important part.

By the way, you are giving me too much credit for obtaining and distributing tracts, papers &c amongst my men, for I did not say that it was myself that done it. Oh, no, but it is a sergeant named Terrill [Turrell], who should receive the credit of it all, for he goes down to Brand Station, and gets the reading every Saturday and Sunday morning, distributes an equal share to each company in the regt and then the officers or sergeants of the companies distribute amongst the men. I received the "Hymn Book" you sent by mail, and am a thousand times obliged for it, although I do not sing myself, I shall endeavor to make it useful by allowing others to use it, that can. The Christian Commission supplys us pretty liberally with soldiers hymn books, and I think nearly every man in our regt is supplied with one, so we are not as bad off in that respect as you probably thought. I have thought of applying to them to send some one to talk to us on the Sabbath, but I will speak to some of them about it myself, or get Sergeant Terrill to do so, if I do not see any of them. But as we are some six miles from this depot, I am afraid they can not very well do it. The Christian Commission is a noble institution and is doing a vast deal of good in our army. They take pains to distribute papers, books and everything useful through the army. Although I suppose the Sanitary Commission* is an equally good institution, yet I have never seen so much of their work, as of the Christian Commission.

By the way, speaking of getting the men together to sing and pray, we do that every Sabbath when the weather permits, as also quite often on pleasant evenings and have singing, prayer and usually some one to speak to us, as there are some 10 or 12 professing

---

*The Sanitary Commission, whose origins can be traced to a meeting of women held in New York on April 25, 1861, saw to the physical needs of the soldiers in regard to diet, clothing, cooks, campgrounds, and everything connected with the prevention of disease.

Christians in our regt who do speak and sing and pray, and at such times the larger portion of the regt turns out to listen, and all of the men, I have reason to believe, have too much good sense to ridicule or sneer at these meetings. And the officers, although none of them take any prominent part in the meetings, yet always feel it their duty to encourage them, more so, I think, than when we had a chaplain. And amongst our new recruits there are more men anxious for these meetings than of old men.

The weather for the last two weeks has been very stormy. On the night of the 22nd, we had a violent snowstorm, and in the morning there was a foot of snow upon the ground, more snow, in fact, than we had seen when we were up in Michigan. But that day the sun came out and by night it was all gone. We have rainstorms about us as often as every other day, so that the ground is in such bad condition, it precludes the possibility of moving at the present time, at least. Today it is raining quite hard, but then this is the season of year we must expect it.

I received the music book you sent me, and am greatly obliged for it. But I must now bring this letter to a close, as I expect to have to get ready this evening for picket tomorrow morning. Give my regards to Rev. Dr. Duffield, and Dr. S.P. Duffield. Also remember me to Henry when next you write. Hoping to hear from you again soon,

> I Remain
> Respectfully Your Friend
> C.H. Salter

> Camp 16th Mich Inft V.V.
> Near Bealeton, Va. April 22nd 1864

My Dear Friend

Your very kind letter of the 18th inst, I received today and am very glad indeed to hear from you once more, and to receive as interesting a letter as that is, and will set right down and write you an answer today, hoping to be able to write on that will interest and please you. Since my last letter was wrote we have remained quietly in camp, nothing unusual has occurred with us. We have been engaged as usual in picket duty, railroad guard, and drilling the new recruits. Our division is scattered along such a long line of the railroad that our guard duty is the most important part of our business.

The 1st brigade is camped in the vicinity of Manassas and the balance of the division is scattered along from there to the camps of our brigade at Beverly Ford and Rappahannock Station, a distance of 20 miles, and the manner in which we have guarded it this winter, we think speaks pretty well for us, as no rebel cavalry or guerillas have been able to do it any damage on our line, whilst we have been guarding it.

The weather this week has been very pleasant, and the country is improving in consequence. The roads are getting in very good condition, and if we were to move now I think we would not find any bad roads to trouble us, or hinder our march. Gen. Grant has been reviewing the troops of our army this week. On Monday, he reviewed the 6th Corps and on Tuesday the 2nd Corps. Our corps was not reviewed, as we are scattered over too large a space to be collected together for review.

We have been making preparations for marching, and last week the suttlers and all citizens were ordered to leave the army. And all of our extra baggage was sent to Alexandria, to be stored, so as to leave us in light marching order, as all of our extra teams &c are to be turned in, and the army will move this summer with less to cumber us than we ever have before. At present, we are anxiously watching to see that expedition from Annapolis get started, as we do not expect to do anything much untill that force has made a demonstration, and, by the way, that force there is much larger than most people are aware of. They have the entire 9th Army Corps there, and a large portion of the old second corps. As many regts of the latter corps who were home on furlough were ordered to join Burnside at Annapolis instead of coming back here, and by the time the expedition joins the forces already on the peninsula, they will have an army full as large as our "Army of the Potomac" and we look to see that new army (which will probably be called the "Army of the Peninsula"), make an advance upon Richmond that will cause Lee to fall back there in a hurry, with the additional benefit of having us follow him up rather faster probably than he will like.

The great sanitary fairs in New York, Philadelphia, Baltimore and the other places seem to be perfect successes.* I see by the accounts in the papers that at the New York fair they have a splendid $1000 sword, which is being voted for at a dollar a vote, and Generals Grant and McClellan seem to get all the votes. At last accounts we had, over 14,000 votes had been cast, and about 7,000 apiece for each of them. Gen. Grant being ahead about 100 votes only. The N.Y. papers say all the ladies are in favor of Gen. McClellan having the sword, as he would not get it soiled or bloody whilst Gen. Grant would if he received it bring it to the field with him and it would be very apt to get wet and soiled here, if nothing more.

The 1st Michigan Infty came here last Monday, having been home on a 35 days furlough, and today, Col. Throop called over to see us. He says they did not get any recruits scarcely, and he was glad to get back to camp once more; said that when the regt arrived at camp and looked around the old familiar place, it seemed like getting back home again. And so it is with most all of us, unless we have some extra ordinary strong tie to bind us at home, we cannot stay away from the army.

Sergeant Terrill, whom I spoke of in my last letter is not a member of my company, but belongs to Co. H. He is from the western part of the state. If ever he should get

---

*As donations to the Sanitary Commission began to decrease, the idea of having a fair as a fundraising event took root in Chicago. For two weeks in October 1863, 5,000 people a day paid seventy-five cents each to visit the fair. This first fair raised almost $100,000, prompting other cities to hold their own fairs.

promoted to be a Lieut., I intend to ask him to tent with me, as I believe it would be of great benefit to me to have the company and influence of such a good Christian as he is. We have another man named Chamberlain, who has done much towards getting up a religious feeling here in the regt, but I expect the latter will soon leave us as he expects to be transferred to the navy.

But I must close now. Please give my respects to Rev. Dr. Duffield, to Dr. S.P. Duffield, and remember me to Henry whenever you write. Hoping to hear from you again soon, I remain, Respectfully Your Friend,

Charles H. Salter

Headquarters
1st Brig., 2nd Cav. Div.
Columbia, Tenn.
April 27th 1864

Dear Mother

I suppose you are back home again by this time, are you not?

You see by the heading of this letter that I am stationed at Brigade Headquarters. When I got back here, I found that by a new regulation they have started a Brigade Hospital, to be kept with the brigade, wherever it moves. It is capable of holding 40 patients. It is formed in regular field hospital style with 7 large hospital tents & one wall tent for the surgeon. 6 of the large tents are used for the sick & the other is the dispensary & there stays the hospital steward. When I returned to the regt, I found that they had been keeping the place open for me & that I had to go to work at once. I don't hardly know, Mother, to take it as a compliment or not for it is certainly the most laborious as well as the most responsible post a hospital steward could well be called upon to hold. They would hardly give me time to see my friends in my regiment, they were so anxious to get me to work up here.

We have a very pretty place for the hospital. It is on the top of a small hill just outside of all the camps & the hill is covered with a nice grove & besides we have brought in evergreens & made a very pleasant spot of it. The sick ought to get well in a hurry here if they can anywhere, but the great difficulty is we are not going to stay here for we received orders to hold ourselves in readiness to move <u>without</u> transportation on the morning of Friday, the 29th, which in common parlance means that we are going to make a forced march & make a quick strike somewhere & from the wording of the order, I should think it was the beginning of the summer campaign. If so, it will be a tedious one, for it is a full month earlier than we began last year. The order was to pack everything in the way of extra baggage ready for storing. The men will not be allowed to carry any thing but their ponchos, & over coats, besides their rations. That alone looks very much as if we were going ahead when we start. Well, I for my part don't care how quick they move if they are only successful, for you know that I don't think that the war can't come to an end any too quick now.

I had a long talk with Dr. Fish, Bacon & Armstrong but can't make much out of them as yet. Armstrong will help me any way he can but his influence does not amount to much & for once my influence failed with Dr. Fish & I think I know the reason. I may be wrong but I wish I had taken that trip out to Flint that I spoke about but it can't be helped now & so we must make the most of the chances that are left. If Ben will write a letter to Dr. Fish & Dr. Bacon, it will do a great deal towards it but he must not let them know that I know anything about his writing & if he can get Mr. Burns to say a good word for me when he writes to Dr. Bacon, it will go a great ways. Any big name will influence Dr. Fish for he would feel very much flattered to think that Dr. Geo. W. Fish was known by some body of high standing in society outside of Flint. The only encouragement that he has gave me is that, by and by, after we get settled, he will do all he can for me.

I suppose that means that he will not let me die in the service. I am very much obliged to him for that, but that is rather long to wait when a man is in a hurry. Dr. Jung, the same one I was with in Huntsville, has charge of this hospital, but I think that this sheet of paper is about full & so I will stop as I don't think I can fill another.

> Good Bye from
> Your Affectionate Son
> Jimmie

April

SATURDAY 2—went out on picket for the first time.

THURSDAY 14—Brigade review.

FRIDAY 15—had Division review.

SATURDAY 16—saw a man drummed through camp.

FRIDAY 22—had a grand corps review by Gen. Grant.

SATURDAY 23—went on picket up on the plank road towards the rapids; saw a man drummed through camp this morning with the words rumseller on his back.

MONDAY 25—A man hung in the 2nd Division for commiting rape on an old woman in Maryland [the man] belonging to the 18 Mass Regt.

FRIDAY 29—went on picket in sight of the rebs.

May

TUESDAY 3—were orderd to pack up and be ready to march at a moments warning; struck our tents at nine oclock at night and started for the rapidan.

WEDNESDAY 4—crossed the rapidan at nine in the morning; marched twenty miles and then went on picket; crossed at earlys ford; staid over night.

THURSDAY 5—marched about six miles and came up with the rebs; went in double quick and commenced fighting and repulsed them; slept on our arms that night.

FRIDAY 6—attacked the rebs at daylight and fought until one oclock and were driven back to our breast works; then the rebs made a charge and were driven back; both Bowdishes were wounded.

SATURDAY 7—lay in the breast works all day and night.

SUNDAY 8—marched about three miles and came to where they were fighting; lay on the battle field all night.

MONDAY 9—changed position; marched about two miles; came up with the rebs again; slept on the battle field.

TUESDAY 10—lay all the fore noon in an open field with the sharpshooters picking at us all the time and in the afternoon, marched about three miles and came to where they were fighting despartly; went in on a charge and were repulsed twice.

WEDNESDAY 11—nothing done but building breast works and exchanging shots all day.

THURSDAY 12—left the works at midnight and attacked the rebs at daylight and drove them out of their works; captured 18 cannon and 4000 prisoners at Spotsylvania court house.

FRIDAY 13—fighting all day.

SATURDAY 14—lay on the battle field and shelled the rebs a little and took two pieces of cannon.

SUNDAY 15—marched around back wards and forth, changing position.

BATTLE OF THE WILDERNESS, MAY 5 TO 7, 1864. SKETCHED BY FRANK BEARD.
(THE PICTORIAL BATTLES OF THE CIVIL WAR, NEW YORK, 1895)

MONDAY 16—the regiment on picket; at night advanced as skirmishers through thick swamp; captured two rebs.

TUESDAY 17—came back to our old position.

WEDNESDAY 18—were routed out about ten oclock and marched about ten miles.

THURSDAY 19—lay all day in an open field; all quiet; were ordered to pack up; just dark; marched back about a mile, then right about faced and came back again.

FRIDAY 20—lay still all day; packed up at ten oclock and started for bowling green; got there at noon, then went to milford station; went on beyond about three miles and built breast works.

SATURDAY 21—got there about three oclock in the afternoon and built works.

SUNDAY 22—went out on picket and staid all night; South anna river instead of pamunkey.

MONDAY 23—packed up early in the morning and marched to the pamunkey river and at night built works; had a pretty hard battle; distance 12 miles.

TUESDAY 24—crossed the river about ten oclock in fore noon and then went out as skirmishers and skirmished until night.

WEDNESDAY 25—went out on skirmish line and built breast works and lay behind them all day and left them and went back across the river; lay on the banks all night.

THURSDAY 26—started for the peninsula; marched all day and all night.

FRIDAY 27—marched all day.

SATURDAY 28—crossed the pamunkey river about three oclock in the afternoon and built breast works; lay behind them all night.

SUNDAY 29—marched about a mile and built more works and lay there all night.

MONDAY 30—started at daylight and marched about four miles and went out skirmishing until night, then staid on picket; drove the rebs out of their rifle pits.

TUESDAY 31—advanced and drove them out of their lines of pits and were relieved at night and went back and built works; lay in them all night.

Villainous, Ga.
May 13th 1864

Dear Mother

Yours is the first letter I have received from home since I left except one from Geo. Maurice & as I have an opportunity to send one through by Dr. Armstrong, who is going home on a leave of absence, I thought I would answer it. All mail matter from the army is stopped at Nashville until this movement is over. I wrote to Father when I was at Chattanooga, but I suppose you will not get it yet a while on that account.

We have just received news that Dalton is evacuated & that we are to move out tomorrow early. I suppose now that we will have a chance to see a few grey coats once more but as for poor me, I shall have to stay in the rear with this brigade hospital, as usual. I suppose that is not exactly in the rear but off from the battle field just far enough from it to be on hand to take care of the wounded if we should be so unfortunate as to have any.

We have been on the march ever since the 30th of last month. On that day we left Columbia, Tenn. It is about 175 miles from here. We have taken it very moderate, only going 18 or 20 miles a day starting early & camping early. General Gerrard is the commander of our division & he seems to understand marching cavalry first rate, for he stops early enough to give the men time to take care of their horses & get their suppers before dark, which is more than we generally get a chance to do.

I had a visit from Benny Briscoe this morning. He is Aid de Camp to General Judah of the 2nd Division, 23rd Army Corps, & Benny's regiment (the 23rd) is in that division. He is looking first rate, as fat & healthy as ever. He wanted to go home, but he can't get sick enough to get a surgeon's certificate of disability. He seems to think that he is altogether too healthy for his own good. I don't think that can be all he wants to do now is to practice looking sick for a short time & it will do just as well as the genuine article. At least, that is my experience. You must send over & tell his folks that I saw him. He left Knoxville the 27th of last month & has been on the left wing of this army since we started this movement, but their corps was changed to the right in order to reinforce McPherson's Corps & I suppose with the intention of flanking the rebels, who have a strong hold in the mountains at a place called Bustard's Roost, which I presume, however, was evacuated at the same time as Dalton.

We will have to chase them now & hold them where ever we can. It is rumored that the rebels have left this part of the country entirely & have taken the road to North Carolina. How true this is will be seen hereafter. We could hear heavy cannonading here until about noon, when it ceased & we have not heard any since.

Armstrong has 20 days to stay at home & it will probably be in Detroit. If he is, he will come & see you, of course, & he will tell you a great deal more than I can write, for I did not know that he was going until after dark & a camp fire don't make the best light to write by & one's knee don't make the best writing desk I ever wrote on. I wrote to have Jerry get me 3 dozen of my photograph taken & send them to me. If Armstrong goes to Detroit, he can send them through by him. I want to exchange with the officers of our regiment. I want those I had taken last. Give my love to all the folks & write as often as possible to your

Jimmie

Villanous, Ga.
Saturday May 14th 1864

Dear Brother

I am disappointed & out of sorts in general, so having nothing to do, I thought I would improve this opportunity to let you know what I have been doing since I left home.

But perhaps you would like to know what put me out of sorts this morning. I will tell you. We expected to be ordered out early this morning & so I got all ready last night for an early start & now we have not received orders to move & expect to stay here, for all I can see, for a month. For if they don't want to use cavalry now, they never will. What is the use of them if they are not to have a chance to show the rebels what they are made of, & when the rebs are on a retreat is just the time to give them our compliments. But I have said enough to let you know what is the matter with me, so I will change the subject.

When I left Detroit, I took a berth in a sleeping car with Ponce & slept all the way to Michigan City, changed cars for Indianapolis & then changed for Jeffersonville. On the road we were stopped by the wreck of a train that had run off the tracks & lay smashed up all over the tracks here. We had to change cars & they forgot to change our baggage & we had to stay over at Louisville 24 hours to wait for it, where we put up at the Planters Hotel. We then took the train for Nashville & arrived there at 6 o'clock, went to the Commercial Hotel & stayed over night; left the next morning at 6 & arrived in Columbia at 12. I found the regiment there & plenty of friends as long as that bottle lasted, which by the way, did not reach Dr. Fish. As I found that it would not do to show any partiality so I distributed it as evenly as possible among my friends as far as it went. I stayed with the regiment 4 or 5 days, when I received orders to report to Brigade Hd Qrs for duty at the brigade hospital, where I have been ever since. I had just got there when we received orders to pack up & be ready to move in the morning, but the order was countermanded & we did not leave Columbia until the morning of the 30th at 9 o'clock & after marching 19 miles, we went into camp at 4 o'clock on the plantation of [the] widow Hughes.

It rained all night & I was fortunate enough to get a chance to sleep in one of the houses on the plantation. The roads were very bad & the wagon train did not get up until the next night, on the 1st, so we stayed there all night on the first. The rain ceased & the roads improved very fast. We started on at ½ past 6 on the morning of the 2nd & after marching 20 miles, we camped at 4 o'clock in the outskirts of Shelbyville. The 11th

Michigan Infantry were in Shelbyville en route for Chattanooga. I went to see Charlie Lum & Dr. Batewell. The Dr. was very busy getting his sick sent through to the front by rail, as they were going to march on farther before they went into camp for the night. Col. Lum was rather the worse for whiskey. In my opinion, it might have been excitement, however.

We started out at 6 on the morning of the 3rd, passed the 11th [Michigan] about 8 miles from Shelbyville; passed through Tullabowa at 1 P.M., left one sick here to be sent back to Columbia. We had 5 in the brigade; went 7 miles beyond "T" & went into camp after a hard days' march of 25 miles on a bad road, at ½ past 4 P.M. The wagons did not arrive until nearly midnight.

We started at 7 the next morning (4th), & after marching 15 miles went into camp at the foot of the Cumberland Mountains. The wagon train went up on top of the mountains so as to be ready for an early start & be out of the way of the cavalry when we started.

Started at 6 on the morning of the 5th & marched 25 miles, breaking down 6 wagons & killed about a dozen mules. It was the hardest days' marching we have done on this march. We did not get into camp until after 9 o'clock. Half of the 25 miles we were on the mountain and besides that, we ran out of corn for the horses, so we had to feed them rails. The night before they only got half rations & they took the rails quite readily. But we were only 3 miles from Stevenson & they sent us out corn & oats before morning.

Left camp at 9 o'clock the next morning (6th) & went into Stevenson, ahead of the division to leave our sick; had 4 in all. We passed through S & out on the road to Chattanooga. After marching 17 miles, we went into camp at Shelmound at 9 o'clock P.M. It was dark & I was tired, so that I did not much mind where I laid down, only that I was not in the dust, which was about a foot deep & when I awoke the next morning, I found I had been sleeping in a grave yard, with a grave as my pillow.

We crossed the Tennessee River twice on that day, once on the pontoon bridge & once on the RR bridge. While the regiment was crossing the latter, the cars came upon them suddenly & ran over about 200 of them before they could get out of the way. But strange to say, out of the whole 200, not one was badly hurt owing to the bridge being built so that the cars run on top & the wagons & foot passengers on the under side or rather the inside of the bridge. It is the first one of the kind I ever saw & I don't think any horse ever saw one either, when the cars went over us. I received a letter from Geo Maurice that day. It was the first one I had received from him since I left.

On the morning of the 7th, the division were ordered to the front at once & the wagons were ordered to Chattanooga & I was ordered to go with them. We did not leave camp until afternoon & only went 4 miles before we went into camp again. I made a visit to McKajackcarn???? before we left Shelmound. I was there once before, but went in on horseback. This time, I went a foot & went into it some distance. It is a big thing; part of the way, we took a boat across a lake.

Left camp at 8 o'clock on the 8th & after marching 17 miles, arrived at Chattanooga at 3 o'clock. Such a hot & dusty march I never did see as that days' was. Chattanooga don't look like the same place it was when I was there before. The grove where we were encamped is all cut down & the hills are all fortified. It is a well fortified spot now & that is about all you can say for it. We were camped on the banks of the Tennessee River, but could not go in swimming on account of the string of dead mules & horses that were laying all around the banks. They make a splendid perfume (night blooming cereas is nowhere). I wrote a letter to Father that day.

We left all our sick in hospitals there, 16 in all, so as to be able to come on with the train, which left the next afternoon (9th), at 2 o'clock & only went 4 miles before we went into camp for the night at Rossville, a small place containing 3 barns & a pig pen, but well remembered by the men who fought the Battle of Chickamauga. It is just on the line of Tennessee & Georgia. I tied my horse in Tenn. & slept in Georgia that night. I wrote letters to Geo & Geo Maurice before we left Chattanooga.

We left camp at ½ past 5 on the morning of the 10th & after marching 20 miles, went into camp once more with our division at Lafayette. We had hardly got the saddles off from our horses before the "general" sounded & of course we expected to be ordered out again, but they thought we had marched far enough for one day & so they let us stay until the next morning & the division went on without us. It rained all night & they did not get into camp until 12 o'clock at night. It was pretty hard on them but a soldier can't expect easy times all the time. As for us that were left, we had houses to sleep in & so had it quite comfortable. I can rough it with the best of them when necessary, but I prefer a house when it can be found without to much trouble.

We left Lafayette at 7 o'clock on the morning of the 11th & after marching 18 miles, we went into camp again with the division at this place, where we have been ever since. It stopped raining just before we were ready to start on the morning of the 11th, which made it cool, comfortable traveling.

On the 12th, (day before yesterday), Gen'l Thomas and Sherman passed by this place bound for the front. The 9th Infantry were with them. I called on Jimmie Hyde & Capt. Baiye???? They were well & confident that the fight was to begin soon. Wiggins & Poria were left back in Chattanooga, in charge of the Military Prison.

The 23rd passed by here yesterday & I had a call from Benny Briscoe, who is looking well. He is on Gen'l Judah's staff of the 2nd Division, 23rd Army Corps.

There, I have wrote myself into better spirits & I think I will quit. No one can blame me now for not giving particulars. I know for the present I will bid you an affectionate farewell & requesting you to proceed to answer this in the course of six months. I remain

Your Affec Brother
Jim

P.S. For the present address
James Vernor
Hospital Steward
Hd Qrs 1st Brig 2nd Cav Div
Dept of the Cumberland

On the Battle Field
Near Spotsylvania Court House, Va.
May 15, 1864

My Dear Friend

Your kind letter of April 29th was received on the 5th inst, and I take the first opportunity I have had [to send] you a letter, to write one in pencil, as we cannot do otherwise,
here on the battle field. I suppose you have heard a great deal about the great battle or
series of battles the Army of the Potomac has had during the last 12 days, more probably, than I am able to tell you, for the movements, and battles, have been so vast and
complicated that I could only keep track of my own corps, the 5th Corps, Gen. Warren,
commanding.

We left our camps along the railroad on the 1st May, and on the 4th, our corps, as the
advance of the army crossed the river, (the Rapidan), at Raccoon Ford, and bivouacked
that night near Robertson's Tavern. Our division, the 1st, in the advance, and the 1st
Michigan, were placed in front as pickets. The next morning at daylight, the rebel army
attacked us with such haste and fury, that they nearly annihilated the 1st Michigan, and
they came in to the division with the rebels right on their heels. But we met them and
drove them back about 1½ miles or so. And then they became too many for us and drove
us back a short distance when the balance of our corps coming up, and the 6th Corps. A
battle was fought, lasting all day long without either side being able to gain any ground,
and miles off to our left, near Chancellorsville, the 2nd & 9th Corps were also engaged
in a hard fought battle, with about the same result. And the next two days we were fighting near the same place with out being able to accomplish much (except to get immense
numbers of our men killed and wounded). Then, on the 8th, before daylight, our corps
left their position and, in the darkness, moved several miles to our left, to flank the rebels
on their right, and at daylight came across them and pitched in, and succeeded in gaining a good deal of ground, driving them some 3 miles, and getting several thousand men
killed and wounded during the day, and at night, as usual, both parties went to work
building up rifle pits and earthworks.

We continued fighting there untill on the night of the 11th & 12th insts, the 2nd &
6th Corps moved to our left, and on the 12th, captured a division of rebel troops with
some 40 or 50 cannon and one major general and 3 brigadiers. A number of the cannon,
however, lay between the rebel line and ours, all day long, without either party being
able to get them, so hardly contested was the fight. But, next morning, our troops gained
them. Then on [the] night of the 13th & 14th, our corps moved to their present position, to [the] left of where we were and opposite Spotsylvania Court House, about 1½
miles east. Here we are entrenched and the rebels also. The 6th Corps is on our left and
the 2nd & 9th are pushing on yet farther in that direction. Thus you perceive, since this
battle commenced, our forces have continually been moving to the left, and the rebels
have been obliged to move to their right to meet us. And as both sides have moved along,
they have also entrenched themselves. We are now, I suppose, some 15 miles from Rac-

coon Ford, and have left a continuous line of fortifications from there to this place, and so also have the rebels. In the meantime, we have been fighting every day and it is estimated, by an officer high in command, [that] we have left enough dead on the route to make a continuous corduroy road of dead back to where we started from. This may sound perhaps wicked, at least shocking, but it is true, never the less, and the men composing our army have all suffered terribly. It has been a harder campaign than any we ever had before or imagined of and the terrible, used up expression on every man's face seems to say, "My God! How long must we suffer?"

Today makes the 12th day we have been fighting, more or less every day, and in the course of that time, many great events have occurred, many great battles have been fought, all inside of one great battle, and a writer fond of noting the movements, scenes, and all the various details of it, might fill up a large book about it. But I am sick and weary of all this carnage and bloodshed, and only thank God that he has in mercy spared my life, whilst I have lost many dear and valued friends amongst the Michigan Regiments. Frank Raymond, 1st Mich., Adjt., was wounded, and several others of my acquaintance killed or wounded. In the 4th Mich., Col. Lombard and many other brave men are gone. In the 24th, Col. Morrow severely wounded; Capt. Hutton killed; Capt. Norton, do [ditto], and many others too numerous to mention. In our regt, one of my best and closest friends is missed—that is R.W. Jacklin, our Adjt, who is either killed or a prisoner, we do not know which.

On the night of Sunday, the 8th, our regt was out at the front, and advancing upon the rebels. It was very dark, and suddenly we found ourselves mixed up with the rebel lines and a terrible scene of carnage and horror ensued. We captured a number of the enemy, and held our ground. But, towards morning fell back, as we were too close to the enemy's works, to remain there in daylight, and it was during this scene that Adjt. Jacklin was missed. The entire loss in our regt up to [the] present time is, I believe, 91 in killed & wounded, and this is very light compared to the loss in most of the regts of our army. One reason for which is that our regt was out as skirmishers when the corps went up to the enemy's right flank on the 8th and did not, in consequence, get up untill the division had passed nearly through that days' fight. I do not know what the loss of our army is, but so far it is estimated to be about 30,000 and the rebels the same, or not much difference.

Gen. Sedgewick, commanding 6th Corps, was killed and now Gen. Meade remains with and commands that corps and the army at the same time. Gen. Grant is, of course, here and commands all the forces. Gen. Burnside commands the 9th Corps, and Gen. Meade the 2nd, 5th & 6th Corps. We hear rumors that Richmond is taken, also Petersburg, and that Gen. Sherman has whipped Johnston, and we do not know whether to believe any of them or not. The rebel army in front of us yet appears to be as large as ours and to keep up a bold front as large as ours, and to be in excellent spirits. Gen. Wadsworth (who ran for Gov. of N.Y. last election), was killed. The loss in our regt may be made a little smaller by the recapture of a number of prisoners by our cavalry, who are now on a raid in [the] rear of the rebel army, and have recaptured 500 of our men.

But, I must now close, as a rain storm is coming on. I hope this letter will reach you all safe, but do not know when it will go. Give my regards to Rev. Dr. Duffield, Dr. S.P. Duffield and remember me to Henry when you write to him. I remain, Truly Yours

Charles H. Salter

Monday May 16th
7 A.M.

I will write a few lines more, as I have not had an opportunity of sending the letter as yet. It has rained now for nearly every day the last week, and the country is terribly muddy, the roads we all abandoned, as it [is] easier to move over the fields and through the woods. The plank road from Fredericksburgh is in such bad condition, that wagons cannot possibly go over it, and the provisions are brought up by mules. We have to lay in the mud every night and expect if our army has to fall back, it will be owing to the mud more than anything else. Yet we expect that the movements of our cavalry and other forces have cut off the rebel supplies and that they will likely have to retreat for want of food, at least it looks as if our Generals were figuring upon that supposition. And a few days more will settle the campaign into something more decisive. C.H.S.

Battle Field near Spotsylvania Court House, Va.
May 19th 1864

My Dear Friend

Yesterday evening we received the first mail we have had in over two weeks, and I was much pleased to receive your letter of the 11th inst. The mail arrived and was distributed to our regt as we were lying behind our breastworks, within musket shot of the main works of the rebels, and I can assure you that never was a mail more thankfully received by us since we have been in the army. I wrote you a letter last Sabbath, in pencil, as that was the best I could do at that time. But today, having some ink, (such as it is), I will try to do better.

Since my last letter we have not moved much, but we have done some hard work, and considerable fighting. On [the] evening of [the] 17th at 8 o'clock, our regt, with the 11th Mass. & 118th Pa., moved to the front, in advance of our pickets, and went to work throwing up entrenchments within ⅜ mile of the main works of the enemy, and a stone's throw only from their picket line. We kept still and worked hard, and by 1 o'clock had a strong work completed. Meanwhile, 16 pieces of artillery had been brought up in our rear, and by morning they too had good earthworks, and when daylight revealed to the astonished gaze of the rebels, what the Yankees had done during the night, they opened upon us a heavy fire from 24 pieces of artillery, thinking to shell us out of our position. But we were too well entrenched for them to hurt us, and our batteries replied to the rebels firing over our heads. And they kept up a lively cannonade untill noon, and then ceased, and during the afternoon nothing was going on but a little picket firing now and then, to keep us in mind that the rebels were there yet. This morning, the rebels appear to be quite peaceable, as over a dozen of them have come out half way, met our boys, and exchanged papers with them, and then going back to their places. Both parties were ready to shoot each other the next minute. The rebel papers, of course, claim a victory for their side in every engagement we have had, and say that the 9th Mass. (of our 2nd brigade), threw down their arms, surrendered, &c, whereas, the fact is, they have not got over a dozen prisoners from that regt.

Our present position is right opposite Spotsylvania Court House, east of it, and about ½ mile distant. We are about in the centre of our lines. The rebel lines run just this side of the village, which is a very small, but a very pretty place, judging from what we can see of it, from our position. The rebel General Longstreet is disabled so that he will not be able to do duty again for 2 months, so says the Richmond papers. They also claim that on the 16th, Beauregard met Butler at Drury's Bluff and defeated him, capturing Gen. Heckman and 1,000 prisoners, and that Butler was retreating. I am afraid there is too much truth in it, and think our gov't should not have sent Butler to fight Beauregard, as Butler is a very good military governor &c, but I think he is no general. We needed some one like Gen. Hooker to send against Beauregard. And they claim that on the same day Breckenridge met Sigel in the Shenandoah Valley, defeated him, and drove him 9 miles. We have seen no account of these battles in our papers, and are anxiously waiting to find if they are true or not. From the rebel papers we first learn that the rebel Gen. Stuart, of the cavalry, was killed in some engagement with our cavalry, by Major Hogan, of a Penn. Regt.

They also claim that Gen Grant gives his troops whiskey to make them drunk before going into battle, and that is not true in any sense, for we have only had whiskey issued twice to the men whilst on this move, and then when they were exposed to bad weather. As I write, the band of the 18th Mass. is here playing, and the rebels are swarming on their earthworks, looking over at us and no doubt wondering at the audacity of the Yankees in coming so close to their works to play. In fact, today we are having the sunny side of war.

You say you cannot see how we get time even to eat sometimes, and to tell the truth, we did not get time to eat for 24 hours at a time, during a portion of this campaign, and became quite faint sometimes from hunger, and often weary from want of sleep. But we are resting now, and preparing for another great battle which is expected soon to take place. And now I will close, hoping to hear from you again soon. I remain,

> Respectfully Your Friend
> C.H. Salter

———————— June ————————

WEDNESDAY 1—went out about four oclock in the afternoon on the skirmish line and made a charge on the rebel works and got drove back; were relieved at dark and marched all night.

THURSDAY 2—marched until eleven oclock in the fore noon; rested and built works; the brigade massed in a hollow.

FRIDAY 3—made a charge on the rebel works at half past four in the morning and wer repulsed with great loss; got up close to the rebs and built works.

SATURDAY 4—lay behind our works all day exchanging shots with the rebs; at night the rebs made an attack.

SUNDAY 5—lay in the same position all again; the rebs attack at night but do not make anything.

MONDAY 6—nothing unusal occurs; our dead of the third are not buried yet and the stench is awful.

TUESDAY 7—firing on both sides about three oclock in the afternoon; a flag of truce to bury the dead.

WEDNESDAY 8—no firing all day; relieved at dark and went back to the third line of works.

THURSDAY 9—sharpshooting all day; Chester Reynolds mortally wounded.

FRIDAY 10—nothing but sharpshooting all day; ordered to be ready to march at twelve oclock; order countermanded.

SATURDAY 11—sharpshooting kept up all day; were relieved at dark by the 6th corps and went back half mile and stay all night.

SUNDAY 12—lay all still all day; march at dark on night march.

MONDAY 13—still on march; halt and make coffee before we cross chickahomy; cross at 4 oclock; march until 11 at night; halt and stay.

TUESDAY 14—start for the James river at 3 oclock pm; cross the river and while we lay on the banks & had a swim in the river; at night go picket.

WEDNESDAY 15—start for petersburgh; fall out and march at my leisure; find plenty of berrys; sleep all night in the woods; had a sleep.

Camp in the Field Near
Etowah River Bridge, Ga.
Monday June 6th 1864

Dear Mother

I take it for granted that you want to hear from me occasionally, although the folks at home seem to think that I don't care about hearing from them there. Yours being the only letter I have had from home since I left & I think if you (no I don't mean you but the rest of my relations), could only know how anxiously we watch for the appearance of the Post Master, they would write oftener. But, I think that will answer for complaints now.

I am going to let you know what we have been doing since I wrote to Charlie & suppose you have received that letter haven't you? I wrote it on the 14th. Well, I had hardly put it in the mail when we received orders to move. We started at 3 P.M. & after marching 14 miles in the direction of Rome, we went into camp at 11 o'clock at night on the farm or rather, only field of a poor Irish man who complained very much because we were spoiling his corn field. The corn was up about 3 inches & if course, was completely ruined. It was 1 o'clock when I laid down & at 3, the bugle called us up. At ½ past 4, we were in the saddle & from that time until 6 in the evening we marched 25 miles. We got within 3 miles of Rome. I think it was the intention to take the place but the rebs had 2 divisions there & we only had one brigade, as the other brigade, Wilder's, was off on our right for some other purpose. We fought them for about an hour when after killing 5 & wounding 7, we fell back to Floyd Springs, one of the fashionable watering places of the South. May 16th we laid still all day & left camp at just dark. After marching all night & making 21 miles, we crossed the Ostenola River on a pontoon bridge. At 6 o'clock on the morning of the 17th, we staid there for 5 or 6 hours, got breakfast & a small sleep & left again at 2 o'clock P.M. When we started, it was raining like fury. It cleared off, however, [and was] quite pleasant before we stopped, which we did after marching 15 miles, within 2 miles of Hermitage. May 18th, we went 11 miles to day, moving very slowly, feeling our way as we went. Wilder's Brigade had the advance. When they came up with the rebels, they sent back for a regiment of cavalry to do the skirmishing. Our regiment was sent out & went out rather farther than was expected. When they met the rebels, they were 3 miles from the column & were fighting about 5 times their number so that the rebels flanked them just as easy as could be. They sent back for support but it was so far away that before they got there, they were obliged to break & run or get captured. Of the two evils, they chose the last, so they turned & ran just as fast as the horses could go for a short distance.

Then they formed a new line, stood & fought for a while & then done the same thing all over again & so on until the support arrived. Then they made up for what they had lost by driving the rebels from the field, just about as fast as they drove in, killing a rebel colonel & several men. Our loss was 3 killed, 11 wounded & 12 missing. Major Robbins, Lt. Carter & Randolph wounded & Maj. Grant captured. We camped upon the battle field at night. We came up to the Etowah River, where we were informed that a division of rebs were making directly for us, to cross the river on a bridge at that place & that we were expected to keep them from crossing, which we agreed to do. So the men went to work & in 15 minutes, had a rail fortification built which would have cost the rebels their whole force to have gone over. But they did a safer thing. They forded the river & we did not even get a sight of a grey coat. We stayed at that place for 3 days. On the morning of the 23rd, we started out at 5 o'clock & after marching 12 miles, we went into camp 2 miles from Van Wirt with the infantry. We had to go very slow to day to allow the infantry to keep up with the line. We were on the extreme right & probably in the rear of the enemy's left most of the time. It was 11 o'clock before we went into camp.

May 24th. We started at 5 this morning. Our regiment was in the advance & after marching 211 miles, we came upon the rebs about 3 miles from Dallas & after driving them into town, we went into camp for the night. We had 3 wounded during the fight— Capt. Lawton & 2 privates. [We] went forward at noon the next day & after marching 5 miles, went into camp again just about as far from Dallas as we were before. Just after we had our tents put up & supper nicely underway, we were ordered to pack up again & in 15 minutes we were in the saddle. We moved right out & just then it began to rain & the way it did come down was not slow, I can tell you. But for all that, I never saw a happier set than our boys were then. It was just after dark & ⅔ of the men were singing & the other third were whistling. We went about 2 miles (which by the way took us 3 hours). We camped in a ploughed field in line of battle with our artillery planted & every thing ready for a night attack. As for your son, he crawled into an ambulance & slept soundly until morning. We were not disturbed although the rebels were not over 2 miles from us.

The next day we changed our position a little for the sake of position merely. I was sent out with an ambulance for a wounded man. We had an escort of a hundred men & when we got to where the man was, we found that ½ of a rebel brigade, 5,000 strong, had just finished passing the house & the other ½ were expected every moment perhaps. That man was not taken to camp in a hurry, oh no!

May 27th. We sent an ambulance out that morning for a man that was shot while on picket & while it was out there, the rebs made a charge & captured it but did not hold it long enough to examine it, for which I am very thankful as my ponchos were in it. Our boys charged back & retook it. We went out 2 miles & tried all day to establish a line of communications with McPherson, but could not do it for the rebs were too plenty just there. We had 14 wounded & 4 killed in the brigade, 2 of them from our regiment. We returned to the same camp we had the night before & went into camp. The next morning we took our sick back about 5 miles to where our wagon train was & established a hospital. During the evening, we heard very heavy firing, which proved afterwards to have been a rebel division charging our rifle pits. They paid dear enough for the attempt, for prisoners, all of which are wounded, say that out of the division only 13 got back to their lines safe. Allowances must of course be made for excitement, but it must have been perfectly angled for in front of the rifle pits of one regiment, they buried 73 rebels. That shows pretty hard work to say the least.

May 29th. We were ordered to take the sick & wounded nearer to the center of our lines at just dusk & it was dark before we were ready to move. We went about 2 miles & stopped by the side of the road to await day light. We had to move back on account of a change in our lines, the right being swung around on the same ground that we had the hospital on. Our division was still the right & had just taken their new position when the rebs, not knowing of the change, made a night attack on our empty rifle pits. They pounded away with artillery until they were tired, when they charged & you can imagine their surprise when they found that they had been shelling an innocent dirt heap. They, of course, thought there was foul play up, so they fell back.

May 30th. We drew our ambulances up in the shade & lay still all day. [We] received orders to take the sick to Kingston & at 3 o'clock in the night, we started & after marching 27 miles, arrived at Kingston at 3 o'clock, where we left our sick & wounded at the depot hospital to be sent North on the cars. They tried to keep Dr. Jung (the surgeon who runs the Brigade Hospital), & myself in the hospital but we begged to be excused. But nevertheless, the next morning we were detailed to stay & such a mess I never was in before. It was perfectly awful. The wounded lay all around under trees & everything else they could get to in the shade & to cap the climax, ⅔ of the wounds had never been dressed & were full of worms.

I worked as hard as I could all day. There were about a dozen surgeons there & I do believe that Dr. & I did as much as any 5 of them. While we staid, I made myself sick & have hardly got over it yet. No one had any particular work to do, only to take hold just where he pleased & consequently the majority did not take hold at all. We went around & asked the men if they had been dressed since they were wounded & found enough that had not to keep us busy. The next morning, June 2nd, we succeeded in getting our sick & wounded on the cars & shortly after we were relieved from duty & ordered to report to our command. Two happier mortals it would have been hard to find, I can tell you.

We went 4 miles out of town to the river where we staid over night at a courier post. We would have went right on but were told that it was not safe to do so, so we thought we would wait till morning & go out with some train that would be going out but the next morning we found that no train was going out, so we concluded to risk it by ourselves & made a bee line for the front, which, after marching 22 miles, we struck on the left center in the rear of the 23rd Corps. We followed to the right until we found Gen'l Thomas' Hd Qrs, when we found that our division had been changed from the right to the left & that they were about 12 miles from their Hd Qrs, so we concluded to stay there over night & go through the next morning. So I at once made for the 9th Michigan & claimed food & lodging from Jimmie Hyde, which he was most happy to furnish. I had a talk with Captain [Samuel] Bangs & then being under the weather, I turned in for the night.

The next morning we started out at about 9 o'clock with the very comforting assurance that the road we were to travel was all exposed to the rebels & just as like as not, we would meet straggling parties. Well that was very fine but neither of us had as much as a pen knife, but we concluded to risk it & we got through safely although a courier who went through just about ½ hour ahead of us had his horse shot under him but we did not see as much as a shadow but arrived here safe after a 15 mile march at 3 o'clock P.M. of Saturday, June 4th, 1864.

The next day we put up our tents & prepared for sick & at present we have 3 sick & wounded—there, if you have the letter I wrote Charlie, you will know what I have been doing since I left home.

I enclose a flag that we captured out of a rebel house. The family had all gone south & deserted the plantation, evidently in a hurry. The flag is one that they used to hang out of the window when the rebels were passing. It shows what fine work can be done down south when they have a mind to. Give my compliments to all who owe me letters & tell them to send them along as soon as possible.

Yr Affec Son Jimmie

Bivouac 3rd Brig. 1st Div. 5th Corps
Near Kidds Mills, Va. June 7th 1864

My Dear Friend

Your kind letter of [the] 25th inst was received a few days ago, and today as I have a few moments to spare, will try to write you. We left our position at Spotsylvania May 21st and marching east to the railroad at Guinness Station. We then moved southwest to Bowling Green, where we staid that night, next day moved on, our regt the advance of the corps, and my co., with three others ahead as skirmishers. The rebel cavalry tried to hinder our advance, and we had considerable firing with them, but drove them back, and made 10 miles that day. Next day we moved on to the North Anna River, the 2nd Corps was to take the main road, whilst our corps went 2 miles above them to cross at Island Ford. Our division, in advance, had but just got across when the rebels attacked us with Ewell's Corps. We hastily formed line and held our ground untill the balance of our corps got over, when we drove the enemy 2 miles, capturing over 1,000 prisoners and they left 260 dead upon the field. We should have done much better than this but night came upon us, and we had to hold up till next morning, when we moved forward three miles, found the enemy strongly entrenched in a good position. And we entrenched also. The next two days we were skirmishing with them and tearing up the Va. Central R.R. We destroyed 10 miles of that and then on the evening of [the] 26th, fell in and moved back across the river. Next morning at 4 A.M., we marched east, halted at 7 P.M., after having marched 25 miles that day.

Next morning we moved on, crossed the Pamunkey River at Hanover town, and after going 2 miles south, formed line & threw up [a] line of breastworks; next morning advanced again, driving the enemy 5 miles, and the next day, advancing, our regt was in advance, only skirmishers ahead of us, and after going 3 miles (driving the enemy every foot of the way). We found them entrenched in a strong position, and our division had a hard battle, without either gaining or losing any more ground, in this days fight our regt lost Major Elliott, mortally wounded (he died that night), and Lt. Burns wounded in [the] left arm, as also 10 men killed & wounded. Next day, the 31st, our regt was out on the skirmish line, fighting all day, and June 1st before we were relieved, our division was ordered to advance, and we went ahead as skirmishers. We drove the enemy's skirmishers back 1 mile to their main line, capturing 2 lines of their rifle pits and holding them, whilst our division came up in our rear and went to work throwing up breastworks of logs, &c, and our regt was relieved by another.

We had but just got back to our main line when the rebels advanced in three lines of battle to attack us. We laid low untill they came within a short distance of us, when we opened fire upon them and for 2 hours a desperate battle ensued. But we finally drove them back to their breastworks just before dark, and so gained another victory. Our regt lost this day, Capt. Hill mortally wounded, Lt. Schwartz slightly, and some 10 men. The next day, we lay behind the breastworks untill, at 2 P.M., we fell in to move to our left to make another flank movement, and the rebels discovered the movement and pursued us, driving in our skirmishers. Our division halted and formed line behind some old works about 1 mile in rear of our last position. We had scarcely got in position when the enemy came on in great force, and for over 2 hours we had a desperate battle, but finally succeeded in driving them back with but slight loss to ourselves. We then remained there untill Sunday night when we fell in, and moved about 4 miles to our left, then on Monday, we heard of rebel cavalry in our rear, and the 1st Michigan and our regt went out to see them, arriving at Allen's Mills. I was sent out with 60 men as skirmishers, and soon met the rebel skirmishers. We drove them back ½ mile, and then established my picket line, and remained there untill relieved during the night, when we returned to our division. Then this morning we moved 5 miles east and are now at Kidd's Mills, about 1 mile from the Chickahominy, and 2 miles east of Gaines, 8 miles from Richmond, awaiting further orders.

The loss in our regt so far has been 120 in killed and wounded, 15 of whom are from my company, "E." I have so far escaped all harm for which I have reason to thank the Lord who has spared me when so many others have fallen. Sergt Terrill is also safe and well. Col. Welch has not returned yet, but is expected soon, when I shall look for that letter you sent by him. Last Saturday we had a company of 64 recruits from Saginaw join our regt, and Col. Welch started with them but for some reason had not yet arrived. The 1st Michigan and our regt have been consolidated (for field service) and is now under command of Lt. Col. Throop, of [the] 1st Michigan, who is a good officer and well liked by us all. Our regt, since receiving these recruits, numbers about 300 men, the 1st about 100 only. Our bivouac today is clear in [the] rear of the balance of our corps, in a pleasant grove, and I do not know what is going on at the front, although we hear considerable firing.

You will have to again excuse pencil writing, as I could not have wrote at all if I had to write with a pen. Please give my regards to Rev. Dr. Duffield, Dr. S.P. Duffield and, hoping to hear from you again soon, I Remain,

> Respectfully Your Friend
> Charles H. Salter

> Bivouac 16th Mich Vet Vol Infty
> Summit, Va. June 12th 1864

My Dear Friend

Having a few spare moments this bright pleasant Sabbath day, thought best to improve them by writing you a few lines.

We yet remain in the same place we were when I wrote you on last Tuesday, and have been resting most of the time since then, and now feel much better than when we first arrived here. This afternoon we have had service by the chaplain of the 21st Maine, and this is the first time we have had service in our regt by a chaplain or minister for a long time, so long that I cannot remember when the last time was.

We are under orders to be ready to move at a moments notice, and expect that we shall move tonight or in the morning. We do not know where we are going but I suspect it is to be down the Chickahominy and across at Bottoms Bridge or somewhere in that vicinity. Our wagon trains have already moved to Tunstall's Station, and if we move to Bottom's Bridge, they will then be directly in rear of us. Our pickets are on the N.E. side of the river and the rebels on the Richmond side, and lately by mutual agreement, they have ceased the mischievous plan of picket firing and are apparently as quiet and peaceable as near neighbors should be. But, if we should attempt to cross, then the aspect of affairs would be changed in a moment, and the apparently sleepy headed rebel sentries would become our devoted enemies.

Our army are all feeling in very good spirits now and after the few days rest we have had are all willing to go ahead and do whatever may be required of us, and now after the campaign of the last month, we have the proud satisfaction of knowing that at last the world acknowledges that the Army of the Potomac is the best and greatest army of our country. And this last week, Gen Grant publicly acknowledged to our generals that he (the Lieut. General commanding all the forces of the U.S.), never knew what real hard fighting was untill he came to the Army of the Potomac. He says he never even imagined when hearing of our fighting here, that it was of the terrible nature he has lately witnessed, and also that our western army never had any such men to fight as we have, nor such able generals to contend against as Lee and his Lieuts., Ewell, Hill & Longstreet. And this but corroborates the opinion we have always had, and that was that the western rebels are nothing but an armed mob, and not anything near so hard to whip as Lee's well disciplined soldiers. And Gen Grant now knows that it is a much more difficult undertaking to take Richmond than it was to take Vicksburg, and acknowledges that Virginia is the worst country in the U.S. or in America to fight in, or to conquer.

Our Colonel (Welch) has not come back yet, and our generals somehow do not seem to like the idea of his being away from his regt, whilst we are fighting nearly every day and no one here but a captain to command the regt, and I am much mistaken if he does not get himself into serious trouble about it. Our brigade commander, Gen Bartlet, and division commander Gen Griffin, are apparently determined not to let the matter go unnoticed and what makes it worse for the Col., is that whilst Major Elliott was lying dead in his grave, (having been killed whilst leading his regt to meet the enemy), Col. Welch was casting reflections upon his character in Detroit, and saying he was not fit to command the regt, &c, whilst every man in our regt, and every soldier in our army that knew Major Elliott, knew that no braver man ever lived than the Major was, and that he had done his duty in ten battles where Col. W had in one. This is the simple truth, and although I suppose I have no business to cast reflections upon a superior officer, I cannot help it. I know that his conduct has disgraced our entire regt, and that had he been here leading his regt, as other Michigan colonels were, our regt would have had a better name, and more notice taken of it, during the campaign by the papers than we have had. As it was, what Detroit paper would notice a regt whose Col. was in Detroit pleasure seeking whilst his officers and men were battling for their country, and giving up their lives on every battle field. But I believe God is just and will surely bring such men to punishment, and in his own good time and way.

Our regt was, for about a week, consolidated with the 1st Mich, but it is now under command of Capt. Fuller of this regt, and the connection with the 1st dissolved. We have yet 300 men for duty, whilst the 1st has but 100. As that was a much smaller regt than ours when the campaign commenced, and we have also received 80 recruits lately, and expect some more yet to come. We have lost about 120 killed and wounded during the campaign, but half of the wounded will be back again in the course of three months.

But I must now close. We have received orders to march at dusk this evening, and must be ready for it. Remember me to Rev. Dr. Duffield, Dr. S.P. Duffield, and to Henry when next you write to him, and hoping to hear from you again soon.

> I Remain, as ever, Respectfully Your Friend
> Charles H. Salter

———————— June ————————

THURSDAY 16—started at trying to find a place to get some thing to eat; at last find a place and get some hoe cake baked; went tip top; jog along; find plenty of cherries and honey; sleep at night under a big tree.

FRIDAY 17—catch up with the regiment and go on picket.

SATURDAY 18—the brigade charge at daylight and drive the rebs half mile.

SUNDAY 19—sharpshooting and shelling all day.

MONDAY 20—shooting as usual; were relieved by the 6th corps at dark; march about three miles and sleep till morning.

TUESDAY 21—orders to be ready to march at a moments notice; march five miles to the left and get a position; our brigade as skirmishers; at night build works; had a man wounded in Co. B.

Bivouac 16th Mich Infty V. V.
Near Petersburg, Va. June 21st 1864

My Dear Friend

Your kind letter of June 12th was received a day or so ago, and very glad was I to hear from you once more. Col. Welch arrived here night before last and gave me the letter you sent on May 18th, only a month on the route, however, I was glad to get it. I wrote you a letter on the 12th inst from Summit.

Our division fell in that evening and moved down the Chickahominy 10 miles to Jones Bridge, crossed over next morning, and went up 2 miles towards Richmond, formed line, and protected the crossing of our army that day. Then at 10 P.M., we fell in, and marching towards the James River 10 miles, halted at 2 next morning; and at 5 started on again, marching to Charles City Court House. We then bivouacked about 1 mile from [the] James River. On the 16th, we crossed the river on transports, and then took up our line of march for this place. After a very fatiguing march of 25 miles, we halted next morning only 2 miles from Petersburg. The 2nd, 9th & 18th had already taken these lines of rebel earthworks, and some dozen or so of small forts, and were pushing on as close to the city as possible. Two divisions of our corps were sent out to the front to assist, our division being kept in reserve. That night there was some terrible fighting out in the front, the 9th Corps being engaged principally, and early next morning our division went out to relieve them. Coming up to a line of breastworks that had been repeatedly charged by both sides the previous night, a terrible sight met our gaze. Our men lay piled up on the outside and the rebels on the inside, most of them on both sides having been killed with the bayonet. It was at this place the 1st Michigan Sharpshooters were engaged with others. I do not think I have seen such terrible fighting, since Gettysburg, as that was. Over 200 dead on each side lay piled up about a line of breastworks, not 100 yards long, but our forces held the place, and were now way beyond.

We advanced a short distance farther & passing the 9th Corps, we became engaged, and drove the rebels back ½ mile, gained possession of the Norfolk Railroad and, that night, crept up to within 300 yards of the rebel earthworks and threw up a line of breastworks and established our skirmish line within 150 yards of them. And next day not a man could show his head above our works, or theirs, but that a dozen balls would whistle around their head and every little while a man would get hit. The artillery on both sides also were not idle but were banging away all the while. We were in sight of Petersburg, and could only see that the rebels had but one line of earthworks left and those had been thrown up since our first attack on the place. The old works were all taken. We remained there two days and last night were relieved by our 3rd Division and came back a short distance into a wood to rest where we now are. We expect to be sent in again tonight, however. The works we have taken here are of immense strength, and I doubt if we could have taken them had Lee's army been here. But when we first arrived, they had not yet got here, and the works were manned by Hardee's Corps, just come up from Johnston's army. We took many prisoners from them and they said they had never seen such fighting or such bold charging by our men as they saw here. We told them if they had been in Virginia all the while, they would know what fighting was, but out west, they never saw any real fighting except where Grant had been.

It seems to me now that Hardee's has come up here, Sherman ought to crush Johnston, and occupy all the cotton states without any trouble. And I hope to hear soon that he has done so. The loss in our regt at this place has been so far about 30 killed & wounded, most of them killed on account of the fighting being on open ground & over the breastworks. Capt. Swan is not hurt but is now in arrest for charges preferred against him by one of our Lieuts.

You say you see we are to be in a brigade. I do not understand what you mean. We have always been in a brigade (3rd brigade, 1st Division, 5th Corps), commanded now by Gen. Bartlet, and all the troops in our army are disposed of in some manner. Our regt was consolidated with the 1st Mich, for a time, but the connection is now dissolved.

Gen. Chamberlain, commanding our 1st Brigade, was mortally wounded here on the 18th inst. He was lately promoted from Col. of the 20th Maine of our brigade. He died a true Christian. Col. Hayes of [the] 18th Mass., (of our brigade also), has lately been promoted to be a general for bravery at [the] Battle of the Wilderness, where he was wounded, but has just returned to duty again, and will command one of our brigades. Gen. Rice, killed at the Wilderness, was formerly colonel of [the] 44th N.Y. of our brigade also, and was promoted for bravery at Gettysburg, where he commanded our brigade after Gen. Vincent was killed. Vincent also was promoted from colonel of the 83rd Pa., and Gen. Ames, commanding a division of the 10th Corps was the first colonel of our 20th Maine. So you see we have had a pretty good number of promotions from our brigade, and [I] think it speaks well for us. Sergt. Terrill is well and with his company.

June 22nd I ceased writing on orders to fall in. We moved about 1 miles off to the left of our former position, moved out to the front, and, after dark moved out to where the skirmish line had been, and threw up a line of earthworks within 250 yards of the rebel line. It was a hard task and took us all night long, as the ground was full of stumps and roots, and we finished just at daylight, completely tired out. And now we have to hug the earthworks close as firing, both artillery & musketry, is going on all along the lines. And I cannot write you much more, so good by for the present. Remember me to Rev. Dr. Duffield, Dr. S.P. Duffield and Henry.

Respectfully Your Friend
C.H. Salter

——————————— June ———————————

WEDNESDAY 22—the rebs shell us all day; they make a charge on the left of our brigade and take 400 prisoners and a battery.

THURSDAY 23—sharpshooting all day; got a letter from home; at night went on picket.

FRIDAY 24—on picket about 8 rods from the rebs; pretty close work; most awful hot; relieved at night by the 5th corps and march about three miles back; go in to camp.

SATURDAY 25—lay in am open all day; about twelve oclock receive orders to pack up and be ready to march at a moments notice but the orders [say] that [we] could not march until dark.

SUNDAY 26—did not march; lay still al day.

MONDAY 27—were ordered to pack up; marched about half mile and went behind works; lay there about 4 hours and then packed up and marched about three miles and went on picket; had a gory time.

TUESDAY 28—on picket; plenty of new potatoes and apple sauce; were relieved and went back to the brigade; stay there all night.

WEDNESDAY 29—put up tents for the officers; about twelve oclock received orders to pack up and be ready to march at a moments notice; march about three miles and relieve the 6th corps; go on picket.

THURSDAY 30—on picket; relieved at night; muster day.

——————————— July ———————————

FRIDAY 1—have to strike our tents and move to the left a short distance and then again.

SATURDAY 2—strike tents again and move about a mile to the right and pitch tents again; I am detailed for picket again; have to go about two miles; very hot;

SUNDAY 3—very warm; on picket; get [to] go back to camp after rations.

MONDAY 4—are relieved and go back to camp.

Bivouac 16th Mich Infty Vet Vol
In Fortifications near Petersburg, Va.
July 4th 1864

My Dear Friend

Your kind letter of [the] 19th June was received on the 24th, and the one of [the] 26th inst arrived on the 1st. I owe you an apology for not answering them, or at least the first one before this, but I have been so busy that I could not possibly get time to answer it untill today. But now I think I shall be able to write you a good long letter today.

My last was wrote the day after we came to the position we now occupy on June 22nd, and that same night I was sent out to advance the picket line in front of our brigade. I had 100 men with me, and advanced under cover of the darkness to about halfway to the enemy's lines, and then commenced to throw up rifle pits to protect our skirmish line. The enemy heard us and opened fire upon us but the darkness hid us and we finished before morning. Works strong enough to protect our small skirmish line, then that day was an extremely warm one, in more sense than one. The rebs tried to make it too warm a place for us, as we were so close to them, we could with perfect ease pick off their gunners, in case they attempted to use their artillery, or, in fact, anyone that showed their heads above their works, and all day long there was a perfect rattle of artillery all along the line, except the battery right in front of us. They could not use their pieces and that night they moved them off to another portion of their works a little further removed from our line. Their infantry kept up a sharp firing from their works on our line all day, but could not drive us from them, and at night we were relieved by another regt and returned to our regt's earthworks.

Since then we have remained in the same position. We have worked nights to strengthen our earthwork untill now we have a very strong line, so strong we feel perfectly confident the cavalry will not dare to charge us if we remain here ever so long. We have also placed an abattis out about 25 yards in front of the works of our brigade, and the rebels could not do anything that would please us more than to see them attempt to charge through that abattis to get at us. We would have such a splendid opportunity of shooting them down at short range. Last week the pickets of both parties in front of us came to an understanding between themselves not to fire any more unless in case of a fight and now all along the line of our corps the pickets pace up and down along this line, without ever thinking of firing at each other, and they are so close together that they can easily converse across the line, and occasionally they meet half way and exchange newspapers, and many little articles as tobacco, knives, &c. Whilst at our earthworks many climb up on them at all times, and take a look over across at secessia, and the rebels do the same without fear. Yet the artillery occasionally bang away at each other, especially if they see a wagon train, or any wagons across in the enemy's lines.

This morning some wagons were seen in rear of the enemy's works, and the battery with our brigade fired some 20 shots at them, and scattered them in pretty quick time. Today being the fourth, we were expecting to have a battle, or at least a great deal of firing along the lines, but so far (at noon), we have had but very little firing and every-thing is as quiet as on ordinary days. We could very easily have a celebration here on our own hook, as we have plenty of powder, by guns, &c, to make all the noise usual on such occasions, but we leave all such business to the citizens at home who are more easily amused by these things.

Here in our regt, all the officers have been busy for the last week making out pay rolls, returns to the War Department, &c, for the last two months and I have had all the writ-ing I could do every day in that time. Untill last night the baggage wagons that had been up close to us were ordered away off to the rear, and I had to send my books and papers away, and now will have plenty time to write letters, if we do not move, or have a battle.

The weather since we have been here has been extremely warm and dry. We have not had any rain for over four weeks, and everywhere in the vicinity of the troops the ground has become light, and by so much moving of troops, artillery and wagons, together with the wind, clouds of dust can be seen hovering over our lines all the while. It is especially worst when we are marching, as nothing disturbs the dust worse than a column of troops moving, whilst the sun pours down scorchingly upon us every day. And all we have to protect ourselves from it is a few bushes we place over and around our trenches. In fact, it is too hot weather for fighting.

Our lines of fortifications extend from the James River, across the Appomattox to south of Petersburg, where our troops hold the Wilderness railroad, thus effectively preventing the enemy from using that road. The army is posted along this line in the following man-ner: commencing on the right of the James is the 11th Corps, then the 18th, 9th, 5th, 2nd, & 6th Corps. The 9th Corps and ours (the 5th) are in the centre, and directly in front of the city from the works of the 9th, the city is plainly to be seen, but between us and the city lies Reservoir Hill, which hides from our view most of the place. We are, however, just about ½ mile from the outskirts of the city. On the right of this line, near the Appomattox, we have batteries placed, which command the bridges across the stream at Petersburg, and as that is the way the rebels have to bring across their supplies in wagons for the troops on this side. It troubles them greatly. They can only bring them over in the night time, and then our cannon fire at them, when ever we have reason to suspect they are crossing.

We are in some places (not to be mentioned), mining to get under the rebel works, and you may expect soon to hear of our blowing up some of these rebel forts, together with the force that may be in them. It is a terrible mode of warfare, but it is the only way we can make a break in the enemy's walls.

By the way, speaking of Jacklin, I supposed you had heard he was taken prisoner in the Wilderness, and afterwards recaptured by Sheridan's cavalry. He rejoined us on May 25th, at the North Anna. You enquired also of the Christian Commission; we do not see much of them, but yesterday the Sanitary Commission visited us in the way of sending to each regt in the army, a lot of canned meats, vegetables, fruit, &c, enough to make one good meal for the army. I understand they distributed 100,000 boxes in this way. That Sanitary Commission is a great institution, and is thought a great deal of by the army.

We are in Gen. Warren's corps (the 5th), as you supposed and our division is Gen. Griffin's (the 1st), and of that, we are in Gen. Barlet's brigade (the 3rd). But I must now close as I have already written a long letter. Excuse [the] poor writing as my ink is very bad. Remember me to Rev. Dr. Duffield, Dr. S.P. Duffield and also to Henry when next you write.

I Remain
Respectfully Your Friend C.H. Salter

——————————— July ———————

TUESDAY 5—go out again on picket.

WEDNESDAY 6—are relieved from picket; orders come that we are to camp for 18 days; the regiment ordered to dig wells.

MONDAY 11—went up to the cars; when I got back found the regt packed up early to move but did not.

TUESDAY 12—orders come about two oclock to pack up; pack up; tore down our works and then marched about two miles and lay all day and night; then marched about three miles and went into camp.

List of killed and wounded in Co. B, 7th Mich,

Killed George Hodges May 6th

Wounded C. Bowdish mortally; L. Bowdish right arm taken off

George Phelps shoulder

James Corwin bruses May 10th

Wounded James Smith [and] Joshua Woffating both slight.

This is the last entry for John Presley's diary. On August 17, 1864, after surviving the battles of the Wilderness, Po River, Spotsylvania Court House, North Anna River, Cold Harbor, Totopotomoy Creek, and the Siege of Petersburg, he was accidently struck by lightning and killed.

16th Mich Infty Vet Vol
In the Trenches, Near Petersburg, Va.
July 14th 1864

My Dear Friend

Your kind letter of the 3rd inst arrived last Sabbath, and today I will try to write you a few lines. I wrote on July 4th, and since then we have had a pretty busy time here.

On the night of the 8th inst, our brigade commenced to dig a line of earthworks out in front of where we were advancing in front of our regt (which had been nearer to the enemy than any other), about 50 yards, whilst other regts advanced 200 yards and straightened out the line, and are now as near as can be estimated, 250 yards from the rebel line, and parallel with them. We have worked hard every night since then, usually all night long, and on [the] morning of the 11th inst, had them completed sufficiently to allow ourselves to move out to them. And now we are at work fixing up a place for a battery of 4 guns, which is to be right in the centre of our regt, three companies having had to move back to the old works to make room for it.

Our line of works are 6 feet high, and 12 feet thick, the dirt that is thrown up being taken all from the outside of the works, thus leaving a large ditch there. And then it is rather a formidable undertaking for a force of the enemy to undertake to climb up those steep walls. But we have no idea that even if they should undertake to charge upon us, they can ever get through the line of abattis we have out in front of our works. On the inside of our works we have a platform raised about 2 feet, for the use of the men in case of a fight and whenever there is any firing going on. But back of the line, on level ground, a person can always stand upright and be perfectly safe from the touch of bullets. The only danger being from the shells which the enemy have just commenced to throw from mortars, they having yesterday brought 13 of them, and put them behind their works, ready for use besides the artillery they had there. To guard against these we are now building bomb proofs, which are large excavations in the ground covered with logs and earth placed over them, and when the shelling commences, the men will get into these unless the enemy attack us, in which case we will have to remain up behind our breastworks.

Just on the right of our regt we have 2 batteries placed in one of the old rebel forts we captured the second day we were here, which we have modeled over and strengthened. Then the next regt on our left, the 83rd Pa, are building works for 6 mortars to be placed in them tonight. These with the battery we are to have will cause a great deal of noise when they get in operation. And as the rebels have full as much artillery opposite us, as we have, we shall probably have a pretty warm time when they all open fire. The rebels now, keep firing at us every day to prevent us from working, but we do not pay much attention to their shots. Our batteries seldom replying, we are not ready yet, and as our work is mostly done in the night time, they do not bother us much.

The men have been so busy upon the earthworks and their bomb proofs, that I have not got my own works for my quarters made yet and shall try to get at it to night. The officers have to have a bomb proof built just in [the] rear of their companies, that is if they want to be perfectly safe. But I shall only have a slight breastwork thrown up, with a shade of boughs over it and place my tent in there, trusting my life in the hands of the Lord who will not take it untill his own good time. I trust and believe.

Thus you see we keep up the siege of Petersburg, steadily pressing on and are not at all affected by the rebel raid up into Maryland. In fact, for the last two days, we have not heard anything about it. But as our 6th Corps is now there, we know that the rebels will soon be driven back, and that this third rebel invasion of Maryland will not amount to anything more than a raid after all, the principal object of which is to call off troops from our army to defend Maryland, and thus gain a respite for themselves here in Richmond & Petersburg. I am sorry they have succeeded sufficiently to take away our 6th Corps. Yet it will serve to rouse up the people of the north to renewed action, and to the great fact that the Army of the Potomac must have more men if they expect us to take Richmond and protect Washington at the same time. Another great object that the rebels have in this invasion is to gather all the supplies they can for their army, as is shown by their gathering cattle, horses &c everywhere they can, and their army here, although not out of provisions by any means, yet is being subsided on short rations for the purpose of making their supplies last as long as possible. And this is causing some dissatisfaction with their men, as some of them desert and come over to us every day. Last night 2 men came over in front of our regt and they looked pretty hard, dirty and ragged & poor.

The weather yet continues to be very warm and we have no rain yet. Therefore the dust is terrible. We should now welcome a rain storm no matter how muddy it would make the ground. It is so warm in the day time we cannot sleep, and the flies are more numerous here than I have ever seen in any place before. They keep us awake even if we [have] cooler weather, and in consequence of so much night work, we are all becoming pretty well worn out. I am for one, and am not much more than a shadow of what I was last spring.

By the way, the 1st Sergt. of my company, Warren T. Angevine, by name, who was wounded at [the] Battle of the Wilderness, May 7th, and was thought at the time to be dangerously wounded, is now in St. Mary's Hospital in Detroit. And I took the liberty of giving him a letter of introduction to yourself, yesterday, as I thought that as he has been with me all through the war, you would like to see him on that account. As he, having been an eyewitness of the battle of the Wilderness and every other battle we had been in before that, could tell you much about it. I hope it will not displease you.

But I must now close. Remember me to Rev. Dr. Duffield, Dr. S.P. Duffield, and also to Henry when next you write to him. It seems that his expectations of an attack to be made on the rebel position were correct, as soon after that they did attack them and were repulsed. But such is the fate of war. We cannot expect to be victorious always. But now I will bid you good by for the present.

> Respectfully Your Friend
> Charles H. Salter

16th Mich Inft Vet Vols
Near Petersburg, Va.
July 21st 1864

My Dear Friend

Your kind letter of the 10th inst has just been received and I am glad to hear from you once more, and today will write you a few lines, if the rebels will keep from shelling us long enough to allow me. I wrote you a letter a week ago today, and since then we have remained in the same position, with nothing of very particular consequence occurring.

Last Friday our mortars, in throwing shell over into the enemy's works, penetrated a magazine, which blew up with a terrible noise, throwing the dirt, timber and pieces of shell high up in the air, where upon our men cheered all along our lines. But the rebels did not appear to be as well pleased about it. We have since learnt that 73 of their men were killed and wounded at this explosion.

On Monday last, during an artillery duel, some of our shells set fire to one of the fine residences opposite us, and it burnt up together with all of its out buildings, after which the rebels ceased firing, thinking probably, that such sort of work did not pay them very well. On Tuesday, we had a rain storm, which lasted all day long, and was very welcome indeed, as we had no rain for about seven weeks, and it would have been better for us to have mud rather than the dust which had become intolerable.

Our 2nd Corps, which is in rear of us acting at present in reserve, has been digging some covered roads from the rear up to our works, so that troops, wagons, &c, can at any time be moved up in perfect security, and without being observed by the enemy. These roads are dug like parallels, in a zigzag direction, from the rear towards the front, dug about 4 feet deep, and the earth thrown up on the side towards the enemy, thus fully protecting any one who may be passing in them, from the enemy's fire. And so we keep to work digging all the while at something or other, and it seems as if there were no end to our labor. It would be perfectly astonishing to any citizen, or any person outside of our army to come here, and see the immense amount of earth we have dug up since we have been here. We thought we done a great deal of such work at Yorktown, but it was very small compared with our immense works here. In fact, I don't think there ever was a siege in the history of modern times that can be compared in magnitude with this, not even that of Sevastopol. And now the rebel raid into Maryland is finally over with, and the disappearance of the rebel forces that participated in it has been as sudden, as their visitation, sweeping carelessly over the breadth of the state, between the Potomac River to the Susquehanna, and advancing simultaneously to the vicinity of Baltimore and Washington. They moved from point to point with impunity, and robbed and plundered every house and every person they came across, and as soon as our forces were ready to meet them, they suddenly retreated, carrying with them large quantities of plunder, and leaving us still to a great extent in ignorance of their numbers, and whence they all came, and where they have gone to. However, the rebel papers at Richmond are beginning to throw some light on the subject. Their great expectations from this bold play were fully up to the panic which it created from Martinsburg to Baltimore. The credulous citizens of Richmond were regaled with a rebel occupation? Of Baltimore! Gained through the assistance of a crushing insurrection in the city; and as if this were not glory enough for one day, they were thrown into ecstacies by the still more glorious? report, that they had captured Washington, including Father Abraham and his Cabinet? But the soldiers of Lee's army knew better than to believe these stories, and probably the citizens do also before this time, and when in a few days (perhaps hours), they hear from Sheridan's cavalry, they will no doubt be very glad to see their raiders come back safely, even if they do not bring any Yankee prisoners or plunder.

For our cavalry started out some days ago to intercept their retreat and have probably come across them by this time. So we shall soon hear from them. I hope soon to hear that Sherman's army has taken Atlanta, for now that he is at last there, he has reached the prize that he has been aiming for. The greatest struggle of his campaign will soon be over, when that is taken, and the rebels themselves think there is no doubt of his capturing the place, as appears from pieces published in their papers.

Our army are all pleased to hear of the proclamation of the President calling for another 500,000 men, (out of which he will probably get 100,000), and hope that the men will probably be furnished. It makes us old soldiers pleased to think how the clerks, and all the nice young men at home are trembling in their shoes at [a] view of the approaching draft. Well! We can afford to laugh, I suppose, as that is something that never troubled us. We are expecting our 6th Corps back here again in a day or two, and then we can go ahead as we were doing before this Maryland raid happened.

Our regt was in a battalion with the 1st Mich, under command of Lt. Col. Throop for a few days after the death of Major Elliott. But the connection was again dissolved, and we are separate again. Our Adjt., Jacklin, has lately been promoted to a captaincy, and is now in command of a company of sharpshooters, who are detailed from the different regts in the division, and are a little battalion separate from any of our regts, so that it makes an independent command for him, and is much pleasanter than being in our regt.

But now, as I have wrote a pretty long letter already, I will close. Remember me to Rev. Dr. Duffield, to Dr. S.P. Duffield, and also to Henry when you write to him. And hoping to hear from you again soon, I Remain,

> Respectfully Your Friend
> Charles H. Salter

16th Mich Infty Vet Vols
Near Petersburg, Va. July 28th 1864

My Dear Friend

Your kind letter of the 19th arrived last Sabbath and was particularly welcome for arriving on that day, as it furnished me some good Sabbath reading, and excellent counsel. And I cannot repay you sufficiently for the many letters you have written me, nor your kindness in giving me so much good advice, yet I will do as well as I can under the circumstances, and write to you as often as the fortunes of war, and my duties will permit.

Nothing of any great importance has transpired here since I last wrote, but we have continued hard at work prosecuting the great siege, and every day that passes brings our works nearer to completion. Last Friday, Gens. Grant and Meade passed along the front line of our works to inspect them, stopping in our earthworks some time to view the rebel fort opposite us, and passed some time in our regtl hd qrs, where quite a crowd of officers collected, all anxious to hear what the commander in chief had to say of the situation, and were gratified in as much as he told us that Petersburg would be ours in two weeks time at the farthest, and I believe he meant just what he said. Both of the generals looked anxious and careworn, more so than I have ever seen before.

Sunday night we had a heavy rain storm that lasted all night long, and was a bad thing for some portions of our troops who have dug their trenches on the inside of their works, as they were flooded out of them, and made very uncomfortable. But for us, as we had our trench on the outside of our works, the water did not trouble us so much, as the men could remain in the tents. Yesterday I went over the left of our line, and back on the flank and found even more fortifications thrown up than I was aware of. Our regt and each of the two regts of our brigade, which are on our left, have earthworks for a battery of 4 light guns each. Then in front of the 1st Brigade, which is on our left, and is the extreme left of the army, we have a fort, now nearly completed, which will have 18 heavy guns mounted in it. It is so close to the rebel picket line that they can throw a stone over into it, and they look over, day after day, and see our men working away, and yet they never fire a gun. They keep quiet because if they should fire at our men there, it would break the truce that now exists all along the line, and moreover, we would then drive them out from the picket line. But we do not wish to break the truce either, untill we get all ready for action, and so let the rebel pickets alone as long as they behave themselves. Their artillery back in their forts keeps firing away every day, and whenever they discover a squad of men of ours standing in an exposed position, they let fly at them. Therefore, we have to be very careful when we go out with working parties.

From this fort, our 3rd Division is off on our left flank, and to protect that point they have erected a fort full as large as Fort Wayne, near Detroit, and a fort that is far better than that one. They have a large brigade of infantry camped in it, and a battery of artillery, and have room for 6 or 8 more batteries, if they are needed. The balance of that division is campd in that vicinity. After viewing their works I returned to my camp

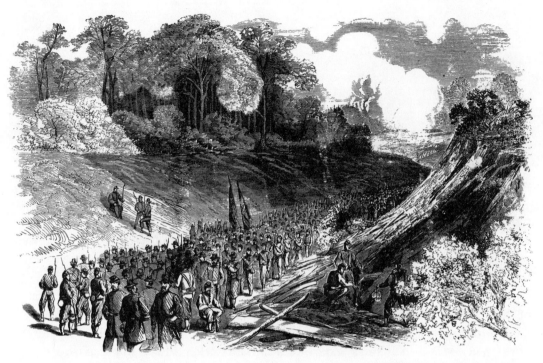

THE SIEGE OF PETERSBURG—THE FIFTH CORPS AWAITING THE ORDER TO ADVANCE, JULY 30, 1864 (FRANK LESLIE'S ILLUSTRATED HISTORY OF THE CIVIL WAR, NEW YORK, 1895)

perfectly satisfied that the rebels could not turn our flank, even if they were to try with ever so large a force.

The 2nd Corps, which has been camped in rear of ours since the 6th went up into Maryland, suddenly broke camp on Tuesday night last, and moved off toward City Point. We have not, however, heard from them since then, but we expect that some flank movement is going on, or that they were sent up to strengthen some portion of the line. Meanwhile, we wait very anxiously to see what has become of them; and at the same time, we ourselves are under orders to be ready to move at a moment's notice.

The mortar battery in rear of our regt is now about completed, all ready in fact, but putting in the mortars, and they will soon be in and be sending over 11-inch shell to the rebs. I have reconsidered my plan for a home and concluded to have a bomb proof as well as the rest, and so have already commenced work on it, and if we do not move, I expect to have it completed tonight or tomorrow.

That was a very curious circumstance that happened about those shirts that your son was distributing. And those Maine soldiers ought to write plenty of letters, at least, to those ladies who made them.

July 29th, 4 P.M. I had to leave off writing yesterday, on being ordered out with a detail of men to assist the artillerists in getting up their mortars. They are all in position now, 6 of them, and all ready for work. Therefore, we shall soon have some heavy firing here, and as the rebels will be very apt to send us some mortar shells back, I have hurried up my bomb proof and now have it finished, and a very good house it makes too. I am afraid I shall not like to leave it now. The men are also now busy building a large bomb proof just in rear of the breastworks, and to form a part of them, so that all of the regt can get in them, and be ready for action at any time.

Well! I will have to close now as I have not much time to write, being on duty as Brigade Officer of the day today. Please give my regards to Rev. Dr. Duffield, and all friends.

Respectfully Your Friend
C.H. Salter

16th Mich Infy Vet Vols
Near Petersburg, Va. Aug 1st 1864

My Dear Friend

Your kind letter of the 25th inst arrived on the 30th, and I am very glad indeed to hear from you once more, although I regret hearing you are so unwell, and hope you are better by this time. I wrote you a letter only last Friday, little thinking at the time that we should have such terrific fighting as we did have the next day.

But so it was, everything had been got in readiness, and at 4 A.M., the signal was given by blowing up a fort in front of the 9th Corps, in which were at the time 3 regts of rebel troops. With a terrific explosion and rumbling noise that seemed more like an earthquake than anything else, huge masses of earth, timber &c went high up in the air, and of the 3 regts in the fort, but 4 men escaped to live of all of them. Immediately after the explosion, Wilcox's Division of [the] 9th Corps charged and took possession of the ruins. The rebels were, at first apparently at a loss what to make of it, but soon bringing up other troops, they charged desperately upon the works, probably a dozen times, but were repulsed with great loss every time. At one time they sent up a brigade of North Carolina troops to charge but when they came near our men, most of them threw down their arms, and gave themselves up. This was the same brigade that tried to come over to our line about 2 weeks ago, but were discovered and prevented from doing so. And, finally between 10 and 11 o'clock, the rebels seemed to give up trying to retake the place and remained quiet.

Then the division of colored troops of the 9th Corps were sent up to assist Wilcox's Division, and, passing to the front of them, formed the first line, and about 1 P.M., the rebels brought up a very heavy force [and] made a sudden charge upon the ruins of the fort. The white officers of the colored troops and the negroes seemed seized with a panic, and to the astonishment of every one, rushed back to the rear, running over the Michigan Brigade and other white troops there, which threw them into confusion, and the result was the rebels captured the place and took a large number of our men prisoners. The 2nd Michigan and also the 20th and 27th lost many men in prisoners, besides a heavy loss in killed and wounded.

In the meantime, our corps was not idle, but as the fort blew up, that was the signal for us to open fire, and in a moment from the entire length of our line over 100 pieces of artillery opened a terrific fire upon the enemy works; heavy siege guns, mortars and field pieces firing as rapidly as possible. We had 18 mortars placed along in rear of our brigade, throwing 32 and 64 lb shells, besides 26 pieces of heavy artillery (siege guns) on our left, and 12 field pieces on our right. These all concentrated their fire upon the fort just opposite us, knocking down the walls, tearing the embrasures all out of shape, and the shell from the mortars coming right down inside of the fort, exploded with a great noise and demolished everything they had there. They had some guns mounted, and the muzzles looking out of the embrasures, which had annoyed us very much ever since we have been here, but that day we took full revenge on them by knocking the guns off the carriages, and apparently rendered them useless. And in the rebel works, not a man could show his head, nor could they even use their artillery, and could only reply to us from their mortars which were, of course, better protected.

Our infantry opened fire also all along the line, and the roar of muskets and artillery combined was greater than any I have heard since Gettysburg. But all this was only a demonstration, as we call it, and only done to prevent the rebels opposite us from going up to assist those at the ruined fort, and we succeeded pretty well too, for the enemy opposite us had to keep close in their bomb proofs and behind their works, and yet we must have killed and wounded many of them, as we could often hear their cries when struck.

But, after the enemy had possession of the ruined fort and the fighting ceased there, we ceased firing also, and then in our vicinity everything became quiet again. And since then, the rebels opposite us have behaved themselves very well. Before that they used to throw a shell over at every little crowd of our men they could see together, but now they do not fire at all. They probably never thought we had so much heavy artillery here, or that we were able to punish them so. But now they are afraid to provoke the 5th Corps to commence firing again.

This morning a party went out from our lines and brought in the wounded from in front of the ruined fort and buried the dead. We had tried to get permission from the rebels to do this before, but Lee, with his usual inhumanity, refused to allow it to be done untill this morning, 48 hours after the fighting was over, and there the wounded lay between the two lines exposed to the hot rays of the sun, and no one to even so much as give them a drink of water, for it would have been certain death for any of our men to attempt to go to their assistance. We sent over several flags of truce, but the rebel generals bothered about one thing or another, making every possible delay they could to prevent us from getting them as long as possible.

The regt is getting paid today, and we are all pretty busy, therefore, please excuse a short letter and poor writing. As I shall have to close now or not get this in todays mail.

Respectfully Your Friend
C.H. Salter

Bivouac 16th Mich Infty Vet Vols
Near Petersburg, Va. Aug 17th 1864

My Dear Friend

Your kind letter of the 8th inst arrived on the 13th, and today I will try, if we do not receive orders to march soon, to write you a letter.

Since my last letter was wrote, great changes have been going on in our army. On the night of the 14th, the 11th & 9th Corps stretched out to the left, and relieved our corps entirely from the front line. A division of the 9th Corps relieved our division and we moved back about ½ mile to [the] rear, into a wood and went into bivouac. Thus, now the 9th and 11th Corps are the only troops occupying the fortifications before Petersburg. Our corps is in reserve, the 2nd Corps, as long ago as the 12th inst left here, went down to City Point and then somewhere! But these movements are managed with so much secrecy now, that I do not yet know where they have gone or what they are doing.

Our present bivouac is in a low, marshy place. We had a heavy rainstorm last Monday which completely flooded our camp to the depth of 6 inches, but the hot sun has since then dried it up again. We, being here in reserve, are liable to be ordered to any part of the line at any moment. Last night we were sent out to the front as an attack was anticipated on our left, but after remaining there ½ hour or so, we were ordered back to camp again. At present, we are under orders to be ready to march at a moments notice, and I have no doubt but that tonight we shall move somewhere, and that the next [event] on the program will be another great battle, in which case the 5th Corps will be found all ready and eager for the fray.

By the way, I cannot say I quite agree with you that Gen. Hooker should have stood having Gen. Howard put over him. I had a letter from a captain in the 14th Michigan the other day, who, in speaking of it says, the most poignant regret was expressed by both officers and men at his departure, which threatened to cause disturbance among some of the regts which had all become strongly attached to him, as all true soldiers will attached to a brave leader, who like Gen. Hooker, never asks his men to go where he will not lead! Gen. Hooker frankly stated his reasons, which were that in the preferment of his junior officer to the vacancy caused by Gen. McPherson's death, he felt an indignity offered him, which as any soldier asking but one of two things—promotion or the grave; it was his duty to resent. Every true soldier fights for promotion. He daily braves death to obtain it and when here it is denied him and awarded to another not more meritorious than he, it becomes time for him to go where his services stand some chance of recognition. Here, we are in hopes he may come to our army yet. I suppose he could come any day if he would take command of our corps, but probably he does not want to serve under Gen. Meade.

I do not know when I can send this letter off, as the mail is not allowed to leave here at present, which shows there must be some movement in progress, and our generals are bound not to allow it to be known any sooner than necessary, and so if you do not yet get this letter for some time, you may know the reason why.

But now I must close, being officer of the day, and here in camp now, I have to be pretty busy. Remember me kindly to Rev. Dr. Duffield, Dr. S.P. Duffield and Henry. And hoping to hear from you again soon, I remain,

Respectfully Your Friend
C.H. Salter

Bivouac 16th Mich Infty Vet Vols
Weldon Railroad, Va. Aug 23rd 1864

My Dear Friend

I have not as yet received a letter from you since my last of the 17th inst, but that is doubtless owing to your trip up the lakes and as I have a few spare moments today, will write you a few lines, not knowing when I shall have an opportunity of writing again.

Our entire corps fell in at daylight on the 18th, and moved off to the left of our army, our (1st) Division in the advance. We arrived at this road about 10 A.M., at a point about 4 miles from Petersburg. [We] found a few railroad guards here whom we captured. Our 2nd, 3rd & 4th Divisions were immediately deployed in line facing towards Petersburg across the road, and our division off on the left flank. The rebels soon made their appearance and attacked our front line in considerable force, and for four hours we had a fierce battle, but the enemy after three separate charges failed to drive our forces, and we gained considerable ground even whilst the fight was going on. However, about 3 P.M. the battle ceased, and we went to work throwing up breastworks. That night I was detailed in command of 250 men of our brigade to establish a picket line out in front of our line, and as it was raining, and very dark, I had a difficult task, but succeeded after a couple of hours in getting my line out about ¼ mile in front of the brigade. The next morning, Gen. Griffin gave orders for the line to advance, and take possession of a road that runs nearly parallel with the railroad, distant about 1 mile west. We advanced in the midst of a heavy rainstorm, and gained the road after a little skirmishing with some of the rebel cavalry, who had held it.

As we had a skirmish line for our brigade of ½ miles in length, it was rather a difficult matter for me to keep them all in order, but I finally succeeded. And then, at 2 P.M., the enemy appeared in heavy force on the right of our corps, where the 9th Corps was to connect with our 2nd Division, and where they had as yet only a skirmish line out, and which the enemy soon broke through and getting in the rear of our 2nd Division, captured Gen. Hays, and a number of our men, how many I do not know, some say 1,000. Gen. Hays was formerly Col. of the 18th Mass. of our brigade. Troops were immediately hurried up from the 9th Corps and our own, and after some desperate fighting, drove back the enemy and regained the lost ground, when our line was there reestablished again. In this battle, as in the one of the day before, the greatest loss in our corps occurred in the 2nd Division, and the 9th Corps lost heavy; in Gen. Wilcox's Division, Major Belcher of the 8th Michigan being killed. When his body was carried off the field, it was pierced by more than a dozen bullets. He has a son, Lt. Belcher, in our regt, who has now gone home with his father's body.

Meanwhile, whilst this was going on, the enemy sent in a strong line of skirmishers, who engaged our picket line, and at one time there was great danger that the right of my line would be drove in or captured, when I hurried up the reserve, 35 men of my regt, strengthened the line, and the enemy ceased further attempts in that direction. But, towards night, a force of cavalry came in on the left of my line, captured one of my men, and attempted to gain possession of the road on which we had our picket line, but I hurried the reserve over there, and after a lively skirmish of 15 minutes, they (the reb cavalry) fell back in confusion, and we captured one of them, with a very good horse and equipments; the man I sent in as a prisoner, the horse I kept and turned in to brigade headquarters, for the especial use of the officer commanding [the] brigade picket line. The enemy disturbed us no more that night but it rained all night long and we passed a miserable night. However, the next morning we were relieved and returned to the brigade after 36 hours duty.

On Sunday morning, the 21st, the enemy thought to outflank us and made an attack on the left, on our division. They suddenly made their appearance in large force, drove in our picket line, capturing some 15 or 16 of them, amongst whom were two men of my company, and the enemy, thinking the 4th Division works were the left of our line, attacked them in front, whilst another force attempted to get on their left and rear. The line of our brigade is 200 yards in rear of [the] 4th Division and probably 4 or 500 yards to the left and could not be seen by the enemy untill they were right upon it. And on they came over an open field on our right, waving their banners and keeping perfect line, whilst our artillery was making fearful havoc in their ranks. But confident of outflanking us, they pressed right on through the gap with one brigade, when our brigade jumped up on our works, and with loud cheers closed in up to the 4th Division, they coming down to meet us, and the rebel brigade surrendered, not one man of them escaped to even tell the story. We captured one Brig. Gen., 4 stand of colors and 100 men, or all that was left of the 4 regts that started to outflank! our 4th Division.

Meanwhile, all along the line of the 4th Division, the enemy were repulsed with great loss, many of the rebels when the charge failed came and gave themselves up. They came on in good order but our fire, both artillery and musketry, used them completely up. In front of one of our regts alone, were 200 dead rebels, and they lost one Brig. Gen. killed, and another wounded and taken by us, besides the one captured by our brigade. They lost large numbers of wounded also whom they carried off to the rear, and although I do not as yet know their loss, but it must have been fully as large as the number of troops engaged on our side, whilst the loss on our side was very small, owing to our fighting behind the breastworks we had put up. In our regt, we had 5 men wounded and a few taken prisoners, who were out on the picket line. It was Hill's Corps, and some of Beauregard's troops from Charleston that engaged us. In all of the three battles of the 18th, 19th, & 21st, and having tried our centre first, then the right, and lastly the left, and been repulsed with severe loss from each attack, they seem at last resigned to giving up the railroad to the veteran 5th Corps, although we hope they will keep on attacking us, for at this rate, they would soon use up their army.

They were using this road before we gained it to bring up most all of their supplies so I was informed by the reb cavalry man I captured, who said Lee was bound to have the road back again at any cost. I told him Lee would probably change his mind after he knew the 5th Corps, the best part of our army, held it. And so, since Sunday, they have not attacked us at any point, and now one division of the corps is here also as our reserve, and we feel confident Lee's entire army could not drive us from it.

The weather has been very wet for the last week. We have had rain every day and the ground has become very muddy and bad for us to move at present, but we gained this point just at the right time, before it became so muddy and we are very thankful for it. I have lately seen several letters wrote from the army here, by your son, whilst he was here and have been much interested in reading them, for they present most truthful and lifelike pictures of scenes and life in our army, but I do not think I have seen all he has wrote, for we do not get hold of Detroit papers here very often.

You will please excuse any mistakes, or poor writing in this letter, for it has been wrote in a hurry. Give my regards to Rev. Dr. Duffield, and all enquiring friends, and hoping to hear from you again soon, I Remain, Respectfully Your Friend

C.H. Salter

Hospital 2nd Cav'l Div
Marietta, Ga. Aug 25 1864

Dear Mother

How I wish you could have been here yesterday afternoon & went up on the Kenesaw Mountain with me. This is the mountain that the rebels held in spite of Sherman & his army for over 3 weeks. It is 1,828 feet above the level of the sea & from the top of it, country for 15 miles in every direction can be seen quite plain. We could see the spires in Atlanta & could see the smoke from our artillery every time it was fired. There is a signal station on the top & the lieutenant in command told us by the smoke of the guns just where our line began & ended & I should think it must be at least 15 miles long. He said the firing yesterday was much more rapid than usual but as the telegraph wires are in order, he did not get any news by signal.

The object of the signals are to keep communications open between the front & Altoona Pass in case the telegraph wires are cut. They also keep a look out over the country & if they see any force of rebels making for this railroad, they signal the fact to the posts on the road so as to have them in readiness to receive them.

The rebel fortification on this mountain, as well as the mountain itself, show the effects of our shells. One place in particular I noticed it was on the sides of the mountain nearest to our works & just under a fort pierced for 3 guns. There was a place about 30 feet square & in that square could not be found a place 2 foot square but had been struck by shell or solid shot. One of the port holes had to be closed up in the fort. Our artillery had got the range of it & the rebs could not use it, so they closed it up. This fort was about ¾ of the way up the mountain.

All of our officers who have been up say that the rebels missed it when they fell back to it for there was a much better position about a mile & a half north of the mountain & that they could have held it much easier than the mountain. The greatest difficulty with the mountain was that they could not depress their artillery sufficiently to do any damage to us in the line of works we occupied. Those works you can look right down into from the top of the mountain. It seems as if they were almost under you. The only way they could shell us was to use very little powder, just enough to give the shell a start & then trust to luck for the rest. Our batterys had such good positions that whenever the rebs would fire a gun, it would be answered from all sides & silenced in short order, so that they did not even have a fair chance for practice.

The road up this mountain is on the north side & was exposed to our fire during the whole siege so that if they took wagons up at all, they must have done it during the night. I recollect their trying to get a train down one afternoon & it was shelled all the way down. I wondered then why they did not run it back out of the way but I see the reason now. The road is very narrow & it is so very rocky on either side that there was but one way to go when they got started.

There is a small spring almost up to the top of the mountain, but the water is not very good. It tastes of iron & is not cold. I think it is nothing but a wet weather spring, for when the water comes from that height, unless it is from the rain we have been having for the last 2 or 3 days, I can not see.

News from the front is scarce as usual. Our brigades have not returned from our expedition of some kind they had started on when I arrived here. The right of our army is reported to have made its way so far south of the city that it rests on the Macon Rail Road. If so, their last road is out & they will have to stand a siege where they are or try cutting their way out & if they try that, it seems to be the opinion of those who ought to know, that Mr. Hood will lose a good share of his company. But this looking ahead at the movements has got to be [so] common that it don't pay, so I will do the opposite & look back & tell you what I have been doing since the 25th of July. I believe that was where you left me, was it not?

Tuesday July 26th 1864

Received orders to get ready for a move at 4 o'clock the next morning, which we did by supplying ourselves with 5 days rations & a good days rest. The next morning, we moved out at 4 o'clock without the sound of a bugle (for fear I suppose the rebs would know we were going), on the main road to Covington in the rear of Stoneman's Division. After going about 8 miles, we separated, Stoneman continuing on the same road & we turned to the right on a road that led to Jonesboro, a station on the Macon RR. We moved on this road 7 miles, when we struck a party of rebels with a small wagon train at Flat Shoals, a point on the Yellow River. We captured the train & a few prisoners & then went into camp. At 3 o'clock the next morning, we were woke up & told that we were surrounded. The men were taken out, dismounted & formed in line of battle, expecting an attack.

They laid there until daylight. We were then ordered to cut our way out & of course, we did. But for some reason or other, we did not meet with much opposition & afterwards found out the reason. The rebs heard of Stoneman & went after him. We moved back about 5 or 6 miles towards Covington & went into camp. I went out about 3 miles after forage. It was almost dark when we returned. We did not move camp the next day & I went out foraging again; went about 6 miles; there was 3 of us & we were told that a patrol of about 25 rebels had just passed there, so we thought, under the circumstances, we would be justified going back to camp.

The next morning we moved on in the direction of Decatur. At 6 o'clock, after moving 5 miles, we went into camp where we staid until the evening of the next day (the 1st), when I received orders to go to Marietta with sick. I had a bad headache, but nothing would do. I must go, so of course, like a good soldier who always obeys orders, I went. It was about 15 miles & we got there about 2 o'clock in the morning. I put the men in the hospital & laid down until day light. That afternoon, Dr. Bacon gave me orders to go to Columbia. I started at 10 o'clock P.M., Aug 2nd & got back here on the morning of Aug 20th & it was a very hard trip, to say the least, as it rained all day on the 20th & 21st. I staid in the house but it cleared up nicely & I went up on the mountain yesterday. Today, Dr. Bacon, who has been sick for about 2 weeks, is going up. We told such large stories when we got back, that nothing would do but he must go. He is almost well again & the trip will do him good.

But I must stop. It is pleasant out doors that I am want to stay in the house. I enclose a photo for my collection. It is the hospital steward of the 7th Pa. Cav.

The flowers are the only kind that I could find on the top of Kenesaw Mountain. I don't know how they will look when they get to Michigan. They were the only thing I could find. I might have sent a rock or a piece of shell but they weigh to heavy for postage stamps.

> Give my love to all & write soon to
> Your Affec Son
> Jimmie

Bivouac 16th Mich Infty Vet Vols
Weldon Rail Road, Va. Sept 2nd 1864

My Dear Friend

Your kind letter of the 24th was received on the 30th, and as today I have a few spare moments, I will write you a few lines not knowing when I can write again.

In my last letter of the 23rd inst, I gave you a hurried account of the fighting of our corps when we took possession of this road, and from that you will perceive you were right in supposing our regt is in the 5th Corps, who done the fighting here on the 18th, 19th & 21st Aug. Gen. Warren, whose photograph I sent you, commands our corps, and has personally superintended every movement connected with the occupation of this railroad. Since I wrote you last we have only had one battle here that occurred on the 25th inst. 2 divisions of the 2nd Corps had gone south on the rail road to below Ream's Station and were engaged in destroying it, when Hill's Corps, and some of Beauregard's suddenly attacked them. The rebels charged twice upon our men only to be repulsed with heavy loss each time, but rallying all their troops and sending a force of cavalry into the rear of our men, they succeeded the 3rd time in driving our men from their position, and, taking probably 6 or 800 of them prisoners. Then night came on and closed the scene, and during the night the rebels and our men fell back to their original positions. This was a fiercely contested battle and the loss on both sides was very great compared to the small numbers engaged.

Our loss was 1,500, including some 6 or 800 prisoners, and 9 pieces of artillery, whilst the rebel loss was said to near 3,000, almost all of them killed or wounded. Two brigades of the 3rd Division and one of the 4th Division of our corps, were on the way to reinforce the 2nd Corps, but having 4 miles to go to get there, did not arrive on the scene of the battle untill after dark, when it was all over. Since then, the enemy have made no attacks upon us, but have remained comparatively quiet. And after all their boasts that they would drive us from possession of this road at any cost, they seemed to be resigned to leaving us in our works, and to have made up their minds that the veteran 5th Corps could not be drove from any position they once get.

We have been busy for the last 5 or 6 days in building two large forts, one in the line of the 3rd Division, and the other in front of the centre of the line of our division, each one is calculated to contain 24 cannon, and from 1,000 to 2,000 infantry, as may be necessary. I think they will both be completed by tomorrow, and then the enemy could not please us better than to make an attack on us.

Yesterday afternoon we heard considerable firing out on our picket line, and we fell in behind our breastworks, expecting an attack, but it turned out to be only a force of the enemy's cavalry, who were trying to drive in our pickets. But they failed entirely in their plans. This morning a force of our cavalry went out intending to go over to the Danville R.R. to destroy a portion of it. But they only went out about a mile when they met a large force of the enemy's infantry, and were obliged to come back, the enemy being too strong for them to force their way through.

We have had so much digging to do since we have been here that we are all pretty well tired out. We are out on picket, or else on fatigue duty just every other day, and those that are not on picket [are] usually out at work 12 hours out of the 24. Yet in spite of this some of our men have found time to put up a large shade of pine boughs for the purpose of holding meetings in, and on the Sabbath, some of the Christian Commission come around and give us a sermon, and we have prayer meetings there every pleasant evening, at which usually from 50 to 100 men of the regt attend. Most all of the regts in our division hold meetings also nearly every night, and I think there is more interest manifested in them by the men than I have ever before seen in the army.

Since the heavy rains we have had, about the time of our arrival here, the weather has been much cooler than before, and therefore much pleasanter, but the country about here is very low and flat; therefore when we have rains, it becomes very muddy.

Enclosed with this I send you [a] photograph of Gen. Bartlet, who commands our brigade. [He] has been in command of it now for nearly a year. But I must now close as it is near time for the mail to leave. Hoping to hear from you again soon, I remain,

Respectfully Your Friend
C.H. Salter

16th Mich Infty Vet Vols
Weldon Railroad, Va. Sept 12th 1864

My Dear Friend

Your kind letter of the 2nd inst arrived in due time, and I take the first opportunity I have since had of writing you a few lines. I am very glad to receive that letter of your sons, and although that happened to be about the only one I had seen before, I am as much obliged to you for it, and many others have read it, as I passed it around amongst my men as a choice bit of reading, and every one who saw it was pleased with it.

Since I wrote to you on the 2nd inst, we have not had anything occur here out of the usual line of our soldier life. We remain in the same position we did then and the forts and other fortifications I wrote about are all completed now, and we are strong enough to resist the combined assault of Lee's entire army should they attack us, which I do not think they will now as the time for that has gone by. Lee knows we have very strong works here, and the rebels, brave as they usually are, cannot be brought to storm any fortifications of any strength at all.

We have just completed a railway from our corps head quarters to connect with the City Point railroad below Petersburg. The cars yesterday ran right up to our corps head quarters on the Weldon road, and the rebel pickets could easily hear the whistle of the locomotive, and I presume, it rather astonished them to think that we had a railroad already built, on an entirely new track in so short [a] time.

There was great rejoicing in our army when we heard of the fall of Atlanta, and Gen. Grant ordered a salute to be fired from every battery in our army that bore upon the enemy! The salute was fired from shotted guns at midnight, and the rebels supposing we were going to make a general assault upon their lines replied with vigor, and for a couple of hours we had a very lively cannonade, but, as usual, nobody was hurt. It was a great and glorious victory and I hope Sherman will keep pegging away at Hood's army untill it is entirely destroyed, and then the rebellion will have nothing to depend upon but Lee's army here, which gives us so much trouble.

The presidential election does not cause but very little excitement or attention here, yet when the time comes to vote, the army will be found to vote upon the side of the Union by a tremendous majority. Gen. McClellan had an immense number of friends in our army before he allowed his name to be used by the "peace at any price party" but although they like him, they do not like the Chicago platform, nor the southern sympathizers, Pendleton, candidate for vice president, as an illustration. Gen. Griffin, commanding our division, has always been a strong McClellan man, (as are in fact most generals of our army), and he has been looking for a long time to see him set up by the war democrats as their candidate, but when he read the proceedings of the Chicago convention, their platform, and saw Pendleton on the same ticket with McClellan,* he said he was sorry to see George in bad company. But if he would accept the nomination of the Chicago convention, he must use all his influence against him. And as Gen. G. is a great favorite with our division, his influence goes a great way. And there is one thought that does more to turn the soldiers against that ticket than nay other, and that is: suppose McClellan should be elected, and soon after die, as did Gen. Harrison, and Gen Taylor, and be succeeded by Pendleton, who has always been a bitter enemy to the soldiers, and a great friend of the rebels, what would be the result? What would the struggles of our army for the last 3½ years amount to! What, in fact, would become of even our country itself! The result is too well known to every soldier in our army, and would be nothing but a tumbling to pieces, of our entire country. The North would fall into half dozen petty powers, compared to which the Southern Confederacy would be a mighty nation, whilst the North would have enacted on her soil the same scenes of battle, bloodshed and destruction, that the South is suffering from now. This is no fancy picture, but it is what our army firmly believes would be the result, and we can plainly see that when even democratic papers, such as their great leader, the N.Y. Herald, denounce the ticket, that it must, in reality, be very bad, or they would uphold it. I enclose a piece written by one of our army, which is a pretty good exposition of our views.

A week ago yesterday, Geo. H. Stuart, chairman of the Christian Commission, was here and addressed our brigade, and every man who could do so attended. He made us a soul stirring address, and everyone liked him. The soldiers all think he ought to be

---

*General George McClellan ran for president on the Democratic ticket and garnered 45 percent (1.8 million votes) of the popular vote but only 21 electoral votes, losing to Lincoln.

a general in our army, he is so earnest in his work. We have in our regt church every Sabbath, when a chaplain from some of the neighboring regts addresses us. And also we have prayer meetings every morning, when it does not rain. For this purpose we have a brush house set up, by making a skeleton of poles and covering it with pine brush for the roof and sides, and it is a very pleasant place to hold exercises in, in dry weather. At brigade head quarters, they have a similar structure, and Col. Gwynn of the 118th Pa., who commands our brigade in the absence of Gen. Bartlet, takes a great interest in promoting the cause of religion in the brigade, as does also Col. Gregory of our 2nd Brigade, whose brigade is camped next to ours.

By the way, during the last week, 6 officers and some 40 men of our regt, whose term of three years had expired, have been mustered out of the service, and have gone home. It made us old vets feel homesick for a while when we see them going. Yet we hope that the war will end in the course of a few months, or a year at most, and then we shall go home also. At best, what is left of us.

Speaking of those envelopes, I had a number printed for the reason that it was more convenient to use especially when, as is often the case with me, I have not much time to write. But, as I have already written a long letter, I will close. Please give my regards to Rev. Dr. Duffield, Dr. S.P. Duffield, and remember me to Henry when next you write. And hoping to hear from you gain soon,

I Remain, as ever,
Respectfully Your Friend
C.H. Salter

Head Quarters 3rd Brig. 1st Division, 5th Corps
Weldon Railroad, Va. Sept 20th 1864

My Dear Friend

Your kind letter of the 12th inst was received on the 17th, and I was very glad to hear from you, and take the first opportunity I have had to write you a few lines. It seems that your letter was written the same day I wrote you last. Since then I have been on duty at our brigade head quarters as Acting Inspector General, and have been kept very busy, I assure you, as I came here at the busiest time of the month, but as I am only temporarily detailed, I expect to go back to my regt again in a few days. I am at present engaged in inspecting the different regts of the brigade, as we do usually once every month. I inspect one regt each day, and have now inspected 5 and have 2 more left yet.

Our corps all remain in the same positions, and nothing has occurred to disturb our usual routine of duty, except a few days ago, when the rebel cavalry came in our rear and took 4,200 head of cattle, or about all the beef we had in the army at the time. It was a very disgraceful occurrence, and will give the rebels enough beef to feed their army for 2 months. The cattle of the army were all ordered to be sent to the rear, and kept together, which is very different from the manner in which they have heretofore been kept, as the cattle have always been kept with the different corps for whose use they were intended. And no sooner had they all been gathered together, with a guard of 300 cavalry, than along comes the rebel cavalry, and drive away our beef, and the 300 cavalry also, I suppose, for we have seen nothing of them since.

We are now engaged in drilling every day, and are kept generally pretty busy. We have company and battalion drill in the morning, and brigade drill in the afternoon, which latter is the only one I am required to attend.

I am obliged to you for the reading matter you sent me, and your letter was very interesting also. Your life has indeed been a long and interesting one, and you have done a great deal of good also. I sincerely hope you may be spared to witness our country at peace with ourselves and all the rest of the world once more. As regards that sentiment of that peace man the other day, is a wrong and mistaken idea. If this war is over, and Mr. Peace man wants to fight England, I don't nor won't nor will you find, I believe, not 10 men in the Army of the Potomac that will. A civil war is something we cannot help. A war with another nation is something we can, and I never will take part in a war with England or any other foreign power, for I do not believe there would be any right or justice in it. And I believe that is what the army generally think. They need not trouble themselves about what they shall do with the army, for the army has always taken care of itself without their assistance, and so it can continue to do so, after this "cruel war is over" without any help from them.

We have, whilst I have been writing, received news of a glorious victory gained by Sheridan over Early at Winchester yesterday, in which we captured 5 pieces of artillery, 9 battle flags, a large number of prisoners, and completely routed the rebels, they being reported flying in confusion. I was this afternoon, left in charge at Brigade Hd Qrs, whilst the brigade is out on drill, and sent the dispatch immediately out to Col. Gwynn, who is commanding our brigade at present, and from the cheering out there, I should judge the dispatch was being read to the brigade. I did think that Sheridan did not do as much as he ought, but from this I judge he moved at the proper time, and struck home, and I guess that the rebels will have to leave the Shenandoah Valley now for good.

You will please excuse a short letter this time. I am kept so busy, I can scarcely think of anything but business. I am greatly obliged for the many letters you write, and, hoping to hear from you often, I Remain,

> Respectfully Your Friend
> C.H. Salter
> Excuse mistakes and bad writing

Head Quarters 16th Mich Infty Vet Vols
Poplar Grove Church, Va. Oct 5th 1864

My Dear Friend

Your kind letter of the 25th arrived in due time and I take the first opportunity I have had to write you a few lines.

I left brig hd qrs on the morning of the 30th and came to the regt to act as major. The same morning, our division and the 2nd Division of our corps left camp, our brigade in the advance, and marched west. After going about 3 miles, we met the enemy's skirmishers, and drove them in, and soon came in sight of a long line of the enemy's earthworks with a strong fort in the centre. We formed [a] line, our brigade on [the] right, 2nd Brigade on the left, and Gen. Griffin ordered us to charge the works. We went forward on the double quick, over a field ½ mile wide. The rebels poured a heavy fire of musketry, grape shot and canister into us, yet the line never wavered nor halted, but pushed right on, untill we arrived at the enemy's works, our regt just on the right of the fort. A private named Scott was the first over and myself second. Our colonel stood on the left of the works, urging the men to get over, when he was shot through the head and fell dead, 2 balls through his head. Yet the men got over, and the rebels left the breastwork we had gained and went into the fort. I led a party of my regt and some others around into the rear of the fort, just as they were hauling off their battery. I succeeded however, in getting one of the cannon, and we closed in at the gateway of the fort, and had a short struggle in there, and captured 47 prisoners, who I sent back to the rear, and now hold a receipt from the Provost Marshal of our division for them.

We did not stop here but pushed right on and gained another slight work about ¼ mile farther on, whilst the 1st Michigan and 18th Massachusetts of our brigade, took another fort about ½ mile to the right from the one we took. We then rested on that line, whilst the 2nd Corps, coming up, passed us and, going out to the front, engaged the enemy, and soon Hill's Corps came up and charged the 9th [Corps], who to our surprise, broke and ran, and we were ordered to advance to meet the enemy. Our brigade yet in the front rank, we moved out by the right flank, every man in his place as if going on parade. Officers mounted, and getting out to the front, came on the right by file into line, my regt being last in the brigade, was thus placed on the extreme left, and the most exposed. We were just in line when the enemy opened fire with a battery, and the solid shot ploughed through the ranks, piling up 7 or 8 dead and wounding many more. And the column reeled like a drunken man, yet none of them ran to the rear. And fortunately at that time we were ordered to move off a short distance to the right, where we got position on the brow of a small hill, the 9th Corps rushing past us to the rear, and our brigade, standing like a stone wall, pouring our fire into friend and foe alike. It was a fearful struggle, and a terrible alternative, but we had to do it or our own ranks would be broken. Soon the rebels were within 10 feet of us, pouring a withering fire into our ranks, but we checked them, and our 2nd Brigade just then came up and, strengthening our line, poured such a fire into the enemy that they fell back, and our batteries just getting into position opened fire on them, and assisted their retreat. At about dusk the fighting ceased, and the victory was gained not by our army, but by our brigade, for if it had not been for the desperate stand taken by our little brigade, the entire 9th Corps would have been driven back in confusion to our old works near the Weldon R.R. Their generals seem to be the most utterly incapable men, and their troops the most cowardly of any in our army. Their corps is much larger than ours, yet they allowed one half the number of rebels to drive them, and had we not been on hand to check the rebel attack, they would have taken prisoners [of] one half of that corps. They do not seem to be good for anything since they have not Gen. Burnside to drive them in.

We lay in line of battle where we fought all that day, and night of the next day, in the midst of a heavy rainstorm, and on the 2nd (Sunday), we threw up a line of breastworks, and buried our own dead and the rebel dead. Then the next day our brigade had to move off farther to the right about ½ mile, and give place to some of the 9th Corps. Then yesterday, we built another strong line of works, where our present camp is, on a ridge or high ground, in a pine grove. We have a very pleasant place for a camp, but expect to have to move soon, so we cannot expect to have any rest here.

Our brigade of 7 old regts went into the fight with but 1,200 men, and had 350 of them killed and wounded. Our regt went in with 175 men and lost our colonel and 9 men killed. [The] major, 3 Lts., and 37 men [were] wounded. I have been in command of the regt since the fight, and have but 1 captain and 4 Lts. left in the regt to assist me, so that I am kept as busy as I can be and have scarcely time to think of anything else.

Gen. Warren and Gen. Griffin both seem to be proud of our brigade, and of the part we took in the battle. I had the honor to be personally thanked by Gen Griffin for my conduct, and I know that I never saw so brilliant a charge in all the war before as we made upon those rebel works, and drove from them, more than our own number. Had we had the 2nd Corps with us instead of the 9th, we could have gained the southside railroad, but we did not and so we have the task yet to do. And I cannot say I am very anxious to push ahead with such men as the 9th Corps with us. Our men all hate them about as much as the rebels.

Speaking of George Cassman, he is here with the regt and well. You must excuse poor writing and haste in this letter. Please give my regards to Rev. Duffield, Dr. S.P. Duffield, and all enquiring friends and hoping to hear from you again soon,

> I Remain
> Respectfully Your Friend
> C.H. Salter

GRANT'S MOVEMENTS SOUTH OF THE JAMES—BATTLE OF POPLAR SPRING
CHURCH—GALLANT CHARGE OF A PART OF THE FIFTH CORPS
ON THE CONFEDERATE FORT, SEPTEMBER 30, 1864
(FRANK LESLIE'S ILLUSTRATED HISTORY OF THE CIVIL WAR, NEW YORK, 1895)

Head Quarters 16th Mich Infy Vet Vols
Near Poplar Church, Va. Oct 15th 1864

My Dear Friend

Your kind letter of the 2nd and 9th insts have been received, the latter arriving only this morning, and as I am not quite so busy today as I have been on any other day since taking command of the regt, I will endeavor to write you a few lines.

I wrote you a letter on the 5th inst, which I hope you have received, and were able to read also, for I wrote in such a hurry then, I am afraid it was a miserable looking letter, but, as it was just after the battle, it was about as well as I could do under the circumstances.

Since then, we have occupied the same camp we did, and although we had no idea of remaining this long when we first came here, yet everything has been very quiet along our portion of the line. Our corps now occupies a line of about 3 miles in length, and extends to about 2½ miles west of the Weldon R.R. We have strong lines of breastworks along our front and have thrown up four more forts already, one of which is on the line of our brigade, and we are at work upon it now, and so we always do as soon as we get possession of new ground, fortify it, make it almost impregnable and then move on to take new ground. Our position is already very strong and soon we will have it so that a small force can hold it, and we will then be ready for a movement towards the Southside Railroad, which is but about 2½ or 3 miles out in front of our works, from which they shelled us the first few days we came here. But now our works are so formidable, they keep very quiet, not wishing, I suppose, to stir up our artillerists any more than necessary.

The 9th Corps is on our left flank, their line forming nearly a right angle with ours, and so protecting our left flank. Being over in the 9th Corps the other day, I was talking of Gen. Parke to Col. March of the 12th Michigan, who said that there was no confidence felt in him amongst the Michigan regiments in the corps, and that they were very anxious Gen. Burnside should come back to them. They say that Gen. Wilcox would handle the corps much better if he had command of it, but being only a division general, he has to obey Gen. Parke's orders.

Yesterday morning we received orders to be ready to march at a moments notice, as the rebel cavalry were expected to make a dash into our rear, but so far we have not seen anything of them.

On our extreme right, north of the James River, our 10th and 18th Corps had some severe fighting about a week ago, and like us gained a few miles more of ground, but now everything appears very quiet again, and I do not expect we shall have any more battles for several days unless the enemy attack us. Sheridan is doing well in the Valley, his last victory being gained by the cavalry under Generals Merrill and Custer. The latter is winning a glorious name for himself, and if his life is spared, will probably soon be rewarded by a Major General's command, and Michigan may well be proud of his record.*

I see in the papers Gen. Sherman's report of his operations during the summer's campaign. It is a splendid record for his army, and is worth a great deal to make up the history of the war. From the news we receive, I should judge that the rebels were making desperate efforts to cut off his communication, but I think if Hood ventures to place his army in [the] rear of Sherman, that it will suit the latter better than anything else.

Since I took command of this regt, I have been extremely busy in making out reports for the last quarter, of the battle, &c, for the different departments, and as when I came here, it was the first time I had been at the regt hd qrs. The colonel being killed, major away wounded, and the adjt away sick, it seemed at first a Herculean task, but calling the assistance of the quartermaster, Lt. Powers, a very able officer to act as adjt, we worked both day and night untill we got everything in order, and now we are getting along very well. I received some communications the other day making the following promotions in our regt: Lt. Powers and Belchers to be captains; and, 2nd Lt Beard to be 1st, and Sergt James L. Laird to be 2nd Lt. The first is acting adjt, the next is on the brigade staff and

---

*George A. Custer, born in New Rumley, Ohio, married Elizabeth Bacon, the daughter of a prominent Monroe, Michigan, judge. Custer led the Michigan Cavalry Brigade, consisting of the 1st, 5th, 6th, and 7th Michigan Cavalry Regiments from 1863 to 1865.

will succeed me as brigade inspector, the next was wounded in the recent battle, and the last is a very smart young man, who ought to have been promoted long ago. I have sent on to our major, recommendations for 2 first Lts to be captains, and all the 2nd Lts to be 1sts, and all the 1st Sergts to be 2nd Lts and so we shall likely soon have a large number of promotions in our regt. But for my part, although I am in command of the regt, there is another captain absent wounded, who outranks me, and so if I do not get promoted to be major right away, I shall not complain. Yet if any other than that one should be promoted over me, it would take me only about 30 minutes to make out my muster out papers, take them to the division mustering officer, and be made a citizen, and call on the 2nd relief to take my place. Having served my three years out now, I am as likely to muster out at any time I please, therefore, my remaining here now is entirely voluntary. Yet the way our regt is now situated, I feel it my duty to remain and take care of it as long as it has so few officers as at present. Our regt, being so small we can only have a lt. col. and major for field officers, as it requires 780 men to muster a colonel, therefore, unless the Governor sends us some drafted men or recruits to fill up, we cannot have a full colonel.

Our major will doubtless be promoted to be lt. col., and who will be major remains to be seen. Captain Fuller of our regt mustered out on Sept 7th, and went to Washington, was going to work for the government as conductor on the military railroad (the Orange and Alexandria road), and yesterday we saw in the papers he had been murdered by guerillas whilst running a train in [the] vicinity of Manassas. The old officers of the 16th seem to be very unlucky, and to be stepping off every few days. The Major, Capt Hill (absent wounded), and myself are the only old officers now left with the regt, either present or absent.

The draft in Michigan afforded us much amusement here in reading the names of those who had drawn prizes! One young man, who has been writing to me ever since I have been a soldier, (figuratively patting on the back and saying good fellow, pitch in), has now been drafted and has what I should term a call to serve his country, in propria persona.

The 300 cavalry who guarded those cattle captured by the enemy, were also captured with the cattle, and nothing has been heard of them since.

I presume you will be very glad to see Henry home, as you say he is soon coming, but I am afraid it is a difficult matter now to go from Atlanta up to Nashville at present. I am greatly obliged to Mr. D.B.D. for the Tribune he sent. It was the first I had heard or seen of the piece about the 16th, and I was considerably surprised, as I have always avoided newspaper notoriety, when I could. But, come to find out it was Captain Powers of our regt who wrote it. He was, at the time, acting quartermaster, and so not with the regt, therefore, did not do full justice to our last engagement that day, when we repulsed Hill's Corps. But he gave me more praise than I deserve, for I did nothing but my duty.

The papers misprint and say Captain H. when it should have been Captain S, there being no Captain H in the regt. George Cassman was much pleased to get the paper, and wishes to be remembered to Mr. D. The Sergt. Tyrell wounded in our regt is not the one whom you have heard me speak of, but another and although not a Christian, a very brave and good young man. The Sergt Tyrell I have spoken of is here, and well as usual. The poetry you sent me is very beautiful, and I am obliged for it. But I must now close, having already written a long letter. Please give my kind regards to all friends. And hoping to hear from you again soon, I remain,

Respectfully Your Friend
Charles H. Salter

Head Quarters 1st Brig 2nd Cav Div
October 17th 1864

Dear Mother

It is some time since I have had a chance to send a letter home & perhaps you would like to know where I am & what I am about. As far as the first, I am in an ambulance, laying flat on my stomach writing this letter. Said ambulance is at the foot of the mountains known as Taylor's Ridge, 20 miles from Rome & about 55 miles from Chattanooga. As to what we are doing, it is more than I am able to say but if you would like to know what we have been doing, I am just the person to tell you.

Saturday Oct 1st. I left the command at Vining's Station & went to Atlanta with our sick where we laid over night. The next morning we moved back as far as the river & found the bridges had both been washed away. We laid over night until the next morning, when we came to where they [the regiment] were. They were not there, as they had just gone out on a scout, so we staid with the train which was ordered to Marietta. The next morning when we arrived there, we found every body excited & half scared to death for the news had reached them that the whole rebel army was in our rear & had cut off our <u>cracker line</u> & was about to take us all in out of the wet which was considered as quite a joak by the army. But <u>stragglers</u> considered it as any thing but a joak, but one they could see was being put upon half rations, for such was Sherman's order & that sent a great many of them back to their commands.

This night (4th), we laid in line of battle at the foot of the Kenesaw Mt. The next morning we moved out 7 miles to the main road on which the whole rebel army, 40,000 strong, had passed to our rear. Here we skirmished with the rebel cavalry or rear guard. We laid there all the next day. I took this opportunity of examining the ground fought over by the 21st Corps (Hooker), when the rebels charged his works that you may know how very heavy the firing must have been. The trees for a full half mile in front of our rifle pits were killed by the bullets, I never saw trees full a foot in diameter that had been cut completely off with a shell & while falling was cut in 3 pieces by two other shots & shell.

Friday Oct 7th. We moved to New Hope Church, a place about 15 miles from our other camp & 2 miles from Dallas. Here we remained until the 10th, when we received orders to go to Rome without delay. We went as far as Stylesboro, when we stopped to get supper. We moved on again at midnight & arrived at Rome at 5 o'clock the next morning, (11th), making a trip of 411 miles. The next morning, we passed through Rome & across the Ostanurda River, finding a force of rebels about 2 miles from town. We pitched into them & drove them about 4 miles where they took position behind strong works & opened on us with artillery. We drew back & went into camp for the night [as] we had no artillery along.

The next morning we moved out, supported by the 23rd Corps. Moving out, we found the rebs formed outside of their works with their artillery in full sight. This was enough [and] our brigade was ordered to charge & away they went, down the road like mad men. Before the rebs could form behind their works, our fellows was upon them & scattered them like sheep. We drove them 10 miles & at last accounts, they were still going. We lost but 5 men in the brigade & took 150 prisoners, killed about 211 & captured both pieces of artillery. The boys were in the best of spirits, for it was the first time they have fought in their favorite manner (a charge), for a long time, for lately we have been dismounted when there was any fighting to do. The brigade was highly complimented for the days' work. The rebel force was 2,000; our brigade numbers somewhere in the neighborhood of 500 <u>Mounted Men</u>.

Friday Oct 14th. Crossed the river & going through Rome; started out on the Knicton Road but left the main road, going to the left of it; moved 21 miles & went into camp. Next morning, moved forward in the direction of Resaca; after moving 21 miles, went into camp 4 miles from this place. All the time we were guarding the wagon train of the army, rumor said to Chattanooga. At all events, when we reached Snake Creek Gap this noon, we received news that the rebs had left for parts unknown & we started off at once for this place. I presume Kilpatrick, on the other side of the wagon train, has done the same thing. We are probably trying to find out where the rascals have gone to but I must stop as it is getting very late. We will probably go to Rome tomorrow. We leave here at half past 6 a.m. If we get to Rome, I will mail this to you then. Good Night.

Your Affec Son
Jimmie

I received letters from George, Nettie, Willie & Ike, all in a heap a few days ago. Also 6 papers with the list of drafted in them. That chain is a fine one & every body that looks at it says so & will not believe that it is home made. In those drafted lists, I found only 32 that I knew. How many will come down here, do you suppose? Jim

Oct 22nd. I have not had a chance to mail this until today. We are sending our wounded from yesterdays' fight to Rome & I will send this with them. The rebels are about played out. We have a rub with their rear guard most every afternoon. We are now about 35 miles from Rome & in Alabama. This road we are on comes from Rome through Summerville to this place & on to Ashville, which is 45 miles from here. But as the ambulances are starting I will stop. Jim

Head Quarters 16th Mich Infy Vet Vols
Near Poplar Grove, Va. Oct 23rd 1864

My Dear Friend

Your kind letter of the 16th inst arrived in due time and I will improve this Sabbath by writing you a few lines. I was sorry to hear you were suffering from a rheumatic attack again, and hope it is over by this time. Speaking of that picture in Harpers [Weekly] of Col. Welch jumping over the works, it is not correct at all, as he never got over the works but was shot whilst on top of them. You would have seen in Frank Leslies of that same date, a picture of our charge as correct as anything possibly could be, where Col. Welch being shot, is falling over backward, and Captain S is by his side, the men rapidly getting over.

By the way, I wrote a letter to your son, D. Bethune, today requesting his assistance in getting promotion in my regt. Lt. Kilets, who is now at home, is figuring for it, and trying to get the Majority of the regt away from me. I wrote a full account of it to Mr. D, giving him the history of this man since he entered our regt, and it is not a very creditable history, I can assure you. As our regt now stands, I am the second captain on the rolls. The first captain is away wounded, intends to leave the service, and I hear has sold out his interest to Lt. Kilets in it. I have been in command of the regt ever since the battle, and the regt here all expect that I am to be promoted to be Major. I think that I have fairly earned it, and therefore do not wish to be disgraced by having a Lieut placed over me, simply because he is a favorite of the powers that be. There are now eight captains in our regt, each one of whom I regard as being much fitter for the position than this man, and certainly much better entitled to it. The regt has not heard of it yet, but if he is made Major, and comes here to take command, I would not give much for the discipline of the regt, for every man in it, thoroughly despises him. And for my part, I shall not put up with any such outrage, but muster out and go home, sooner than put up with the insult.

I did not know anything about what was going on untill last Friday, when my orderly sergt returned from Detroit, and informed me of it. This is the young man I wrote you about who was wounded in the Wilderness and has been home this summer. I expect a commission will be on here for him very soon, as 1st Lieut. I have sent on for it. The commission for company officers are sent on by the governor on recommendation of the commanding officer of the regt, but the commissions for field officers are not. The governor reserves the right to make those promotions himself, and that is the reason I have wrote to Mr. D about it and requested him to see the Governor, as the Governor can give me the commission of Major if he wishes, even if the commanding officer of my regt does not recommend me. For this reason, I wish you would speak to Mr. D, and urge him, if he can do so consistently, to use his political influence in my favor, as I am willing and anxious to fight for my country, as long as my services are needed. But I do not believe in allowing myself to be imposed upon, whilst so doing.

Speaking of the battles that returned soldiers had been in, it is a strange coincidence I have been in just the same number, viz, thirty-two; therefore, I think he too must have been in this army, and been out in the service ever since the commencement of the war as I have.

We are expecting here very shortly to make another advance movement, to gain possession of the Southside railroad this time, and then we shall doubtless have a terrible hard battle, for the rebels are in strong force out in front of us and will fight desperate for the possession of that road. They have strong works there also, but if we could only gain possession of that road we could afford to go into our winter quarters. And in possession of the Weldon Railroad and Southside also, the rebels could not supply their troops in Richmond with supplies all winter, and would, in consequence, be obliged to evacuate the place before spring. I hope, and pray, that if we advance again, the 9th Corps will do better than they did last time, as our brigade is on the left of our corps, and right of the 9th and would have to bear the brunt of the battle (as we did last time), if they should run again.

But I must now close. Please give my regards to Rev. Dr. Duffield, Dr. S.P. to Henry and all friends and hoping to hear from you again soon, I remain,

Respectfully Your Friend
Chas. H. Salter

Hd Qrs 1st Brig 2nd Cav Div
October 25 1864

Dear Brother

That chain is a beauty & every body says so that sees it. You did right in not trying to get it mounted cheaper, for looks is what I was after & not the expense. By the way, you did not say what it cost to have it mounted. How much was it?

I have not received any letters since I got yours & that was about 2 weeks ago. Then we received all our back mail & my share was letters from Ike, Willie, Nettie & you & 6 papers, in which I found 32 that I know that was among the drafted. How are you conscripts? I wonder how many will come down here. I understand that subs bring pretty high figures in Detroit. Have you found out whether you are drafted yet or not?

Perhaps you would like to know where we are—what we have been doing for the last 24 days. We have been continually on the move after the rebel army, which is said to have been in our rear, trying to cut off our cracker line, but I imagine they have found it more of a job than they took it to be, for as fast as they tore up the rails, they were driven off & the road fixed almost before they are out of sight. If it was their intention to starve us out, they came a little too late, for we have about 40 days rations on hand when they started & were informed of their movements 2 days before they struck our railroad. Since that time, the cavalry have been in pursuit of them & have succeeded in picking up 5 fights with them, mostly with Wheeler's Cavalry, acting as rear guard for the retreating rebels.

In one of these fights, our brigade made 4 successful charges, driving the rebels about 10 miles, when they received reinforcements from their infantry. During those charges, we captured 2 pieces of artillery & about 200 prisoners; our loss being 1 killed & 5 wounded. We have since we started after these fellows marched 287 miles, making an average of 12½ miles a day. Last year, during the Wheeler raid, we averaged 10 miles a day.

We are (that is our brigade, the rest of the division were sent off at 3 o'clock this morning on a scout), camped on the side of the Little River in Alabama, about 8 miles from Gaylesville & by the side of the Lookout Mountain. We came here last night & expected to go away this morning. We came from a gap in these mountains about 10 miles below here. When we found the rebels in a strong position with infantry & artillery, & as we have no infantry support & no artillery, we fell back & came to this place. A corps of infantry moved up to take our position & we, I suppose, are to cross the _____ & give him a touch in the rear. That is where the rest of the division has gone, I think, & I should not wonder if we should go after them before night, for it is some thing uncommon for us to lay still for 24 hours.

We are having very pleasant weather to travel in but the nights are awful cold. It takes 3 blankets to keep a fellow warm & that is altogether to many for this time of the year, don't you think so? But you don't take your rest out in the open air &, of course, don't notice the cold. If you did, you would say that we might congratulate ourselves that it did not rain. Well, we do, cold before wet, anyway.

I don't expect to hear from home as often now as I did while you were there. I think some of them might write once a week at least, if they would only try a little.

But I must stop for I want to write a letter to Ike. No knowing when I shall have another chance to write or when I shall be able to send this off, unless I can find some one who is going to Rome & send it by him. Our regiment is on courier duty between here & Rome, or at least between the army & it.

> Good bye. Write often to
> Your Affec Bro
> Jim

Head Quarters 16th Mich Infy Vet Vols
Near Poplar Grove, Va. Nov 6th 1864

Dear Friend

Your kind letter of the 29th inst has been received and I am very glad to hear from you once more, and to hear that you are gladdened by having Henry at home after his long absence. But to judge from what you write, I should think there was some idea of his going back again. I hope if he does go back, he will go in a higher position than the one he has occupied for the last three years, for I believe he is deserving of promotion if anyone is.

Since I wrote you last, we have had a movement, as I suppose you are aware. We left camp before daylight on the 27th, and our corps moved about 3 miles to the left from the position of the 9th Corps; the 9th Corps filled in the interval between us and our works here, whilst the divisions of the 2nd Corps advanced still farther to the left from us. We skirmished with the enemy all day long, and took up our position quite close to their works there that guard the Southside railroad, untill towards night, when the 2nd Corps received orders to fall back. And in so doing, the enemy attacked them and nearly surrounded one division, but our troops made a charge and cut their way out. Although our loss was quite heavy at that point, we took 900 prisoners. When that division of the 2nd Corps cut their way out, our corps remained there untill next morning, when we also received orders to fall back. But our brigade was to cover the retreat, and was deployed as skirmishers on the front line and remained there untill noon, when as all of our corps had gone back, we fell back slowly. The enemy's cavalry followed us close enough to watch us, but did not come close enough to engage us, and about 4 P.M., we arrived back in our old camp. And so ended the greatest reconnaissance our army ever saw.

We expected as much as could be, when we started that we would attempt to take the Southside road, and we never expected to return to our old camps again, but such seems not to have been the intention of Gen. Grant. Since then, we have been at work putting up winter quarters, and in a few days our regt will have quarters good enough to live in all winter, the regt hd qrs excepted; we have been waiting untill the men should get theirs completed.

The commission from the State of Michigan to take the votes of the 1st and 16th Michigan arrived here last Wednesday, and has been staying with me, and we are busily engaged in making preparations for the election, which is coming off this next Tuesday. Our regt, as you are probably aware, came out as a democratic regt, so called, but I am morally certain that in this election, we will cast a good big majority for Lincoln and Johnson. All the officers in the regt but two go in for the union side, and one of them has already sent in his resignation, on the ground of incompetency to command a company. I forwarded it, approved and recommended for the good of the service.

I received a letter from your son Bethune, who told me he had seen Adjt Gen Robertson, who assured him, Capt. Hill had been promoted to be Major, on the ground of seniority. I had not heard Capt. Hill was to be Major, but knew that Lieut. Kilets, our acting adjt, was figuring to get it, and it was to prevent him from being promoted over me that I wrote to Mr. Duffield. Had I known or supposed Capt. Hill was to be promoted, I should not have said a word, for Hill is a good officer, one who outranks me, and being the senior captain, is entitled to the promotion. But I expect that Major Hill is soon to be transferred to the Invalid Corps, as he is disabled from a wound received last June, and cannot be fit for field service again. Then the question of the Majority will occur again, and as I am now the senior captain, I look upon it as belonging to me. And I expect this man Kilets will try to get it when the opportunity occurs. But, I shall now wait patiently and see what is going to be done. I wrote to Mr. Duffield telling him all about Kilets, who he was, &c.

I am under many obligations to you for your kindness in this matter, and the interest you have taken in my affairs. I did not expect you would write to Col. Partridge about it, yet am just as much obliged to you for so doing. I shall write again to D. Bethune in a few days, as soon as election is over. Remember me to Rev. Dr. Duffield, and all enquiring friends, and please tell Henry I should like very much to hear from him. And hoping to hear from you again soon,

> I Remain,
> Respectfully Your Friend
> Charles H. Salter

Head Quarters 16th Mich Infy
Near Poplar Grove Church, Va. Nov 20th 1864

My Dear Friend

Your kind letter of the 8th inst arrived in due time, and I take the first opportunity I have had this week of writing, to drop you a few lines.

We are yet in the same camp we were when I wrote you two weeks ago today, and nothing unusual has occurred with us. Our election took place just the same as they are carried on at home, with the difference that here we had no noise, entertainment or confusion, such as is usual in civil life. Our regt, I am sorry to say, gave their majority for McClellan, the vote standing 78 for Lincoln to 81 for McClellan. The First Mich. gave a majority of 9 to McClellan also, but all the other Mich. Regts. in our army gave large majorities for Lincoln, and in fact, ours are the only two regts I have heard of yet as giving majorities for McClellan.

There were many reasons for this vote in our regt, but the principal one is that two officers of the regt worked as hard as they could to get the men to vote for McC., and did influence a great many of them in that way. They were not fighting officers, but were a captain on the brigade staff, and our quartermaster, men who never go near the field of battle, and it was all that class of men, who are not with the regt, that carried it for the Copperheads. We had some 20 men detailed in a regular battery who came over and voted in a body for McC., as also did all our men detailed at brigade head quarters, in the wagon trains, &c. I felt mortified to think that the old regt, after fighting the rebels for three years, should then vote for the northern friends of rebellion, but it cannot be helped now.

I have been busy this past week in building a house for my winter quarters, and only got it finished to move into last night. The size of the building is 16 ft. long by 12 wide, and built up with log sides 6 ft. high and a canvas roof; planks hewn out of logs for a floor, and boards from the house of Col. Pegram of the rebel army for tables, chairs, and shelves. I have a good brick fire place, and if we remain here all winter, shall be very comfortable, but it is yet uncertain about our winter quarters, as we hear Butler's canal is now finished. And yesterday, portions of the 2nd and 9th Corps moved off in that direction, and we are expecting soon to hear of heavy fighting there, although the weather has been very unfavorable. For the last two days, we have had a heavy rain storm, and the roads are getting very bad. If it had been good weather this last week, we very likely should have moved before this.

Our division had orders to have a review tomorrow at 2 in the afternoon. But I am afraid if this rain storm continues, we cannot have it. I am glad to hear that the loyal states went so nearly unanimous for old Abe, it was even better than any of us here expected. Only Kentucky, New Jersey and Delaware left out in the cold.

I should think Henry would find it very dull business in the law study after having been in the army so long. It sometimes seems to me that I never could settle down into civil life again, after the exciting life I have had for the last three years. I deposited my second vote for old Abe, this election, as I am proud to say I voted for him the first time also in 1860.

Our division Gen. (Griffin) has just been promoted to be Brevet Major General, which is a very justly deserved promotion, as he has commanded our division now for over two years, and is a brave man as well as a skillful general. Our brigade commander, Gen. Bartel is also one of the oldest brigadier generals in the service and we look for him to be promoted soon.

But I must now close, as it is time for the mail to leave. Please remember me to Rev. Dr. Duffield, Henry and all enquiring friends. And hoping to hear from you again soon, I Remain,

Respectfully Your Friend
C.H. Salter

Hd Qrs 4th Mich Cav
Louisville, Ky.
November 23rd 1864

Dear Father

Your very welcome letter came to hand some time ago but owing to my new position, I have been unable to answer it. The fact is, I find I need quite a little touching up to be able to perform the duties of my new office. But I flatter myself that I am doing as well as any of the new beginners & better than some of them. That, however, is only my own opinion of the matter.

We have to get up at 5 o'clock & the officers are then drilled by the colonel for about an hour. Then we take breakfast & at 9 o'clock, take the men out & drill them until 11 o'clock. At 12 comes dinner & then 2 hours more drill. You see we do not lack for exercise. We have quite enough of it & some think too much.

I was officer of the day yesterday & was very highly complimented for the improved looks of the camp. I had a force of 60 men at work on the grounds all the morning & it made quite a difference.

The officers have most of them (the married ones, of course) sent for their wives & we expect to have a merry time if we are allowed to stay here a week or two. Lt. Mackey's wife is here now. She is a Detroit girl. Charlie will remember her [as] Miss Gowdy. By the way, tell Charlie that I have received notice that Miss Buckley is living about a mile from here with an aunt. She sent word by Doc that she would be very happy to see Mr. Vernor but I have been so busy that I could not call yet but will soon. I want some new clothes first & as we expect to be paid in a few days, day after tomorrow, I believe, I think I will postpone my call till afterward.

We have not been paid since Oct 31st, [18]63, just one year & we begin to feel the want of some money but have made up our minds to grin & bear it until pay day. I have the advantage of most of them, having on hand most of the necessary articles & therefore am not forced to patronize the sutlers, who just at this time are making money fast; only $8.00 for a shirt & $5.00 for a pair of gloves, other things in proportion. The more necessary they are, the higher the price, of course. We are living first rate just now & will live better after a day or two. How I wish some one of you could come down & pay me a visit. It is rather cold but I can give you good quarters in a tent if you will come or any one else. Now is your time to see camp life; only two days travel to get here.

The Ladies of Louisville have made arrangements to give us a Thanksgiving Dinner tomorrow but I have not heard how it will be done, whether we will be marched to town or they will bring it out here. But I must stop.

Give my love to all the folks & write as often as possible to

Your Affec Son
Jimmie

Hd Qrs 4th Mich Cav
Louisville, Ky.
Sunday November 27th 1864

Dear Mother

I was astonished when I opened your letter to find that you did not know where I was. I don't think it can be my fault for I have written home quite often, I think & I was quite sure that I kept you posted at home as well, if not better, than I did George; but perhaps he gets letters oftener & I am quite sure he does than any other of my correspondents, for the simple reason that I make it a point to answer letters the first chance I get after I receive them & if he gets more answers than any one else, there is a good reason for it. He writes oftener, I presume, since he left Detroit. I have not received as many letters from there as usual & I am sure there are lots there that might write, if they only would think so.

I have not had one of Libbie's good letters since I can recollect. I used to rely on them for the Detroit news entirely, but now I have to get what I can from the papers, that thanks to Jerry, come quite often. As for Fannie, I have come to the conclusion that she has quit entirely. The only thing I can hear from Charlie is that men returning from furlough come in & tell me that they met a brother of mine in the Q.M. Dept. & that he told them to tell me that he was well. That is all very well, as far as it goes. I am always glad to hear that he is well but why don't he write & tell me what is going on as he used to when I first came out. I hope he don't think I have been so long from "D," that I have forgotten every body I ever knew there. The fact is I asked to come back there one of these days, say in about 9 months from now & I want to keep as well posted as possible. I shall be far enough behind the age any how.

You ask "when will you come home." I mustered for the unexpired term of the regiment, which will be the 28th day of August, 1865, just 9 months from tomorrow, to a day. We were allowed to do so by reason of an order stating that officers mustering in regiments that had more than six months to serve could muster for the unexpired term of the regt, or for 3 years, as they chose & I, of course, took advantage of that order & so will be enabled to get out of the service with what is left of the men I came in with.

We are having very nice times here. Last night I made a call on Mrs. Clark & while there, our band came over & gave us a serenade. After they played several pieces, they proposed that we should all get ready & go over & call on Mrs. Eldridge (Capt E's wife), so we went, six couples in all & gave them quite a surprise. From there, the band went up to where Dr. Armstrong & wife are stopping but as it was late, we did not go with them. We are expecting to have a lively time while we stop here. There is some talk of getting up a few dancing parties at the different homes. If they do, I will be just in town, won't I?

But I must stop. Give my love to all from
Your Affec Son
Jimmie

P.S. Dr. Armstrong wishes to be remembered to you. Jim

Head Quarters 16th Mich Infty
Near Poplar Grove Church, Va.
Dec 4th 1864

My Dear Friend

Your kind letter of the 20th arrived in due time, and the morning being Sabbath, I will take the opportunity to write you a few lines. Since my last letter was wrote, we have been kept very busily engaged in drilling, and Sunday is the only day that I have any leisure time to myself.

We yet remain in the same camp we were in, and have all our quarters now completed, all comfortable, and good enough to live in all winter in case we should be allowed to remain.

The Inspector General of the Army made a general tour of inspection throughout the 2nd, 5th & 9th Corps, and paid particular attention to our camp, and reported it as the best arranged camp in the army, and our quarters as the best of any in all the camps he had inspected, and noted the fact that the commanding officer of said regt was only a captain, whilst the other 7 regts of the same brigade, all commanded by field officers, could not show camps to compare with ours.

Our men's tents are all sided up with logs 5 feet high, and are 12 feet long by 6 wide, with a good fire place in each tent, where they do their own cooking, and in the tents, usually three, but not more than 4 men are quartered. The company streets are all graded, and constantly kept clean. Each street has a row of evergreen trees set out on each side of it. Then the companies have each a cook house of the same size as the men's tents. And the company officers have large, comfortable quarters, and our regt hd qrs is as good as they have at either Brigade or Division hd qrs. Then, out in front of the camp, we have a strong earthwork, where in case of an alarm, either day or night, the regt quickly falls in, each company in its place.

We have [heard] however, rumors of an intended move by our army this week as it is expected, that the enemy has sent a portion of his army down to Georgia to meet Sherman. In fact, it is certain that they have sent Hampton's division of cavalry there, for it had usually been kept on the rebel right, or our left, and the last week Gregg's division of cavalry went down the Weldon road 20 miles, destroyed the track for that distance, and done a vast amount of damage to the country but saw nothing of Hampton's cavalry. We fear more damage will be done to Sherman's army, by this division of cavalry than twice the number from Hood's army could do, for they are the best troops, without exception, that the rebels have.

We are very anxious to hear from Sherman, but can get very little news from his army. News from Gen. Thomas' army is encouraging. It seems he is enough for Hood.

This last week we had a review of our brigade by Gen. Griffin, our division commander. Our eight regts number from 150 men to 400 each only, and there were about 2,000 men out of the review. Our 1st & 2nd Brigades are each composed of two new regts only, but have the same number of men. That shows a great contrast between new regts and those composed only of veterans. We are to have a review of our division this week if we do not move.

I am very busy putting my regiment through a regular course of drill, the old officers having nearly all left the regt and the present officers being nearly all new ones; it is much harder for me than it would be otherwise, but we are getting along very well.

I am having a chapel built for the use of the regt and have it now nearly completed. It is built in our usual manner of logs, and a canvas roof. [It] has a fire place and we are going to make a floor and seats in it this week. It is 24 feet long by 16 wide, and is about large enough for our small regt.

Since I have been in command of the regt, some member of the Christian Commission has come up and addressed us each Sunday by my request. And I try to do everything I can to induce the men to keep a proper observance of the Sabbath, which is something new to our regt. Please remember me to Rev. Dr. Duffield, Henry and all enquiring friends. And, hoping to hear from you again soon, I remain,

> Respectfully Your Friend
> C.H. Salter

Hd Qrs 4th Mich Cav
Louisville, Ky. Dec 11th 1864

Dear Brother

I sent word by Jerry to tell you that I would take back all I wrote in my last letter as far as it concerned you, for the sight of your letter was enough to do the job. It seemed quite like old times to hear what is going on in Detroit. You said the club members were to have a pin & promised me a description of it when you got one. Have you got it yet? If you want to see a real fine one, you must go to Morrison & Conklin & look at those they are getting up for us, if they have not sent them on yet. Jerry saw one when he was here. The Col. wore it.

Those Segars are prime, in the opinion of both the QM (Perry Davie) & myself. I could not make him believe that he was to have only one, however, & he is of the opinion that all the trouble he has with the QM Dept after he is out of the service, will not amount to much. But I suppose that is the way with all new QMs. They think they can see their way clear through. Perhaps he will think different in the course of a year or so.

I suppose you have heard that we have been pressing horses here in Louisville. You ought to have been here to see the fun.

Wednesday night we received orders to be ready to move with rations for 36 hours at 4 the next morning, where to or what for was more than any one could find out, so all we could do was to get ready & trust to luck for the rest. At 4, we started & went toward the city. When we arrived at Broadway, one battalion went to the right, another to the left & the other (mine) straight down to the river & in a very short time, we had all Louisville surrounded. We formed a line of picket all the way around it & when the citizens woke up, they found themselves taken in & about to be done for. About 8 o'clock, the work commenced. The dismounted men of our brigade & the 1st Brigade proceeded down town & began to pick up the horses with which the streets were lined—of course there was a rush to get out of town but what was their surprise when they thought they were safe outside of the city, when they were ordered to halt! We were not allowed to take any horses ourselves but we kept them from running off & the men that were on that duty did the taking part. We got about 2,000 the first day & such forlorn looking streets I never saw. The boys were not inclined to show much mercy on the hacks, I can assure you & the streets were full of all sorts of conveyances, from drays to private carriages.

I was on picket at the Portland Ferry & used the ferry house for horses. I had plenty of sport with men who thought it would be a nice thing to run their fine horses across the river but they changed their minds for some reason or other when they came to go on the boat.

It was late last night when we were ordered back to count & we did not get in until most midnight. It snowed quite nice last evening & we passed several sleighs on our way to camp. The snow was only about 3 inches deep but here they have to make the most of what little they get.

Blind horses & mules (or as Jerry called them, Jackasses), are in great demand to day.

There is no order for us to move yet. The order for this impressments of horses came direct from the War Dept. at Washington to us.

We are trying to get up a small dance here among the officers who have wives & those who are acquainted with young ladies in the neighborhood. I don't know how we will make out. I come in on both or either. Think of me occasionally when you are keeping time to the violin &c

Write soon and often to
Your Affec Brother
Jim

The brother of Lt. Backus was here for a couple of days but I was on picket & did not get a chance to see him. He started for home this morning. You know him, I think, don't you?

Put these photos with my collection.

Good night
Jim

Head Quarter 16th Mich Inf V V
December 13th 1864

My Dear Friend

Yours of the 4th inst has just been received and I learn with regret of the severe illness of Mr. D. Duffield, and hope it may not prove fatal, and hope to hear soon that he has entirely recovered.

Since I wrote you last our corps has, as you have probably heard ere this been down south on a grand raid, and has destroyed the Weldon road for about 50 miles south of Petersburg. We left our comfortable quarters near Poplar Grove Church on Tuesday, the 6th, and moved about 5 miles to east of the Weldon road, and bivouacked over night in a large open field where our corps was gathered together, and the next morning at daylight, we started, and marching nearly due south, halted at night about 2 miles from the Nottaway River, after marching 20 miles. Then at 2 next morning, we moved on and through Sussex Court House and then over to the railroad, arriving at near Jarrett's Station. We then worked untill 12 o'clock, tearing up and destroying the railroad track. And our division alone destroyed about 5 miles that evening, then the next day, we marched to within 2 miles of Hickford, a village near the North Carolina line, destroying the track as we went along, and bivouacked over night. We suffered some for about 36 hours from a cold hail and snow storm, but next morning the 10th, we started back. The roads were very muddy, and the weather cold and disagreeable.

We came back the same route we went down and arrived last night at our starting place, where we are now bivouacked in a wood about 4 miles south of our front line of works. We destroyed the railroad to a point said to be 60 miles from Petersburg, and left only a few miles of track uninjured in the vicinity of Stony Creek, a place about 15 miles or so from Petersburg. And the rebels cannot rebuild it again this winter, if they were left alone whilst doing it. We also left a track of fire on our return march by burning up nearly every house and barn on the route. In fact, we destroyed everything on our route through the country that could be of use to the rebels in any way, shape or manner.

The winter was cold and stormy and the march was a very hard one. We suffered considerable, in fact, we never were exposed to such hard weather before on any march. But now, we have come back. We are not to go into our old quarters, but are bivouacked in a wood, and are getting ready to go off on a march again. We do not know where to, however. It seems as if we were not to be allowed to go into winter quarters at all, but to keep up the campaign all winter. It seems hard, but I suppose we shall have to stand it as long as we can.

We were going to Weldon or Wilmington, and were glad of it, for we wanted to get to a warmer country than this, for we feel the cold as much here as if we were in Michigan, but we were doomed to disappointment in that we had besides our corps, the 3rd div. of the 2nd Corps along with us, but all the troops were under command of Gen. Warren, our corps general.

I hope this war will end soon. Excuse pencil writing and this dirty paper, but it was the best I could do at present. Remember me to all enquiring friends.

Respectfully
Your Friend
C.H. Salter

For Major Salter, the war ended a month later. This is his last letter to Mrs. Duffield. On January 15, 1864, he took his discharge near Petersburg, Virginia, and returned to Michigan. As was subsequently revealed in his pension application, Major Salter suffered a severe hernia in August 1862 on a forced march from Harrison's Landing, Virginia, to the Second Bull Run battlefield. He evidently served with this injury until his discharge.

Camp 4th Mich Cav
Near Gravelly Springs, Al.
Jan 29th 1865

Dear Mother

Here we are at our present journey's end after a march of 330 miles, executed in 29 days. Out of those, we laid over 4 days at Nashville & 3 at Columbia. We have traveled over some of the worst roads I ever saw & as for cold, I never suffered so much from it as I have on this march.

We are now fixing up winter quarters at this place. Most of our wall tents were lost coming down here by boat but Clark & I was lucky enough to get an old one & have fixed it up quite comfortable. It is reported that we will stay here several months, but I don't think we will.

We are camped on the top of a hill & a pretty high one too, I can tell you, near the Tennessee River, 2 miles from Gravelly Springs & 6 from Waterloo & in the northwest corner of Alabama. It is 10 miles from here to Eastport, Mississippi.

We are not living as well as we were when Jerry came to see us, for the simple reason that the whole army is out of rations & have been several days. Most of the officers acknowledge that this is a little the worst time they have seen for <u>grub</u>. The infantry at Eastport have been out of rations. This is the 7th day & for us it is the 4th. We are all living on horse food (corn). Yesterday, the Brigade Commissary sold to each officer 2 lbs of meal. The men had issued to them about 6oz per man; before that they had been living on whole corn, either boiled or parched. Some of the boys were lucky enough to forage quite a lot of meat the day before we came in here, but that is all gone now. We should not have it quite so bad if the orders were not quite so strict. But foraging under any circumstances is forbidden. If they would move us across the river & give us permission, we could soon get all the rations we needed but foraging is not known down there.

I was amused the day we came in here. Some of my boys came upon a wagon filled with meal & flour & if they did not make that wagon look sick, I am no judge. Come to find out the articles belonged to Gen'l Wilson & he had the whole command searched for the offenders. But it was a very unsuccessful one. He only recovered enough of his own supper out of the whole load. "Wilson Bread" was eaten by a good many hungry men that night.

We received a mail yesterday but [I] was not among the favored ones. It takes a little longer for our letters to come & go now as they have to go to Louisville, then down the Ohio & up the Tennessee River.

Things look to me as if we would not lay here long & I should not be surprised if we should be ordered off before we have lain here a month.

We count the days now, only 7 months—that is not long. Give my love to all & let me hear from home often in the next 7 months as possible.

Your Affec Son
Jimmie

Hd Qrs 4th Mich Cav
Chickasaw Bluffs, Ala.
Sunday March 19th 1865

Dear Father

It is some time since I have written to you & so I will do the best I can under the circumstances and give you my farewell letter before leaving this part of the country. I hope you will not think that I might have used ink but if the truth must be told, I don't feel competent to write a letter with ink tonight. It is so much easier to write with pencil.

We move from here at day light tomorrow morning. The train moved out this evening. There is 4 divisions going, all cavalry. 2 divisions move on the Cherokee Road & 2 on the next one to it. We take the Cherokee. We are to move (so it is said), to Montgomery. We are ordered to take 24lbs [of] corn for each horse to be used during the 1st 4 days & march, which will be through a very poor country. Orders say that we shall move rapidly & that the loads must be light as possible. All baggage has been sent to the rear. I kept my valise, however, contrary to orders but I guess I can get it along. I thought if I sent it home, I should never see it again until I went home & I have got nothing that I shall want then & I may as well be having the use of them while I need them as not.

I wrote a letter to Jerry day before yesterday but it got mislaid & I don't know whether it got into the mail sack or not.

We leave here with 10 days rations carried by the men. Besides that, we have in the wagons, 60 days rations of coffee & 30 of sugar and salt. Of course, it is the intention to take the rest from the country as we go along & if we don't know how to do that to perfection, no one does—there was some talk of our regiment being dismounted & left here, using the horses for other regiments, our time being so near out, but I am happy to say there is no truth in it, for I have always wanted to get further South than I have been & if I don't do it in the next <u>5 months</u>, I never shall, for a trip to this country is the last I should ever think of taking.

There is no telling when we shall get another chance to send or receive a mail but don't let that keep the folks from writing, for letters directed as usual will follow us to any place we may [go] to. I was in hopes of getting a letter or two from home before we left but we will not get another mail here unless some one is left behind to bring it up.

We are having beautiful weather and if it continues, we'll have a fine march of it. We will have about 20,000 men, about 2,000 of which is dismounted but have all the necessary equipments & it will not take long to mount them. After we get started, once on something we are not at all particular on what.

But I must stop & bid you good night, for a good night's rest is worth a considerable to a fellow who has to sit in the saddle all the next day.

Your Affec Son
Jimmie

This is James Vernor's last letter that is extant. He led his Company, "M," through several subsequent engagements, such as Selma and Montgomery and the Wilson raid ending at Macon, Georgia. He was discharged in July 1865 and returned to Detroit in time to celebrate the Fourth of July. In an interview much later in his life, he had this to relate about an incident near the end of the war:

"I was serving at that time, the Fall of 1865, as second lieutenant of the 4th Michigan Cavalry, the regiment, you know, that captured the president of the Southern Confederacy. We had reached Macon, Georgia, and one night I was sent out with a company to chase some guerillas who had captured three of our men. When we got back the next morning, we found that the rest of our regiment had been sent after Jefferson Davis. He was captured at Abbeyville, Georgia, as you know, and the way I got the souvenirs I now have at home was this;

"There was a man in our cavalry who had deserted from the Southern army and, knowing Jefferson Davis' horse, he captured it while our men were taking Davis. I was told afterwards there was $5,000 in gold in the holster (one account says ammunition horn), on the saddle, but when the man rode into our camp on this horse, the holster contained only some empty cartridge shells. It was not till later that I secured one of those gold pieces. I had to pay him $28 for a $20 piece.

One of the privates in my company has secured Jefferson Davis' dressing gown, but I succeeded in buying it from him for $15. It is one of those old fashioned, big-figured cashmere affairs, coming down below the knees."

There was a reward of $100,000 posted for the capture of Jefferson Davis and a commission appointed by the War Department decided that the 4th Michigan was entitled to the money. When the appropriation came before Congress, however, the 1st Wisconsin Cavalry made a claim to it as well, one which was upheld and the money was split between both regiments. The money was distributed in 1867. The 4th Michigan Cavalry gained a national reputation for the capture and is the regiment responsible for the capture of the Confederate president.

Afterword

At the conclusion of hostilities, only one of the four men whose words make up this book was still in uniform. James Vernor was discharged with his regiment upon its return to Detroit on July 10, 1865. The regiment was paid and then disbanded. There were a few people on hand to welcome them back; no doubt not as many as there were to send them off to war. Perhaps Charles Salter was one of the crowd of appreciative civilians there when they arrived.

George Vanderpool returned to Muskegon to recover his health. He married a girl from New York named Ellen and had at least two children, a daughter, Dora, and a son, Frederick. He went into banking with a partner, Herbert Field, in early 1869, establishing the firm Vanderpool & Field in Manistee, which is located about eighty miles north of Muskegon. The business flourished until September, when Field disappeared. After an extensive search, the body was found on the shore of Lake Michigan. Circumstantial evidence pointed to the remaining partner, and Vanderpool was subsequently arrested, tried, convicted, and sentenced to life imprisonment at Jackson, Michigan, after a sensational trial that put Manistee on the map.

Within a few months of serving his sentence, Vanderpool's lawyers and friends secured for him a new trial and venue and he was tried for a second time in Kalamazoo.

This time the result was a hung jury, standing seven to five for conviction. Yet a third trial was held at Hastings in Barry County; the jury returned a verdict of not guilty. By 1880, George Vanderpool was living in Tiffin, Ohio, with his family and working as a shoemaker. Sometime after that, he moved back to Fulton County, New York, where he lived until his death in 1924.

Charles Salter returned to Detroit to restart his career in the grocery business. Apparently his injuries did not keep him from leading a relatively normal life, as on September 17, 1867, he married Frances I. Hanscom in Romeo, Michigan. They had three children by 1880. His injuries did keep him from earning a living at his chosen profession and he applied for and received an invalid pension from the federal government. Charles died of apoplexy on March 23, 1892, at the age of 55 and is buried in Woodmere Cemetery in Detroit. His passing did not gain notice in the newspapers.

James Vernor returned to Detroit at war's end. He opened a drugstore in partnership with Charles L'Hommedieu at the corner of Woodward Avenue and Clifford Street. By 1870, he bought out his partner's interest and became the sole proprietor. He had been working on a formula for a new ginger ale before joining the army. In 1868 he began selling this concoction as a sideline to dispensing drugs and by 1870 it was becoming more of a full time job than the pharmaceuticals. The soft drink that bears his name (Vernors Ginger Ale) made his fortune.

James married Emily Walker Smith in 1873 and had a son, James II. Being a civic minded businessman, Vernor ran for and defeated the incumbent alderman of the second ward in Detroit in 1888, beginning a 36-year political career that included 24 years on the Common Council. James Vernor retired from public office in 1924 and died on October 29, 1927, at the age of 84.

Appendix

A Brief Chronology of Civil War Battles

——————————— 1861 ———————————

APRIL 12—Confederate forces at Charleston, South Carolina, open fire on Fort Sumter in the harbor. Garrison commander Major Robert Anderson, unable to reply effectively to the bombardment, surrendered the following day. Casualties: Union—1 killed, 3 wounded.

JULY 18—Battle at Blackburn's Ford. An attempt by the Union army to cross Bull Run was repulsed by Confederate forces; this result decides McDowell on the flanking maneuver he used at First Manassas. Casualties: Union—83; Confederate—68.

JULY 21—First Battle of Bull Run. First major land battle of the armies in Virginia; McDowell crossed at Sudley Ford and attacked the Confederate left flank; timely arrival of Rebel reinforcements saved the day. Casualties: Union—2,950; Confederate—1,750.

AUGUST 10—Battle of Wilson's Creek, Missouri. The Union Army of the West attacked Confederate troops on Wilson's Creek, 12 miles southwest of Springfield, and was forced to retreat with losses. The Confederate victory buoyed Southern sympathizers in Missouri. Casualties: Union—1,235; Confederate—1,095.

——————————— 1862 ———————————

FEBRUARY 6-16—Forts Henry and Donaldson. Combined army/navy assault and the first major action under U.S. Grant's command; the fall of the forts opened up the Tennessee River to Union transportation. These victories ensured that Kentucky would remain in the Union and opened Tennessee to Union advance. Casualties: Union—2,331; Confederate—15,067.

FEBRUARY 25—Union occupation of Nashville, the first state capitol to fall to Union forces.

MARCH 3-8—Battle of Pea Ridge, Arkansas. Confederates under Major General Earl Van Dorn attempt to outflank Union positions at Pea Ridge without success. This ensured Union control of Missouri for the next two years. Casualties: Union—1,349; Confederate—4,600.

MARCH 9—USS *Monitor* versus CSS *Virginia*, Hampton Roads, Virginia. The first battle between two armored ships ended in a draw; the CSS *Virginia* withdrew. Casualties: Union—409; Confederate—24.

MARCH 23—Battle of Kernstown, Virginia. In the Shenandoah Valley, Jackson attacks 8,500 Union troops with 3,000 soldiers and is repulsed with serious loss. Casualties: Union—590; Confederate—718.

APRIL 5—Peninsula Campaign begins. McClellan attacked a small Confederate army under John Magruder at Yorktown, Virginia, at the start of his march to Richmond; the results were inconclusive. Casualties: 320 total.

APRIL 6–7—Battle of Shiloh, Tennessee. Major battle begins as Confederate General Albert Sidney Johnston attacks Grant's army before it could unite with Buell; major Union victory. Casualties: Union—13,047; Confederate—10,699.

MAY 31–JUNE 1—Battle of Fair Oaks (Seven Pines). General Joseph E. Johnston attempted to overwhelm two Federal Corps that seemed to be in an isolated position. Timely Union reinforcements prevented a Confederate victory. Casualties: Union—5,739; Confederate—7,997.

JUNE 6—Memphis falls to Union forces. Another combined army/navy assault ends in Memphis surrendering to Union forces. Casualties: Union—1; Confederate—180.

JUNE 25–JULY 1—Seven Days' Battle. A series of battles fought this week: Mechanicsville, June 26–27; Gaines' Mill, June 27; Savage's Station, June 29; Frayser's Farm, June 30; and Malvern Hill, July 1. Casualties: Union—15,849; Confederate—20,614.

AUGUST 29–30—Second Manassas. Under General John Pope, the Union army launched a series of attacks against Jackson that were repulsed with heavy casualties on both sides; rear guard action by Union forces prevented a complete rout. Casualties: Union—16,054; Confederate—9,197.

SEPTEMBER 17—Antietam. Hooker's Corps' assault on Lee's left flank began the single bloodiest day in American military history. McClellan refused to commit more forces on the offensive, which allowed Lee to fight him to a standstill. Casualties: Union—12,410; Confederate—13,724.

SEPTEMBER 22—Emancipation Proclamation. Antietam gave President Lincoln the opportunity to announce his preliminary Emancipation Proclamation, freeing all slaves in the rebelling states, effective January 1, 1863.

OCTOBER 8—Battle of Perryville, Kentucky. Braxton Bragg's autumn invasion led to this battle, as the Union forces under Rosecrans converged at this small crossroads town. The Confederates eventually retreated, leaving Union forces with a victory. Casualties: Union—4,211; Confederate—3,396.

DECEMBER 11—Battle of Fredericksburg. Union engineers laid down five pontoon bridges across the Rappahannock River, enabling the army to cross and assault Lee's entrenched army in a series of futile frontal attacks, resulting in staggering casualties. Casualties: Union—12,653; Confederate—5,309.

DECEMBER 31–JANUARY 2—Battle of Stone's River, Tennessee. Bragg's defeated army retreated to Murfreesboro and prepared to go into winter quarters. Rosecrans followed and on December 29 went into camp within hearing distance of the Confederates. At dawn on the 31st, Bragg attacked and both sides fought it out until Bragg left the field on January 4. Casualties: Union—11,577; Confederate—9,865.

1863

MAY 1–4—Battle of Chancellorsville. Hooker's attempt to turn Lee's left flank was almost successful had the Union commander not lost his nerve. Pressed by Lee, he assumed a defensive posture and left his left flank exposed, which Jackson promptly crushed. This was Lee's greatest victory. Casualties: Union—16,792; Confederate—12,764.

MAY 18—The Siege of Vicksburg begins. Grant's army converged on the city of Vicksburg, on the Mississippi River, trapping Lieutenant General John Pemberton's army.

JUNE 9—Battle of Brandy Station. Just before Lee's advance north into Pennsylvania, Lee's cavalry engaged their opposite numbers in a 12-hour melee of men, horses, and sabers. The Union cavalry had finally stood up to Stuart's best.

JULY 1–3—Battle of Gettysburg. For three days in July, more men fought and died than in any other battle fought on this continent. Lee's invasion of the north failed. Casualties: Union—23,049; Confederate—28,063.

JULY 4—Vicksburg surrenders. The surrender effectively cut the Confederacy in half. This victory led to Grant's appointment as General-in-Chief of all Union forces. Casualties: Union—4,550; Confederate—31,275.

JULY 8—Capture of Port Hudson, Louisiana. Union Major General Banks, cooperating with Grant's Vicksburg campaign, laid siege to the Confederate stronghold at Port Hudson. After 48 days and the fall of Vicksburg, the Confederate garrison surrendered, opening up the Mississippi River to New Orleans to Union transportation.

SEPTEMBER 19–20—Battle of Chickamauga. Confederate General Bragg, determined to reoccupy Chattanooga, attacked part of Rosecrans' army. Finding a gap in the Union lines, they drove Rosecrans and one-third of the Union army from the field. Union General George Thomas took command, consolidated forces, and held against further determined assaults and retreated from the field. Casualties: Union—16,179; Confederate—18,454.

NOVEMBER 23–25—Battle of Chattanooga. Bragg laid siege to Rosecrans in this city, cutting off supplies through October 1863. Grant, now in command of Western armies, reestablished supply lines and began offensive operations, defeating Bragg at Missionary Ridge. Casualties: Union—5,824; Confederate—6,667.

FEBRUARY 17—CSS *Hunley*. On the night of the 17th, the attack submarine CSS *Hunley* sank the Union frigate USS *Housatonic*. The *Hunley* sank to the bottom shortly after, and all crew members were lost.

MAY 5–7—The Battle of the Wilderness. The opening battle of Grant's sustained offensive against the Army of Northern Virginia. The fighting was fierce but inconclusive. Grant did not retreat but advanced by the left flank. Casualties: Union—18,400; Confederate—11,400.

MAY 7—The Campaign for Atlanta begins. General Sherman departed Chattanooga and was promptly assaulted by Confederate forces under Joseph Johnston.

MAY 8–21—Spotsylvania Court House. A two-week battle, actually a series of battles along this front. Nearly 20 hours of ferocious combat. Casualties: Union—18,000; Confederate—12,000.

MAY 23–26—North Anna River, Virginia. A continuation of the Overland Campaign, as Grant divided his army into three parts to attack in an inconclusive flanking movement.

JUNE 1–3—Cold Harbor, Virginia. Sheridan's cavalry seized the crossroads at Old Cold Harbor and repulsed some Confederate infantry. Union infantry came up, assaulted the Confederate lines, and were slaughtered. Casualties: Union—12,000; Confederate—2,500.

JUNE 18—Siege of Petersburg. The siege began after a failed assault to take the city, as Lee rushed reinforcements to defend. Casualties: Union—8,150; Confederate—2,970.

JUNE 27—Kennesaw Mountain, Georgia. Johnston withdrew his army to a position astride Kennesaw Mountain; Sherman assaulted the dug-in Confederates with high casualties.

JULY 20—Peachtree Creek, Georgia. Johnston had withdrawn his army south of Peachtree Creek, about 3 miles from Atlanta. Sherman's troops, arrayed in three assault columns, attacked and forced the Rebels to fall back. Casualties: Union—1,600; Confederate—2,500.

JULY 22—Atlanta. General John B. Hood, replacing Johnston, attempted to hit the unprotected Union left and rear but was repulsed with high casualties. Casualties: Union—3,722; Confederate—8,000.

JULY 30—Battle of the Crater, Virginia. The Federals exploded a huge mine underground beneath Pegram's Salient, blowing a gap in the Confederate position. The break was sealed off with high Union casualties.

AUGUST 8—Capture of Mobile Bay, Alabama. Admiral David Farragut's Union fleet sailed past the forts guarding Mobile Bay, effectively closing that port to blockade runners.

OCTOBER 19—Battle of Cedar Creek, Virginia. A dawn attack by Jubal Early routed two Union Corps in the Shenandoah Valley. Major General Phillip Sheridan arrived from

Winchester to rally his troops and launched a crushing counterattack at Cedar Creek. Casualties: Union—5,665; Confederate—2,910.

NOVEMBER 8—Abraham Lincoln reelected. Sheridan and Sherman's victories helped ensure Lincoln's reelection to the presidency.

NOVEMBER 16—Sherman's March to the Sea. Cutting himself completely off from his supply lines, Sherman cut a path 300 miles long and 60 miles wide through Georgia.

DECEMBER 15–16—Battle of Nashville. In a desperate attempt to get Sherman out of Georgia, Hood moved toward Nashville. George Thomas all but destroyed Hood's Army of the Tennessee. Casualties: Union—3,061; Confederate—4,462.

DECEMBER 20—The Evacuation of Savannah, Georgia. Sherman stormed Fort McAllister on December 13, 1864, after a month's march and captured Savannah eight days later.

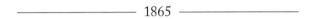

1865

JANUARY 13–15—Fort Fisher, North Carolina. Admiral David Porter's bombardment led the way for Union troops to capture Fort Fisher.

FEBRUARY 17—The Capture of Columbia, South Carolina. Sherman moved from Georgia to South Carolina, destroying nearly everything in sight.

MARCH 19–21—Battle of Bentonville, North Carolina. Johnston attacked the Union XIV Corps with incomplete success due to Union reinforcements. He withdrew toward Raleigh. Casualties: Union—1,646; Confederate—3,092.

APRIL 1—Five Forks, Virginia. Lee ordered Pickett to hold the vital crossroads at Five Forks. Sheridan's cavalry pinned him down, while the Union V Corps overwhelmed the Confederate left flank, forcing the evacuation of Petersburg and Richmond.

APRIL 6—Sailor's Creek, Virginia. Nearly one-quarter of the Confederate army was cut off at Sailor's Creek by Sheridan's cavalry and the II and VI Corps. Most of them surrendered.

APRIL 9—Appomattox Court House, Virginia. After a short Confederate advance against Union lines, Lee surrendered in the parlor of the McLean House. Casualties: 10,780 total.

APRIL 15—Lincoln assassinated. On April 14, while watching a play at Ford's Theater in Washington, D.C., President Abraham Lincoln was shot in the back of the head by John Wilkes Booth. Lincoln died the next day.

MAY 10—The Capture of Jefferson Davis. While attempting to escape the country, Confederate President Jefferson Davis was captured by elements of the 4th Michigan Cavalry.

Select Bibliography

PRIMARY SOURCES

Burton Historical Collection, Detroit Public Library

   Civil War Correspondence

   Duffield Family Papers

   Philip Kearney Papers

   George Vanderpool Papers

   Vernor Family Papers

SECONDARY SOURCES

Crawford, Kim. *The 16th Michigan Infantry.* Dayton, Ohio: The Morningside Press. 2002.

Daniel, Larry J. *Days of Glory: The Army of the Cumberland, 1861-1865.* Baton Rouge, Louisiana: LSU Press. 2004.

Eicher, David J. *The Longest Night: A Military History of the Civil War.* New York: Simon & Schuster. 2001.

Ferguson, Ernest. *Chancellorsville, 1863: Souls of the Brave.* New York: Knopf. 1992.

Michigan Adjutant General's Office. *Record of Service of Michigan Volunteers in the Civil War, 1861-1865.* 47 vols. Kalamazoo, Michigan: Ihling Brothers & Everhard. 1905.

Robertson, Jno., compiler. *Michigan in the War.* Lansing, Michigan: WS George & Co., State Printers and Binders. 1880.

Sears, Stephen W. *For Country, Cause and Leader: The Civil War Journal of Charles B. Haydon.* New York: Ticknor & Fields. 1993.

Sears, Stephen W. *To the Gates of Richmond: The Peninsular Campaign.* New York: Ticknor & Fields. 1992.

Wert, Jeffrey D. *The Sword of Lincoln: The Army of the Potomac.* New York: Simon & Schuster. 2005.